CAMBRIDGE STUDIES IN LINGUISTICS

General Editors · W. SIDNEY ALLEN · EUGENIE J. A. HENDERSON · FRED W. HOUSEHOLDER · JOHN LYONS · R. B. LE PAGE · F. R. PALMER · J. L. M. TRIM

Early syntactic development

In this series

EARLY SYNTACTIC DEVELOPMENT

A CROSS-LINGUISTIC STUDY WITH SPECIAL REFERENCE TO FINNISH

MELISSA BOWERMAN

Bureau of Child Research and Department of Linguistics
University of Kansas

CAMBRIDGE
at the University Press · 1973

Published by the Syndics of the Cambridge University Press
Bentley House, 200 Euston Road, London NW1 2DB
American Branch: 32 East 57th Street, N.Y.10022

Library of Congress Catalogue Card Number: 72–83596

ISBNs:
0 521 20019 9 hard covers
0 521 09797 5 paperback

Composed in Great Britain
at the University Printing House, Cambridge
(Brooke Crutchley, University Printer)
Printed in the United States of America

Contents

Appendices

Acknowledgments

Many people have contributed to this study of children's early syntactic development, which is, in essence, my 1970 Harvard University doctoral dissertation. I am especially grateful to Dr Roger Brown, who advised me throughout my years of graduate study. His insightful approach to problems in language acquisition has greatly influenced me, and his interest, encouragement, and counsel have been invaluable to the execution of this research.

I also want to thank Dr Eric Wanner, who helped me with problems of grammar writing and provided useful suggestions on many other matters; Dr David McNeill, who read initial reports on some of the material in the study and offered helpful comments and criticisms; and Drs Dan I. Slobin and Susan Ervin-Tripp, for their interest and support.

The special dividends of my study have been the native speakers of Finnish I have met. I am very grateful to Olavi Nuutinen, for so patiently and knowledgeably unraveling many of the mysteries of his language for me, and to Mrs Kirsti Bridges, for her clarification of many aspects of spoken Finnish and her help with the transcriptions. I particularly want to thank the families of Seppo, Rina, Katja, and Katarina, the four Finnish children whose language development I have followed, for their hospitality and long-term cooperation with every phase of the research. Only Seppo and Rina are reported on in the present study. I anticipate using data from the other two children in analyses of more advanced linguistic development. In addition, I am grateful to Kendall and her family for providing me with the opportunity to observe the language development of an American child.

This research was supported in part by PHS Grant HD-02908 from the National Institute of Child Health and Development; Roger Brown of Harvard University was principal investigator; and by PHS Training Grant NS-05362 from the National Institute of Neurological Diseases and Stroke to the Bureau of Child Research, University of Kansas. Their aid is gratefully acknowledged.

A very special thanks goes to my husband, William R. Bowerman, who provided much valuable help on matters of both content and form.

TO MY PARENTS
GEORGE AND MARY FOSTER

Glossary of notations used in presenting speech events

..   Indicates a pause within an utterance without terminal intonation contour.

—   Indicates a broken-off or interrupted utterance.

——   Indicates an utterance or a part of an utterance which was unclear and could not be transcribed.

( )   Parentheses in both a Finnish utterance and its English translation indicate that the enclosed word or portion of a word was slightly unclear and may have been incorrectly transcribed. Utterances with very dubiously transcribed sections were excluded from the samples. Parentheses which appear only in the English translation of an utterance and not in the Finnish original simply indicate words which are necessarily present in a grammatical translation, but which do not have counterparts in the Finnish utterance.

⟨ ⟩   Angle brackets indicate that the enclosed part of a word was not actually pronounced by the child. Seppo in particular often omitted sounds or entire syllables from the last part of words. For example, *apina* ,'monkey', was always rendered as *api*, and *saappaat*, 'boots', as *saappaa*. *Palo-auto*, 'fire-car' ('fire engine'), was often simply *palo*.

:   Indicates intervening utterances by child or parent or both.

>   Indicates a particular utterance, usually in a sequence of utterances, which is the example referred to in the text or title of the table.

" "   Double quotation marks indicate that the word so marked is not a legitimate Finnish word, but, rather, is either Seppo's idiosyncratic pronunciation or substitution for a Finnish word, or is a 'baby' word provided by his mother. Words which are widely used by children but not by adults are simply translated as 'doggie', 'piggie', 'moo-cow', 'teddy bear', 'bunny', etc., and are not otherwise marked.

[xi]

The names of participants in speech events are abbreviated as follows:

S	Seppo
R	Rina
K	Kendall
M	Mother
D	Daddy
B	Bowerman (the investigator)

I   *Introduction*

Since Chomsky first outlined his view of the abstractness and complexity of linguistic structures (1957) and stressed the difficulties involved in trying to account for the child's acquisition of language by reference to such concepts as 'association', 'generalization', and 'differential reinforcement' (1959), a growing number of scholars influenced by his formulations has devoted attention to the intriguing problem of how children learn to talk.

The investigations initially inspired by Chomsky's theory of grammar were concerned primarily with describing how children acquire English, but their findings led logically to the question, 'are there universals of language acquisition, i.e. similarities in the way all children acquire language regardless of the particular language to which they are exposed?' Until recently, we have been handicapped in our efforts to explore this question by a lack of comparative material. Hypotheses about language acquisition universals have been based mainly upon data from English-speaking children. A limited amount of support from other languages for these proposals has come from diary studies kept by parents on their children's linguistic development, but such studies, being responsive to the diarist's interests, are too selective to allow the thorough analysis of many of the problems which now concern us.

Within the last few years, however, investigators who combine an interest in language acquisition with a knowledge of exotic languages have begun to expand our cross-linguistic data base by venturing into the field equipped with tape recorders. The result has been a small but growing number of studies, based on speech samples collected by the impartial recording of everything a child produces for a given period of time, which report on aspects of the first language acquisition of children learning languages other than English; e.g. Samoan (Kernan, 1969), Luo (Blount, 1969), and Japanese (McNeill, 1966a; McNeill and McNeill, 1966). Further progress in the investigation of universals of language acquisition will depend both upon the collection of data from still other languages and upon the careful comparison of the cross-linguistic material now available, a task which has barely begun.

In the present study, I present and analyze data from a longitudinal investigation of the early syntactic development of two Finnish children, Seppo and Rina, and compare their speech at two stages of development with that of American, Samoan, and Luo children. The four languages represented belong to different language families (Finno-Ugric, Indo-European, Austronesian, and Eastern Sudanic respectively), and have very different structures. To the extent that languages differ structurally, similarities in the linguistic behavior of children learning them may be attributed to the operation of general principles of language acquisition rather than to exposure to similar structures. Thus, the descriptions of cross-linguistic similarities and differences presented here provide material for evaluating those hypotheses about universals of language acquisition which have already been suggested, and for generating some new proposals.

The following section (1.1) discusses some issues which currently interest investigators who are exploring similarities in the way different children acquire language. It is designed to acquaint the reader with some of the questions to be considered in the subsequent analyses and with the theoretical frame of reference used. The next section (1.2) is a description of the study. It includes an outline of the data used, a discussion of the period of development to be considered, and a brief description of the way in which the language acquisition data from the Finnish children are analyzed and compared with material from children learning other languages. This introductory chapter concludes (1.3) with a brief outline of the organization of the material in the remaining seven chapters.

1.1 Universals of language acquisition

Recent hypotheses about universals of language acquisition have been derived from two main sources: communalities in the empirical data on the language behavior of children learning English, with a small amount of cross-linguistic support, and linguists' proposals about universals of language. Both sources reflect the increasing impact of current linguistic theory upon students of human behavior.

1.1.1 Hypotheses based on language acquisition data. Chomsky's early writings emphasized that knowledge of a language cannot be viewed simply as knowledge of a repertoire of sentences. Rather, every

speaker has somehow internalized a set of rules which underlie sentence construction in his language. While such rules are seldom known consciously, they are nevertheless the basis of the speaker's ability to produce, understand, and make judgments about the grammaticality of the infinite number of possible sentences of his language.

The task of the child learning to talk, according to this view of language, is to discover from the finite corpus of utterances to which he is exposed the underlying set of rules governing sentence construction in his language. Most of the child's own utterances at various stages of development are considered to be the products of a rule system of his own discovery or invention rather than random combinations of words or repetitions of previously heard utterances. Thus, rather than being regarded as a passive associator or imitator, the child is looked upon as an active participant in the learning process. Many linguists and psychologists believe that in acquiring language the child formulates and tests hypotheses, ultimately revising or discarding those which are inadequate to account for new linguistic data. Chomsky (1959) notes that 'the young child [who learns a language] has succeeded in carrying out what from a formal point of view, at least, seems to be a remarkable type of theory construction'.

The term 'generative grammar' is used with 'systematic ambiguity' to refer both to the native speaker's internally represented theory of his language, or the rule system he has constructed, and to the linguist's account of this (Chomsky, 1965, p. 25). In writing a generative grammar for a language, a linguist is thus 'in effect proposing a hypothesis concerning [the speaker's] internalized system' (Chomsky, 1968, p. 23). The knowledge of language structure ascribed to the speaker by the linguist is represented in a generative grammar by a system of rules capable of generating (that is, characterizing, or assigning a structural description to) the indefinitely many well-formed or grammatical sentences of the language while at the same time blocking the derivation of ungrammatical sentences.

In the early 1960s, students of language behavior began to investigate the process by which children arrive at the implicit rules governing sentence structure in their language. Their work resulted in a carefully collected body of data from children learning English which has served as the basis for several hypotheses about universals of language acquisition. Three groups of investigators (Braine, 1963; Brown and Fraser, 1963; Miller and Ervin, 1964) found that early word combinations are not random. These researchers proposed simple generative grammars to account for the regularities of word choice and word order which they had discovered. Grammars written for unacquainted children, when subsequently compared, were found to be strikingly similar. The common elements of the grammars became formalized in the literature as the 'pivot–open class distinction' or the 'pivot grammar' (McNeill, 1966*b*, 1970; Slobin, 1966*c*). An analysis of diary studies of children acquiring languages other than English led Slobin (1966*c*, 1968) to hypothesize that the pivot grammar might be a universal first grammar regardless of the particular language being acquired.

A second hypothesized universal of language acquisition based primarily on empirical evidence from English-speaking children, with a small amount of cross-linguistic support, is that early child speech is 'telegraphic' – that it consists of strings of content words like nouns, verbs, and adjectives, and lacks inflections, articles, conjunctions, copulas, prepositions and postpositions, and, in general, all functors or 'little words' with grammatical but not referential significance (Slobin, 1970).

Still another hypothesis based on empirical data is that children used fixed word order in their early constructions. Slobin, in discussing evidence concerning word order from English- and Russian-speaking children, concluded that there must be something in the human capacity for acquiring language that 'favors beginning language with ordered sequences of unmarked classes, regardless of the degree of correspondence of such a system with the input language' (1966*a*, pp. 134–5).

1.1.2 Hypotheses based on universals of language. Chomsky's theory of grammar has increased interest in universals of language acquisition not only by stimulating empirical research but also by postulating a relationship between universals of language structure and the nature of the child's capacity to learn language. According to Chomsky,

A theory of linguistic structure that aims for explanatory adequacy incorporates an account of linguistic universals and it attributes tacit knowledge of these universals to the child. It proposes, then, that the child approaches the data with the presumption that they are drawn from a language of a certain antecedently well-defined type, his problem being to determine which of the (humanly) possible languages is that of the community in which he is placed (1965, p. 27).

What the child brings to the language learning situation, according to this view, can be characterized as a language acquisition device (LAD), the contents of which correspond to linguistic universals. The input to LAD, or the speech the child hears, is processed in accordance with the child's prior knowledge of these universals. According to Katz,

the role of experience is primarily to provide the data against which predictions and thus hypotheses are judged. Experience serves not to provide the things to be copied by the mind, as on the empiricist's account, but to help eliminate false hypotheses about the rules of language (1966, p. 278, fn. 28).

The fact that LAD is held to consist of just those aspects of language which linguists find to be universal seems less remarkable when viewed the other way around: languages may share universal features in the first place precisely because of the contents of LAD. Whatever characterizes the language acquisition capacity of human beings has left its mark on the structure of all natural languages by restricting the form of language to that which is learnable by humans (McNeill, 1966 *b*, p. 50).

It follows from this view of the nature of children's language learning capacity that hypotheses about universals of language acquisition can be formulated directly from what is known or becomes known about language universals, even in the absence of empirical evidence from language acquisition studies. If a particular feature is common to all languages, we can hypothesize that children have some *a priori* knowledge of this feature and perhaps organize their hypothesis formation and testing accordingly. McNeill has proposed that children have an innate knowledge of at least two aspects of linguistic structure thought by some to be universal: a universal hierarchy of grammatical categories and a knowledge of the 'basic grammatical relations', including the concepts 'subject of a sentence – predicate of a sentence', 'main verb of a predicate phrase – object of a predicate phrase', and 'modifier of a noun phrase – head noun of a noun phrase' (1966 *b*, pp. 28–49).

Other students of child language ascribe less specific structural information to LAD than McNeill does. For example, Slobin suggests that a child is born not with a set of universal categories but rather with a set of procedures and inference rules. Linguistic universals result from the working of this innate cognitive competence but are not the content of the competence itself (1966 *b*, p. 87). Similarly, Fodor hypothesizes that children are equipped with a set of inference rules or analytic procedures for processing input which produce candidate grammars that satisfy formal substantive universals (1966c). Fodor notes, however, that these procedures for language acquisition might conceivably be learned rather than be innate.

This review of hypotheses which have been made about language acquisition universals indicates that different hypotheses focus on different aspects of the language acquisition process. For example, the pivot grammar is a proposal that from a formal point of view the utterances produced during the initial period of word combining are identical across children and across languages. One could extend this hypothesis to later periods of development by proposing that all children pass through a similar sequence of developmental stages, each stage being marked by the production of particular kinds of utterances. In contrast, Slobin's proposal that children initially use fixed word order regardless of the degree of flexibility of word order in the language being learned belongs to a different class of hypotheses, that there are characteristic priorities in the way children formulate hypotheses about the structure of the language they are acquiring. Some of these priorities might be manifested rather subtly and would thus be more difficult to discover than global similarities in the kinds of utterances produced at various stages of development.

The data presented in this study of the learning of Finnish will help us to evaluate hypotheses about several different kinds of universals, whether they are derived from empirical studies of children's linguistic behavior or from linguists' proposals about language universals.

1.2   Description of the study

1.2.1   The structure of Finnish. The new material in this study of early syntactic development comes from tape recordings, taken in the home, of the spontaneous speech of two Finnish two-year-olds. Finnish was selected for this study because it is considered historically unrelated to English and to most of the other languages for which there exist language acquisition data from either parental diaries or from tape-recorded speech samples. Some of the structural features which distinguish Finnish from better-known European languages are vowel harmony, consonant gradation, a negative verb, lack of a special intonation for interrogative sentences, and a complex system of inflections for the nominal system involving fourteen cases. An overview of some of the most important features of Finnish, especially those which are relevant to the present study, is presented in Appendix A.

1.2.2 The period of development considered. This study deals with the earliest period of the acquisition of grammatical structure, that labeled 'Stage I' by Brown (1970, in press). Stage I is bounded at the lower end by the very beginning of word combining, when the average length of a child's spontaneous utterances first rises above one morpheme, and at the upper end by the point at which the average goes beyond two morphemes. This is a period of several weeks or months for most children. These limits are not intended to mark a 'natural' stage of development but are simply a convenient way to segment the continuous language acquisition process so that samples of children's speech may be analyzed and compared.

Brown used mean length of utterance (MLU) to define this period because it has been found to be 'the best single index of the level of speech development' (Brown, Bellugi, 1964). MLU is related to chronological age, since older children have longer MLUs on the average than younger ones, but there is not a perfect correlation. Brown and Fraser suggest that developmental sequence can be viewed as 'a Guttman scale with performance following an invariant order but not pegged to particular ages. The sequence can be covered at varying rates of speed; the rate would be a function of intelligence and learning opportunities' (1964, p. 72). For example, they found that in a sample of 13 children, all children with MLUs below 3.2 omitted 'be' in utterances in the progressive tense (for instance, 'I going') while all those with MLUs above this included 'be'. Some of the children who omitted 'be' were older than children who included 'be'. MLU has been found especially useful as a developmental index early in language development but it becomes more variable and less useful later on (Brown, Cazden, Bellugi-Klima, 1968).

Since MLU has been developed and used primarily as a guide to the level of linguistic development of English-speaking children, it has not been known whether similar MLUs mark similar developmental stages across languages. Therefore, to determine the usefulness of MLU as a means of matching samples from different languages, I did a rough preliminary comparison of the speech of the Finnish children to that of American children studied by Brown (1970, in press); Bloom (1970);

and myself. At similar MLUs, the children's utterances looked very much alike. Many constructions were virtually translations of each other. No differences were so striking as to indicate that the samples were not comparable in terms of the level of syntactic maturity represented. This suggests that MLU may have wide applicability across languages as a measure of linguistic development. After this preliminary analysis, MLU was used as a guide in making up samples of the Finnish children's speech which were deemed comparable to those of the American children. Chapter 2 gives a more detailed account of how the data from the Finnish children were collected and of the way in which the samples were prepared.

After the Finnish samples had been compiled, additional data became available from children acquiring Samoan (Kernan, 1969) and Luo (Blount, 1969). A preliminary inspection of these samples indicated that they too fell within Brown's Stage I and could be directly compared with the Finnish and English data. This material has therefore also been included in the analysis to permit more extensive cross-linguistic comparisons. Table 1 lists all the children whose speech samples are compared to each other and gives relevant information about the samples.

I have divided the total set of thirteen speech samples into two groups representing earlier and later developmental substages within Stage I. These are called here 'early Stage I' and 'late Stage I'. The MLUs of the early Stage I samples, where known, range between approximately 1.30 and 1.50 morphemes. Those of the late Stage I samples range between about 1.60 and 2.00 morphemes. Superficially, the most important difference between the two sets of samples is that the great majority of utterances in the early Stage I samples are no longer than two morphemes, while the late Stage I samples contain numerous three-morpheme strings. The two substages are considered separately in most of the analyses of this study to allow the question of whether all children pass through a similar sequence of developmental stages to be investigated in more detail than would have been possible if all the Stage I samples had been treated as a single group.

1.2.3 Writing grammars for children. Samples of child speech can be subjected to numerous kinds of analyses. However, as Brown, Cazden, and Bellugi-Klima observe, 'the most demanding form in which to pose the question of the child's knowledge of structure at any time is

TABLE 1. *The children used for comparison at two stages of development*

Child	Language	MLU	Age (months)	Collection of the data	Investigator
			Early Stage I: MLU between approximately 1.30 and 1.50		
Seppo	Finnish	1.42	23	2 hrs, taped over 3 wks	Bowerman
Kathryn	English	1.32	21	7½ hrs, taped in few days	Bloom (1970)
Gia	English	1.34	21	7½ hrs, taped in few days	Bloom (1970)
Eric	English	1.42	22	8½ hrs, taped in few days	Bloom (1970)
Kendall	English	1.48	23	1½ hrs, taped in 2 days	Bowerman
Sipili	Samoan	1.52	30	6½ hrs, taped over 1 wk	Kernan (1969)
6 children	Luo	unknown	19–31	tape recorded	Blount (1969)
			Late Stage I: MLU between approximately 1.60 and 2.00		
Seppo	Finnish	1.81	26	1½ hrs, taped over 3 wks	Bowerman
Rina	Finnish	1.83	25	2 hrs, taped over 3 wks	Bowerman
Adam	English	2.06	27	2 hrs, taped	Brown (1970, in press)
Eve	English	1.68	18–19	3½ hrs, taped over 6 wks	Brown (1970, in press)
Sarah	English	1.73	27–28	3 hrs, taped over 6 wks	Brown (1970, in press)
Tofi	Samoan	1.60	26	taped over 1 wk	Kernan (1969)

to ask for a generative grammar that represents his knowledge' (1968, p. 30). For this reason, I chose to analyze data from the Finnish children primarily through writing generative grammars for them at each of the two stages of development.

According to the conception of generative grammar outlined above, the form of a particular grammar is adequate only to the extent to which it accurately represents the knowledge of sentence structure available to a speaker of the language.[1] In the present study, three different theoretical frameworks for writing generative grammars are evaluated with regard to how well they appear to satisfy this requirement for child speakers. They are *pivot grammar, transformational grammar,* and *case grammar.* Assessing the adequacy of each grammar's formulations involves making and attempting to justify numerous judgments about the kinds of concepts, categories, and rules of concatenation which underlie children's early linguistic behavior.

While rules of grammar are proposed only for the Finnish children, their speech is compared with that of the American, Luo, and Samoan children within the theoretical frameworks provided by the three approaches to grammar writing. The relative ease with which the formulations of a given grammar can be applied to the speech of all four sets of children is an important factor in determining the overall usefulness of the grammar as a vehicle for representing the linguistic knowledge of children.

Competence and performance

Early attempts to write generative grammars for children (e.g. Braine, 1963; Brown and Fraser, 1963; Miller and Ervin, 1964) were criticized by linguists on the grounds that studies which rely on children's spontaneous speech reveal little about underlying knowledge of linguistic structure (e.g. Chomsky, 1964; Lees, 1964). In linguistic theory, a sharp distinction is made between *competence,* or the speaker's knowledge of his language, and *performance,* or 'the actual use of language in

---

[1] There is currently much debate among linguists and psychologists about whether the rules of grammar which have been proposed for English (or any other language) are, in fact, isomorphic to the kind of knowledge speakers have of their language (e.g. Fodor and Garrett, 1966; Watt, 1970). Nevertheless, the conception of a grammar as a representation of a speaker's linguistic knowledge – of the way in which he understands sentences to be constructed (although not necessarily of the psychological steps he takes in actually producing and comprehending utterances) – is a useful one, and is adopted in this study as an ideal against which various approaches to writing grammars for children can be assessed.

concrete situations' (Chomsky, 1965, p. 4). According to Chomsky, 'linguistic theory is concerned primarily with an ideal speaker-listener, in a completely homogeneous speech-community, who knows its language perfectly and is unaffected by such grammatically irrelevant conditions as memory limitations, distractions, shifts of attention and of interest, and errors (random or characteristic) in applying his knowledge of the language in actual performance' (1965, p. 3). A grammar is intended to be 'a description of the ideal speaker-hearer's intrinsic competence' (Chomsky, 1965, p. 4).

Because the early child grammars were based exclusively on speech production, they were regarded as inadequate representations of children's competence. Not only does reliance on production allow many sentences which even the child might consider ungrammatical – although he produced them – to enter into consideration, but it also excludes evidence from comprehension, another source of information about competence. Chomsky notes that 'one can find out about competence only by studying performance, but this study must be carried out in devious and clever ways, if any serious result is to be obtained' (1964, p. 36).

Since the first presentation of grammars for children, however, students of language acquisition have gained an increased appreciation of the amount of information about competence obtainable from samples of spontaneous speech. The early investigations simply listed the utterances collected from children and did distributional analyses of the privileges of occurrence of words. But many additional clues to competence can be found in the nonlinguistic contexts of speech events, the linguistic interaction between parent and child, the relationship between successive utterances of the child, and the comparison of the child's speech to that of his parents. For example, information about the child's knowledge of constituent structure is contained in his responses to parental Wh questions (what, where, who, why, etc.). Does the child give the right sorts of constituents as answers? Constituent structure is also revealed through substitutions of pronouns for noun phrases and of words like 'there' for locative prepositional phrases in the child's or parent's antecedent utterances. The analysis of the extent to which grammatical morphemes such as inflections or prepositions are present in contexts in which they are obligatory in adult speech is also a way of getting at the child's underlying knowledge (Cazden, 1968; Brown, in press). Other aspects of competence are revealed in comparisons of the relative frequencies with which parent and child produce various construction patterns, word orders, grammatical morphemes, and so on. Samples of spontaneous speech, if thoroughly and ingeniously explored, are a rich source of information about linguistic competence.

In writing grammars based on spontaneous speech samples, one can often take into account aspects of linguistic behavior which are probably attributable to performance limitations rather than to competence. Not every sentence need be considered equally 'well-formed'. False starts, hesitations, broken-off sentences, and repeated words are frequently identifiable as errors, as in adult speech, because they are one-of-a-kind and often have unusual intonation patterns. Grammars written for children generally attempt to account only for sentences thought to have been formed in accordance with rules the child has formulated for sentence construction. In this study, the term *construction pattern* is used to refer to particular structural descriptions of sentences – such as 'subject–verb', 'possessor–object possessed', or 'two-word utterances with "allgone" in final position' – which can apply to sets of one or more individual sentences. Most investigators who have written grammars for children have judged construction patterns to be productive (rule-governed) only if sentences corresponding to them occur with some frequency in a speech sample, and the particular words in these sentences are variable. This is because it is difficult to think of another explanation for them. In contrast, although a construction pattern which is represented by only one or two different utterances in a sample *may* have been generated by productive rules, there are plausible alternative explanations: that the sentences were either memorized routines or 'mistakes' from the child's point of view. Grammars based on spontaneous speech samples may sometimes underestimate competence because certain sentences which were, in fact, generated by productive rules are excluded from consideration, but many important aspects of competence can nevertheless be represented.

A few studies of the relationship of comprehension to production have indicated that children understand more than they can produce (e.g. Fraser, Bellugi, Brown, 1963; Shipley, Smith, Gleitman, 1968). This suggests that children have some knowledge of linguistic structure which is not revealed in their productions. Grammars written to represent competence should theoretically give an account of this knowledge. We do not yet know how to write a grammar which accounts for both the child's production ability and his comprehension ability. However, it is not clear that the notion of competence as a single system of rules underlying both production and comprehension is as applicable to individuals acquiring a language as it is to 'ideal speaker-listeners', persons who have completed the process. When there is a large discrepancy between what a person can understand and what he can produce, formulating a single grammar intended to account for both abilities is not only difficult, but could also obscure important regularities – which may be similar across individuals learning different languages – in the way the abilities to comprehend and to produce sentences evolve and are related to each other at various stages of development. The study of the emerging competence which underlies children's ability to construct sentences, as distinct from the knowledge they employ in comprehending sentences, is thus an important part of any comprehensive investigation of how language is acquired. The grammars written for the Finnish children in this study, then, are intended to represent neither competence as it is defined for the adult speaker, nor merely performance, but, rather, that knowledge of linguistic structure which lay beneath their ability to produce utterances.

1.3　Outline of chapters 2 through 8

Chapter 2, which follows the present introductory chapter, describes how the Finnish speech samples which constitute the primary data of this investigation were collected and prepared for analysis. The chapter also includes a summary of some of the most important quantitative characteristics of the samples, such as the percent of imitations, the type/token ratio, and the lexicon size, and compares the figures which characterize the Finnish samples with those which describe samples from English-speaking children at an equivalent stage of development.

In chapter 3 the adequacy of the *pivot grammar* as a representation of children's linguistic knowledge is explored. The grammar is tested both for its ability to represent data from English-speaking children, including those upon whose speech it was originally based, and its applicability to children learning Finnish and other languages. The pivot grammar, which takes into account only information contained in the superficial form and arrangement of words in utterances, is found both to provide an inaccurate account of the characteristics of children's utterances and to be fundamentally incapable of representing as much knowledge of linguistic structure as children can justifiably be credited with. Chapter 3 concludes with an argument for the necessity of taking into consideration the meanings as well as the superficial forms of children's utterances.

Transformational grammar, as outlined by Chomsky (1965) and applied to child language by McNeill (1966*a*, 1966*b*, 1970, 1971), Brown, Cazden, Bellugi-Klima (1968) and Bloom (1970), is an approach to writing generative grammars which provides for the representation of information about structural meaning as an integral part of its theory. Because the theoretical and practical aspects of grammar writing have been worked out in some detail in transformational theory, the main exposition of the characteristics of the Finnish children's speech and the comparisons with children learning other languages are conducted within this framework. Chapter 4 presents a transformational grammar for Seppo, based on his early Stage I speech sample. Seppo's speech is then compared with that of American, Luo, and Samoan children at a similar stage of development. In chapter 5, grammars based on late Stage I speech samples are presented for both Finnish children, Seppo and Rina, and comparisons are made with American and Samoan children. Some general conclusions about the characteristics of early and late Stage I speech are reached in these two chapters.

Chapter 6 is a discussion of some of the disadvantages of using transformational grammars to describe children's linguistic knowledge. Representing knowledge with a transformational grammar involves giving formal representation, by means of the subconfiguration of the elements of phrase-markers, to a set of 'basic grammatical relations'. However, it is argued that there is insufficient evidence in child speech to justify our crediting children with an understanding of the basic grammatical relations and of the constituent structure upon which these depend. Thus, writing transformational grammars for children forces us to posit a form of linguistic knowledge which we have not yet demonstrated that children possess. There is in fact a certain amount of evidence (admittedly as yet slight) that the structural components of the rules underlying children's earliest two- and three-word utterances may be semantic concepts like 'agent', 'action', and 'object acted upon' rather than grammatical concepts like 'subject', 'predicate', and 'direct object'. If this is the case, a grammar written for children should be able to give an explicit account of the semantic functions of sentence elements. A transformational grammar of the sort described by Chomsky is not designed to do this, and so may be basically unable to reflect children's linguistic knowledge adequately.

In chapter 7, the potential value of another approach to grammar writing, that of *case grammar* as proposed by Fillmore (1968), is investigated and assessed. Case grammar is found preferable to transformational grammar in that information about the basic grammatical relations and the constituent structure they entail does not need to be represented unless there are good reasons to do so. In addition, it provides an appealing account of many of the important semantic features of child speech. However, case grammar is found to have its own drawbacks.

It is concluded that none of the approaches to grammar writing evaluated in this study provide an entirely satisfactory system for representing the early linguistic knowledge of children. However, some suggestions about what characteristics such a grammar would have to possess are outlined in chapter 8, based on the view of the syntactic and semantic characteristics of early child speech arrived at in chapters 4, 5, 6, and 7.

2 Data collection

2.1 The children

The Finnish data consist of tape-recorded speech samples from two children, a boy, Seppo, and a girl, Rina, who were $22\frac{1}{2}$ and 24 months old respectively at the start of the study. During the time period to be analyzed, I made weekly visits to each child's home and took half-hour recordings of the child's play and interaction with his or her mother.[1] Other family members were occasionally present as well.

Ideally, data should have been collected from children of monolingual Finnish families living in Finland to avoid contamination from other languages. Instead, the taping took place in the homes of families who had recently left Finland to spend a period of time in the Boston area while the fathers did advanced graduate work. The parents of both children spoke English, although Rina's mother was not fluent when the study started. In addition, most of them spoke Swedish and/or German. Whether the parents' familiarity with languages other than Finnish had any effect on their spoken Finnish is difficult to determine. My impression is that it did not. The conversation within the home, in the absence of American visitors, was conducted almost entirely in the dialect of Finnish spoken in and around Helsinki. The only exception to this was that Seppo's mother occasionally used the English words 'please', 'yes', and 'no' in place of their Finnish equivalents, although she never used them in construction with Finnish words. Seppo eventually learned these words, evidently not distinguishing them from his Finnish vocabulary. For example, during the time period being considered he used both the Finnish word for 'no', *ei*, and the English 'no' in single-word utterances, apparently in free variation. Rina had an older brother, age 5, and Seppo a brother, 10, and a sister, 7. Initially, these children spoke only Finnish, although Seppo's siblings gradually began to learn English in school. Neither Seppo nor Rina played with American children at this time. The speech to which they were exposed, then, was almost exclusively Finnish.

[1] The taping of Rina continued for about 8 months and of Seppo for almost two years. Later tapes were usually longer than a half-hour, and, in Seppo's case, were taken less frequently in the second year.

2.2 The taping situation

During the actual taping, I made an effort to avoid speaking English with the mother as much as possible, to keep the situation defined as a Finnish-speaking one. In addition, I tried not to become involved in the child's play unless absolutely necessary, since my accent in Finnish and imperfect grammar might possibly have confused or influenced him. This effort was quite successful with Seppo, who was content to let me sit quietly to one side and take notes of the situation as he played with his toys or interacted with his mother. With Rina it was more difficult, as she began to look forward to my visits with great anticipation and was much more interested in interacting with me, the benevolent auntie and novel playmate, than in talking to her mother. In addition, it was difficult to take notes in Rina's presence, since the appearance of a pen in my hand invariably occasioned the demand for another pen and an insistence upon drawing. Only when my pen was put away could the topic of conversation return to other matters. Therefore, notes were usually made after each recording session and were based on the taped conversation and on my recollection of the non-linguistic situation at the time of each utterance.

The taping sessions did not cover a wide range of the children's daytime activities. Bathing, toileting, dressing, and playing outside were not included. Meals and snacks, spontaneous play with toys and household objects, either with or without the mother's active companionship, and looking at pictures in books or magazines constituted the main activities. In Rina's early tapes, looking at Donald Duck comic books and pointing out various characters and objects, drawing, and trying to obtain food were major activities. Seppo initially spent much time playing with his toy cars, looking at Richard Scarry's *Best Word Book Ever*, a picture book with many small illustrations of animals involved in different activities, and playing with a set of small picture books shaped like blocks. Later, he still conversed about cars and pictures a great deal, but also played more with other toys, especially a toy mouse without a tail and a set of car keys. After the first few tapes for each child, I always brought a bag of toys and games, some familiar and some new, in an attempt to elicit discussion about new topics. This was usually very successful. The children looked forward to opening the bag themselves and seeing what new toys or activities they could choose from. This was an especially valuable spur to speech production from Rina, for without outside stimulation she tended to talk about only one or two topics or to become so active that taping was impossible. Rina's mother could successfully elicit conversation for any period of time only by asking Rina to name different pictures. This rapidly became boring to Rina and resulted in a disproportionately large number of stereotyped naming responses. Seppo and his mother functioned more smoothly as a conversational team even in the absence of new toys and games. Rather than merely naming pictures in his books, he spontaneously described what the characters were doing and answered questions about these activities. In addition, he played more happily by himself than did Rina and talked about what he was doing.

2.3   Transcribing the tapes

The tapes were transcribed by the investigator. Everything said by or to the child was included, as were notes about the object of the child's attention and other aspects of the nonlinguistic situation. I am not a native speaker of Finnish, but my comprehension improved rapidly after a few sessions with each child and by the end of a few months I became fairly confident of my ability to make accurate transcriptions. All the tapes transcribed in the early months were carefully rechecked when I had become more fluent. The tapes used for the samples analyzed in this study were then doublechecked. Seppo's tapes were much easier to transcribe than Rina's. His speech and that of his mother was slow and clear, and I could easily identify unfamiliar words and look them up in the dictionary or ask his mother about them. Rina's speech, in contrast, was rapid and breathless, and her pronunciation was faultier than Seppo's. Initial consonants were often omitted and different vowel qualities were not always distinguished. After some tutoring from her mother, however, I became familiar with her style of word alteration and was usually able to understand her. Rina's mother also spoke rapidly, with many run-together and broken-off sentences. Because these tapes were more difficult for me than Seppo's, the transcriptions were carefully checked over by a native speaker of Finnish. Some of the early transcriptions for Seppo were also checked, but this was discontinued since there were very few errors.

The speech of the mothers was transcribed in standard Finnish orthography, which is quite phonemic. Careful note was made, however, of differences from standard textbook Finnish in colloquial pronunciation; these were numerous and often involved inflectional suffixes. The speech of the children was generally transcribed in Finnish orthography, but copious phonetic notes were also included, especially about features such as vowel and consonant length (both phonemic in Finnish) and vowel quality (important in Finnish vowel harmony).

2.4 Compiling the samples

Speech samples were compiled from the continuous weekly tapes to allow grammars to be written for discrete 'stages' of development and to facilitate comparison between children at equivalent stages and between the stages of individual children. As noted in 1.2.2, the particular developmental points I selected for analysis were partially determined by the nature of existing samples from English-speaking children. In particular, I anticipated comparison with data from Adam, Eve, and Sarah, three American children whose language development has been followed in a longitudinal study conducted at Harvard by Brown and his colleagues (Brown, Bellugi, 1964; Brown, Cazden, Bellugi-Klima, 1968; Brown, 1968, 1970, in press; Brown, Hanlon, 1968; Bellugi, 1967; Klima, Bellugi, 1966; Cazden, 1968; and many working papers and unpublished materials).

Brown's study involved taping the children in their homes weekly or every other week, under circumstances very similar to those described for the Finnish children. To guide the compilation of comparable samples from each child, Brown chose 'target' MLU values at each of five developmental points: 1.75, 2.25, 2.75, 3.50, and 4.00. These values were arbitrarily pre-selected except for the first, which was approximately the MLU of the earliest tapes taken. For each child, five samples of 713 utterances each were made up from consecutive tapes, the MLUs of which averaged to about these figures.

To allow me to make detailed comparisons between the Finnish and the American children, I compiled for each Finnish child a speech sample, also of 713 utterances from consecutive tapes, to correspond as closely as possible to the earliest samples of the American children at MLUs of about 1.75. These samples fall within the developmental period we are calling 'late Stage I'. For Seppo, the sample was taken from weekly tapes 14–16 and part of 17. The sample for Rina was taken from tapes 1–4 and a small part of 5. Although each sample includes speech from a time span of three to four weeks, it was considered as a unit for purposes of analysis, just as though all the utterances had been produced on the same day. This seemed justifiable, because internal analysis of the samples showed very little qualitative difference between the first and last tapes included.

The MLU value of Seppo's late Stage I sample was computed at 1.89 and Rina's at 1.95 when every segment which is a morpheme in adult Finnish was included in the count. These values are similar to those of the American children's samples: 1.68, 1.73, and 2.06. However, it was difficult to decide whether certain words, which were very frequent in the samples, should be counted as two morphemes or as one. In adult Finnish, prolocatives like 'here' and 'there' and their interrogative counterpart 'where' consist of two morphemes: a pronoun plus a locative case ending. For example, *tuo-ssa*, 'there', is literally 'that-in', *tä-ssä*, 'here', is 'this-in', and *mi-ssä*, 'where', is 'what-in'. These are thus identical in structure to nouns inflected with locative case endings, such as *talo-ssa*, 'house-in'. There is no evidence, however, that the children analyzed these prolocatives into two components, since the locative case endings occurred with no other words at this stage. Rather, the prolocatives had probably been learned as units, just as American children learn 'here', 'there', and 'where'. If these prolocatives are counted as one morpheme in the children's samples, Seppo's MLU drops to 1.73 and Rina's to 1.71. But if a decision is made to count prolocatives as one morpheme initially, at some point in the child's development the decision must be reversed, since adult speakers understand these words to be composed of two morphemes. How to pinpoint the appropriate time to start counting prolocatives as two morphemes is difficult. In this study, a compromise has been made between counting prolocatives as one morpheme and as two by averaging the MLU values obtained in the two methods of counting. Seppo's sample at this stage is thus said to have an MLU of 1.81 and Rina's of 1.83.

Earlier data existed for Seppo. These appeared comparable to those from Bloom's (1970) three English-speaking subjects at MLUs of 1.32, 1.34, and 1.42, and from Kendall, an American child whose development I have followed, at MLU 1.48. A second sample was therefore compiled for Seppo, which consists of 713 utterances from weekly tapes 2–5 (1 was omitted because the speech output was very low and unrepresentatively simple). The averaged MLU of the sample is 1.42. When prolocatives are counted as two morphemes it is 1.43 and when counted as one it is 1.41.

In compiling the Finnish children's samples, I included every consecutive utterance which was completely transcribed and did not seem
to have been interrupted or broken off, with a note as to whether it was
spontaneous or a direct imitation. A direct imitation was defined, as in
the samples from Brown's subjects, as a complete or reduced rendition,
in the same word order, of another person's utterance which had
occurred within the three utterances preceding the child's. Utterances
which were not already separated by an interlocutor's remark could
usually be segmented on the basis of pauses or intonation contours.
Occasionally, sequences of words which may, in fact, have consisted
of two or more utterances were considered as one because they were
run together under one intonation contour and there was no way to
determine where to draw sentence boundaries.

In addition to the children's samples, I compiled a speech sample
from each Finnish mother to help answer certain questions about the
input to the child. These proved especially useful in the analysis of
the word orders used by the children. Each sample consisted of 1000
utterances taken from tapes which were not used in the children's
samples but which were as close in time as possible. For Rina's mother,
the tapes used were the latter part of 5 and 6-8. For Seppo's mother,
they were tapes 8-13. All consecutive utterances which were addressed
to the child or the child's siblings, but not to adults, were included
(there were very few utterances in the latter two categories), except for
those which were direct imitations or expansions of the child's immediately preceding utterance. These were omitted so that the speech
sample obtained would represent as well as possible the output of the
parent's own rule system as modeled to the child, rather than the
child's rule system reflected back to him. The former, presumably, was
the goal towards which the child was working and the baseline against
which his performance can best be compared.

2.5 Quantitative characteristics of the samples

In this study we are primarily concerned with the qualitative characteristics of children's speech. These will be considered in detail in the
next five chapters. However, it is also possible to describe speech
quantitatively. The statistics generated by such an analysis are difficult
to interpret in themselves; the real interest lies in comparing them
across children learning the same and different languages. As comparable

quantitative data from additional languages become available, we should begin to get a sense of whether the figures given below for Finnish and American children are general: whether, for example, the percentage of imitations, the lexicon size, and the type/token ratio at MLU 1.75 are similar across languages. Such a finding would suggest that there is a language-independent sequence of developments directly determined by the child's inherent capacity for language learning.

The statistics are presented in Table 2. Figures for Seppo and Rina at MLUs of 1.81 and 1.83 respectively can be compared directly with those for Brown's three subjects (Brown, unpublished materials). There are no figures available to compare with those for Seppo at MLU 1.42, but the statistics of this sample are included to show the change over time and for the sake of future studies.

The MLUs, relationship of age to MLU, and size of samples have already been discussed. The type/token ratio is a measure of utterance diversity within the samples. An utterance token is one utterance; there were 713 tokens in each sample. An utterance type is a distinctive utterance. There may be several tokens of a single type, for example, five occurrences of the type 'there ball'. If every utterance in a corpus were distinct, the type/token ratio would be 1. In samples of the speech of one adult to another, the ratio probably approaches this figure. In the children's samples, however, many utterance types were repeated, both in succession and at different times during the taping sessions. The type/token ratio tends to increase toward 1 as MLU rises because the more the child matures linguistically the less often he repeats words or combinations of words. The type/token ratios of the Finnish children fell within the range covered by those of the American children at similar MLUs: 0.37 (Sarah) to 0.71 (Adam).

The number of morphemes in the longest utterance in a sample is called the upper bound. This value ranges from 4 to 7 across the Finnish and American children at an MLU of approximately 1.75. The value was 5 in the first Seppo sample. It would have been lower except that Seppo sometimes repeated words several times in 'utterances' which perhaps really consisted of two or more utterances, as in 'away again away again away'. Because his upper bound at MLU 1.42 is inflated in this way, it is not matched by the linguistic maturity it suggests. Most utterances were only one or two morphemes long.

At an MLU of approximately 1.75, from 4 to 18 per cent of all utterance tokens were direct imitations of the interlocutor's speech.

TABLE 2. *Quantitative characteristics of the Finnish and American speech samples*

	Seppo	Seppo	Rina	Adam	Eve	Sarah
MLU	1.42	1.81	1.83	2.06	1.68	1.73
Age (months)	23	26	25	27	18–19	27–28
Utterance types	297	437	338	505	309	265
Utterance tokens	713	713	713	713	713	713
Type/token ratio	0·42	0·61	0·47	0·71	0·43	0·37
Upper bound	5	5	5	7	4·25	4
Number of imitations	173	79	112	37	88	136
Percentage of imitations	24	12	15	4	12	18
Lexicon size	112	226	136	201	169	193
Number of nouns	57	103	74	103	103	142
Number of verbs	31	65	32	37	36	21
Number of adjectives	3	8	5	15	6	13
Number of locatives	3	14	9	7	3	7
Number of pronouns	2	9	8	7	5	?
Functors required	32	98	168	127	91	81
Functors present	1	8	16	7	14	15
Percentage of functors present	3.1	8.2	9.5	6	13	16

The percentage of imitations was even greater in the earlier Seppo sample: 24 per cent. The lowest number of imitations, 4 per cent, was produced by Adam, the child with the highest MLU. Imitation seems to decrease as MLU rises and so may be another index of linguistic maturity.

The figures for lexicon size do not indicate the absolute number of words known by the children but only the number which occurred in the samples of 713 utterances. This number varied somewhat across children. The figures are not quite comparable, since for the American children, all lexical items were included, even direct imitations which never occurred spontaneously, while for the Finnish children, only nonimitated lexical items were counted. Comparable figures for the Finnish children would therefore be somewhat higher, especially for nouns, the words most often imitated. Parts-of-speech in this count were defined as in the adult languages. All five children had far more nouns than words in any other grammatical class. Verbs came next, trailing by a wide margin. Adjectives, locatives ('here', 'there', 'away', 'down', etc.), and pronouns were the next most frequent for all the children, with exact rank orders differing but the absolute numbers rather similar. Words from other classes, such as adverbs, interjections, and rejoinders ('yes', 'no', 'hi', etc.), were few in all the children's samples.

The percentage of functors present, or the number of functors present divided by the number of functors required, is an index to the 'telegraphic' quality of children's speech (see 1.1.1). Functors, defined as articles, inflections, copulas, conjunctions, prepositions and post-positions, auxiliaries, and other grammatical morphemes, were largely absent in all the samples. Strict standards for 'required' functors were maintained in the counts. Words in isolation were never considered to require functors, even if they were reductions of parental utterances in which functors were present. Rather, contexts in which functors were regarded as obligatory were defined on the basis of the linguistic characteristics of word combinations, following Cazden (1968) and Brown (in press). For the Finnish children, for example, noun inflections were considered obligatory on all nouns which were the direct objects of verbs or which occurred in contexts like 'two' + Noun or 'all' + Noun. Noun–noun combinations like 'chick shoe' or verb–noun combinations like 'take store', in which one word appeared to have a locative function as judged from nonlinguistic context, did not constitute 'required' contexts for locative noun inflections, since decisions about what and how many functors were missing depended heavily on the semantic interpretations assigned to the utterances rather than on their strict linguistic characteristics.

Functors were absent with the most consistency in the early Seppo sample. Only one, a dubiously transcribed genitive ending, was present in a total of 32 required contexts, or 3.1 per cent. At an MLU of approximately 1.75, the Finnish and American children supplied between 6 and 16 per cent of required functors, still a small number. The 'telegraphic' characteristics of the early speech of American children are thus matched in the Finnish children's speech, even though Finnish is a more richly inflected language than English. Omission of obligatory functors may well be a universal feature of the earliest stages of word combining. However, evidence from Luo and Samoan children, to be discussed in Chapter 4, indicates that children learning certain languages may begin to use functors at a much earlier stage of development (as measured by MLU) than do children learning English or Finnish. The significance of this is not yet known. One possible interpretation of these early functors is proposed in 4.6.

Why obligatory functors tend to be absent in early child speech is not well understood. Several possibilities have been suggested. Functors are low-information words compared to contentives, and, if omitted, can usually be filled in by the listener. The omission of functors, therefore, results in utterances which are maximally informative for their length. It is conceivable that children omit functors because they are operating under a constraint on sentence length and want to convey the most information possible (McNeill, 1966b). However, maximally informative sentences may result by coincidence from other factors. Brown and Bellugi (1964) outline some possibilities. For example, children may retain content words like nouns, verbs, and adjectives because these, unlike functors, are reference-making words and are often taught and practiced one at a time. In addition, stress usually falls on content words rather than on functors in adult speech, and children may therefore somehow overlook functors. This stress difference is as true of adult Finnish as of English. The initial absence of functors from children's speech and the developmental sequence in which they emerge are aspects of language acquisition which require more study.

To summarize, there is a striking similarity between the Finnish and the American children on most quantitative measurements of the characteristics of their speech samples. Differences, where they occur, seem to be as great among children learning the same language as across languages. The Finnish and the American children appear to have been approaching the language learning task with similar propensities insofar as these are tapped by quantitative measures. In the next chapter, we will turn to a closer inspection of some of the qualitative features of child speech to see whether the pivot grammar is an adequate way to represent the early linguistic knowledge of children learning English, Finnish, and other languages.

3   *The pivot grammar approach*

Prior to the early 1960s, studies of child language typically dealt with such topics as vocabulary growth and proportion of words in various traditionally defined grammatical classes (see McCarthy, 1954, for a review). These studies analyzed child speech with categories developed to describe the adult language rather than approaching the data without preconceptions to determine whether other concepts might not be more appropriate. One result of the recent influence of linguistic theory upon the study of language acquisition is that investigators have begun to look at children's utterances somewhat as though they had been produced by speakers of an unknown language. An important step in a grammatical analysis leading to grammar writing is to discover the syntactic classes of a language. Syntactic classes are defined as groups of words the members of which share privileges of occurrence with each other and have different privileges of occurrence from words in other classes. Grammar writing involves in part the specification of rules for permissible arrangements of such classes in sentences. The syntactic classes of a language can be discovered through a distributional analysis of the privileges of occurrence of words in a corpus of utterances (Harris, 1951). Such an analysis is contentless, taking into account only the form and arrangement of words and ignoring the semantic or syntactic meanings of the utterances in which they occur.

In doing distributional analyses to discover what syntactic classes children, in fact, use, if these differ from those of adults, three sets of investigators working independently on children learning English discovered some similar phenomena (Braine, 1963; Brown and Fraser, 1963; Miller and Ervin, 1964). Common features of their findings have been summarized and discussed in the literature as the 'pivot' and 'open' class distinction. This distinction has been considered one of the few well-substantiated characteristics of early child speech in English and has been proposed as a possible universal of language acquisition (Slobin, 1966c, 1968).

At least two hypotheses about what would cause children to impose a pivot–open classification on words in their vocabulary have been advanced, both of which appeal to the child's innate knowledge of linguistic universals (McNeill, 1966*a*, 1966*b*, 1970). The need for such hypotheses depends upon whether the pivot–open model really provides an accurate account of early child speech. This basic issue requires some re-examination. Careful analysis of the original literature upon which the model is based suggests that much simplification has taken place in subsequent discussions of the pivot–open class distinction. Data from different children collected by different investigators have sometimes been collapsed together, and descriptions initially intended to apply to only one or two children have been extended as though they applied to all the children studied. This has obscured many of the characteristics of the original data, allowing some important aspects of them to be forgotten and others distorted.

Before we look at data from other languages for confirmation of the hypothesis that the pivot–open distinction is universal in early child speech, we must be clear about the characteristics of the model we are testing in order to know what would constitute proof. Deciding whether the model represents the early linguistic knowledge of English-speaking children accurately is an essential first step. If it does not, then we must think of new ways to characterize child speech which will allow us to make more insightful comparisons between the speech of children learning English and those learning other languages.

3.1 Definition of the pivot grammar

Several summaries of the characteristics of pivot and open classes appear in the literature. Slobin gives the following description:

For almost all children for whom sufficient data are available, the earliest stage of two-word utterances can be characterized by the definite structure called 'pivotal constructions' by Braine (1963). Even with a fairly small diary corpus one can, on distributional grounds, separate two classes of words occurring in two-word utterances. There is a small class of what have been called 'pivot-words' by Braine or 'operators' by Miller and Ervin (1964), and a large, open class of words, many of which were previously one-word utterances. For example, a child may say things like *bandage on*, *blanket on*, *fix on*, *take on*, and many other sentences of this type. The word *on* is a sort of 'pivot' here – it is always in the second position, and a large collection of words can be attached to it. The child may also say things like *allgone shoe*, *allgone outside*, and *allgone pacifier*. In this case one can say that there is a pivot in first position – *allgone* – which is followed by a large class of words in the child's speech. On distributional grounds, then, it seems that one of the classes is small and contains words of high frequency in the child's speech. The membership of this class is stable and fairly fixed; these words can be called pivots because other words can be attached to them. A pivot-word may be the first or the second member of a two-word sentence – but whichever it is, its position is generally fixed. The membership of the pivot class expands slowly – that is, few pivots enter each month. The other class is large, open, and contains all the words not in the pivot class. All of the words in this open class also occur as single-word utterances, but some of the pivots never do (1966c, pp. 12–13).

Not all early utterances consist of combinations of a pivot and an open class word. Two open class words can also enter into construction, and these, unlike pivots, do not have fixed position with respect to each other.

McNeill's description of the pivot and open classes is similar to Slobin's but he adds that pivots never occur as single-word utterances and do not combine with each other in two-word constructions, even when they come from pivot classes which occupy complementary sentence positions (1966b, p. 23, 1970, pp. 1076–7). He sees these two features as the most compelling argument that the pivot–open distinction is really a grammatical system: 'It is impossible to think of such a development as not reflecting a restriction on the use of words – that is, as not reflecting a grammatical system of some kind. In fact, the pivot–open distinction is a reflection of the children's most primitive grammar' (1970, p. 1078).

According to these descriptions, a distributional analysis done on a corpus of utterances from the earliest stage of word combination reveals that all the words used in construction can be divided into two or three syntactic classes. These include one or two pivot classes (depending on whether the child has only a first or a last position pivot class or both) and an open class. The words in each class are different for different children, but the privileges of occurrence of the classes themselves are the same across children. The pivot class or classes are small and the words in them occur more frequently than words in the open class. Pivots have fixed position and can occur only in combination with open class words, while open class words can stand alone or combine with each other in any order in addition to combining with pivots.

From these characterizations of the pivot and open classes, it follows that the early syntactic knowledge of children can be represented by a grammar which generates their utterances with rules concatenating pivot and open classes according to their distinct privileges of occurrence. Following these rules results in the following 'permissible' sequences (McNeill, 1970, p. 1077):

$$P_1 + O$$
$$O + P_2$$
$$O + O$$
$$O$$

The grammar does not generate P or $P + P$ strings, since these are considered ill-formed according to the child's own system.

Students of language acquisition have sometimes referred to words which a child uses with greater-than-average frequency and in fixed position as 'pivots', and the utterances in which they appear as 'pivot constructions', apparently without considering whether these words and constructions actually conform to the formal criteria which the terms 'pivot' and 'pivot construction' imply. When used in this way, the concept of 'pivot' has little more relevance to child speech than to adult speech. Adult constructions like 'the' + Noun could also be considered pivotal in this sense, since 'the' occurs with very high frequency and always precedes nouns, but little insight into the speaker's knowledge of language structure is gained by such an interpretation. The important issue is not whether children have constructions of this type in their early speech, but whether a pivot *grammar* is an accurate representation of their linguistic knowledge. The rules of the pivot grammar should exhaustively or almost exhaustively account for the utterances found in a speech corpus. If they cannot do so, or if the characteristic privileges of occurrence claimed for pivot and open classes are often violated in actual linguistic behavior, the structure of the pivot grammar collapses and we are left with a rule no stronger than Sentence → (Word) + Word, which is no grammar at all. These cautions must be kept in mind in evaluating the usefulness of the concepts of 'pivot class' and 'open class'.

3.2 Adequacy of the pivot–open model: review of the original literature

Let us turn now to the data of the original studies by Brown and Fraser, Miller and Ervin, and Braine, to see to what extent the pivot model as it is described in the literature is congruent with the facts. The discussion is divided into three parts:

1. Characteristics of the pivot class.
2. Characteristics of the open class.
3. At what stage does the pivot grammar operate?

After this analysis of the original studies, we shall look first at more recent evidence from English-speaking children and then at alternate interpretations of the 'pivot look' of early child speech before examining data from other languages to test the hypothesis that the pivot–open distinction occurs universally in early linguistic development.

3.2.1 Characteristics of the pivot class. Some of the problems involved in identifying pivot and open class words are suggested by a dialogue which took place in a conference on 'Language Development in Children' (Smith, Miller, 1966, p. 94):

SLOBIN: One of Braine's children has the statement 'want do', which Braine classifies as pivot + open. But the same child also uses 'do' as a pivot in utterances like 'baby do', 'daddy do', and so on.

McNEILL: That's obviously the outcome of Braine's decision to classify 'do' as both a pivot and open word.

FODOR: It is required by the fact that you can't have two pivots in the same sentence. You can't have both 'want' and 'do' as pivots.

McNEILL: Braine could have called 'do' an open-class word throughout.

McNeill felt that perhaps 'do' should have been called an open class word because it lacked what in his view is an essential property of pivots: never occurring in combination with other pivots. But 'do' in Braine's data had other characteristics of a pivot: fixed position and high frequency. Identifying pivot words involves satisfying several conditions at once: fixed position, high frequency, never occurring alone, and never occurring with another pivot. By insisting on most or all of these criteria, one may exclude from the pivot class words which share many characteristics with words defined as pivots and few with open class words. All these properties do not characterize all the words identified as pivots or their equivalents in the original literature. Evidently they have come to be considered the essential features of pivots because the descriptions given by one researcher have sometimes been added to those given by another, whose data may have been somewhat different. The result is a composite which fits no one's data completely. Let us examine some of these criteria separately to see how well they are motivated by the data.

3.2.1.1   Do pivots have fixed position?

Fixed position has been the single most important defining property of pivots as they are discussed in the literature. Braine especially was unwilling to call any word without this characteristic a pivot. However, words which do not have fixed position but which resemble pivots in other respects do occur in children's speech. In Braine's data, there were some words with variable position which occurred with a variety of complements in more constructions than did the words identified as pivots, for example, 'allgone', 'bye bye', and 'all done' in Andrew's corpus. Some of these were pivot words for the other children.

In Miller and Ervin's data, both of the children discussed had words identified as 'operators' (usually considered the equivalent of pivots) which did not have fixed position. Christy's class I ('this', 'this a', 'that') occurred 76 times initially and 5 times finally. Her class III ('here', 'there') occurred 9 times initially and 13 times finally. Susan's class II ('this', 'that', 'this-one') occurred 31 times initially and 9 times finally. Rather than fixed position, these classes had only position preferences of varying strengths. In the original data, then, there were many words which combined freely with a variety of other words in a large number of constructions but without fixed position.

3.2.1.2   Do pivots occur alone?

The idea that pivots do not occur as single-word utterances seems to have originated with Braine's statement that whereas all the words which appeared in a frame with a pivot could also occur alone, some of the pivots never did. Others did, however, for example, 'more' in Andrew's sample. Pivots which occurred alone also occurred with other pivots in the complementary position. These words seem to have had properties of both the pivot and the open classes, and Braine suggested that they be assigned double class membership.

Neither Miller and Ervin nor Brown and Fraser mentioned that their equivalents of pivot words did not occur as single-word utterances. Some of them clearly did. In Brown and Fraser's data, for example, Evie's pivots 'allgone', 'broken', 'fall down' and 'tired' appeared both in final position after many different noun phrases and in isolation. This is reflected in the optional and required selections in the rules given by Brown and Fraser (parentheses indicate optionality):

Utterance $\longrightarrow (C_3) + (C_2) + C_4$
$C_3 \longrightarrow$ 'a', 'the', plus human terms.
$C_2 \longrightarrow$ 'bear', 'bird', 'block', 'boat', etc.
$C_4 \longrightarrow$ 'allgone', 'broken', 'fall down', 'tired'.

It would be surprising if certain pivots in Miller and Ervin's data, like 'here' and 'there', did not occur in isolation as well as in combination with other words, since such utterances are common in the speech of many children. To insist that a pivot must be a word which never (or very rarely, compared to other words in the vocabulary) appears as a single-word utterance would be to exclude from this class many of the words identified as pivots or their equivalents in the original data.

Although not discussed in the original articles we have been considering, the noun modifier classes of Adam and Eve, children subsequently studied by Brown and Bellugi (1964), have been extensively cited as examples of pivot classes (McNeill, 1966a, 1966b, 1970). One source of the idea that pivots do not occur in isolation or in combination with each other has evidently been the fact that these modifiers did not, at least not often. However, it is a mistake to consider these true pivots. They were not isolated on the basis of distributional analyses. Rather, Brown and Bellugi's plan was to discuss the development of noun phrases, and they simply classified as modifiers all those words which occurred with nouns in a modifying relationship. The speech of Adam and Eve at this time was relatively advanced, with a mean utterance length of close to two morphemes and, for Adam, occasional utterances of up to seven morphemes long. Distributional analyses of their speech samples would have revealed not a pivot class (consisting only of noun modifiers) and an undifferentiated open class, but at least noun, verb, and modifier classes, each with characteristic privileges of occurrence. The modifiers were like pivots only in the loosest sense of the word, in that they were a smaller class than the class with which they combined (nouns), and the individual members of the class occurred more frequently, usually in initial position. Only a small proportion of all two-or-more word utterances consisted of modifiers plus nouns and could be described as 'pivot constructions' even in this loose sense. Adam and Eve had developed well beyond the point at which they might have used pivot grammars, and to identify their modifier classes with the pivots of Miller and Ervin, Braine, and Brown and Fraser is to obscure many fundamental distinctions. The fact that Adam's and Eve's modifiers did not occur in isolation or with other modifiers

3

(without a final noun) is perhaps no more surprising that that an adult's modifiers do not do so either, and does not constitute evidence that legitimately identified pivots lack these privileges of occurrence.

3.2.1.3 Do pivots occur together? The idea that pivots cannot appear together in two-word utterances is also not well substantiated by the original data. Miller and Ervin's subject Susan had 10 combinations of the operators in class II ('this', 'that', 'this-one') with the operators in class I ('on', 'off'). Braine's subject Steven, who had the pivots 'want', 'get', 'do', and 'more', among others, produced such sentences as 'want get', 'want do', and 'want more'. Andrew, who had as pivots 'more', 'down there', 'see', and 'I', produced 'more down there' and 'I see'. Braine, as we saw, proposed that words like 'get', 'more', and 'do' be classified as both pivot and open class words, and be considered open when in construction with pivots. McNeill suggested instead that they simply be classified as open in all contexts (Smith and Miller, 1966, p. 94). No matter how they are classified, the fact remains that words which have so many of the characteristics of pivots that they are considered pivots in some contexts do occur together.

To summarize, it appears that many of the pivots discussed in the original literature cannot be accurately described as words with fixed positions which do not occur alone or in combination with each other. One can insist on such a definition when identifying pivots in order to preserve the rules of the pivot grammar as they are now conceived, but this seems arbitrary and forces many words which look rather like pivots in some respects to be classified as open class words. Many interesting patterns are thereby obscured. For example, Christy's constructions containing 'here' and 'there' (Miller and Ervin's data) and Evie's constructions with 'broken', 'fall down', 'tired', and 'allgone' (Brown and Fraser's data) would have to receive the structural interpretation O+O, and would be indistinguishable from less regular and productive combinations of open class words.

3.2.2 Characteristics of the open class. The open class, as it is commonly conceived, is 'a part of speech mainly in a residual sense, and consists of the entire vocabulary except for some of the pivots' (Braine, 1963, p. 13). It is thus made up of a group of words which belong to different grammatical classes in the adult model. Whether all words which are not pivots should be considered undifferentiated is questionable. The existence of some ambiguity on this point is reflected in McNeill's statement that 'apart from the pivot–open construction, early two-word sentences can involve the juxtaposition of O, sometimes with words from a single O class and at other times with words from different classes' (1966*b*, p. 21). What we symbolize by O as a single, undifferentiated class, the members of which all have identical privileges of occurrence, we often implicitly think of as consisting of several classes. O + O might represent, for example, noun–noun, noun–verb, or verb–noun combinations. Do children in fact not distinguish at all between the various adult classes of which their open class is composed? There is evidence that they do, and that we therefore underrepresent their syntactic knowledge when we classify all non-pivot words as O and assign all combinations of these the description O + O.

Braine (1963) found that the O class of one of his subjects, Gregory, could be subdivided into substantives and verbs. One pivot, 'it', could follow only verbs. The O classes of the other two children, Braine argued, were undifferentiated. This is debatable. If O is a single, undifferentiated class, then any O should be able to combine with any P. But in Andrew's and Steven's speech, certain pivots in fact occurred only with nouns. For Andrew, these were 'hi', 'other', 'off', 'by' and 'come', or 5 out of 11 pivots. For Steven, they were 'get', 'see', 'whoa', 'more', 'that', and 'here', or 6 out of 11. Verbs and adjectives as well as nouns did occur with other pivots. Braine's argument that words in Andrew's and Steven's O classes were undifferentiated and had identical privileges of occurrence was based on the observation that some of their non-pivot words occurred in identical linguistic contexts. In Andrew's corpus, for example, the non-pivot words 'fix' and 'wet' both occurred with the pivots 'all' and 'no'. Since it is unreasonable to insist that all O words appear with exactly the same set of pivots in a small sample before identical privileges of occurrence can be assumed, Braine suggested that O words which have a slight overlap of contexts be regarded as potentially having a complete overlap. We must expect actual overlap to be slight, he claimed, because in theory the set of O words that occurs with a given pivot is a random sample from the whole class of O words, which consists of at least 250 members. If the words which appear with given pivots are indeed a random sample of all non-pivot words, the odds are very great against so many of Andrew's and Steven's pivots occurring exclusively with words classified as nouns in adult English. It is more likely that these children distinguished between noun and non-noun words at least in some contexts, and that the rules of their grammars specified that certain pivots be combined only with nouns. If this were not the case, then Andrew and Steven should sometimes have produced such bizarre combinations of P and O as '*hi* shut', 'shut *by*', 'broke *come*', 'through *off*', and '*whoa* high' (pivot word italicized). Nothing like these occurred in the samples and they seem extremely unlikely because it is almost impossible to imagine what a child might mean by them. In contrast, it is easy to interpret the quaint but actually occurring utterances like 'byebye dirty', 'no down', and 'allgone lettuce' which Braine points to as evidence that strangeness to adult ears is no criterion by which to judge the probability of children's utterances.

Miller and Ervin observe that 'the difference between operator [pivot] and non-operator classes is relative rather than absolute. The non-operator words tend to be grouped into large classes but the division between the classes is sometimes difficult to make' (1964, p. 22). They found that they could not group the vocabulary items remaining after Susan's operators were selected out into a single, undifferentiated class. Certain patterns suggested that at least nouns, verbs, and possibly adjectives should be distinguished. The two-class model was also inappropriate for Christy. Words identified as operators in her corpus preceded only nouns and adjectives, with only two exceptions. This was not the entire remaining vocabulary, as it should have been if the simple pivot–open distinction were accurate. Verbs, prepositions, and adverbs also occurred, combining with each other and with nouns.

In summary, dividing words in children's vocabularies into pivot and open classes is much more difficult than has usually been thought; in many cases, it may be entirely impossible if we insist on using for classification all the commonly mentioned definitional criteria. The facts of early child speech are more complex than the pivot–open model indicates. In the speech of the children from whom the model was originally drawn there were high frequency words with fixed position, high frequency words without fixed position, words of either type which appeared alone or did not appear alone, and words with any of the above characteristics which occurred in combination with each other or never in combination with each other. Lower frequency words combined with each other or the above-mentioned words in a number of ways. To impose a pivot–open classification on these words is to allow the definitions of pivot and open classes to control how data are classified rather than permitting the data themselves to suggest what classifications are necessary. This is ironic, since the original studies from which the concepts were derived were motivated precisely by the desire to analyze child speech without preconceived categories.

3.2.3 At what stage does the pivot grammar operate? The pivot grammar is usually described as representing children's syntactic knowledge during the 'earliest stage' of grammatical development. How early is 'early' and for how long does it continue? The lower limit is easy to set, since the child's knowledge of grammatical structure, as revealed through his production, cannot be studied until he begins to put two words or morphemes together. The upper limit is more elusive. There has been a tendency to treat young children's utterances as comparable, all falling into the category of 'early child speech', even when the MLU values of the individual speech samples from which they are taken range from only a little over one (the start of word combining) to up to two or more morphemes. The amount of time and grammatical development required to raise average utterance length from one to two morphemes should not be discounted. By the time average utterance length is two morphemes, the child is also capable of programming sentences five or six morphemes long (Brown, unpublished materials), an accomplishment far beyond his reach at the initial stage of word combination.

Of the children studied in the three articles we have been considering (Braine, 1963; Brown and Fraser, 1963; Miller and Ervin, 1964), only Braine's were truly at the beginning of grammatical development. He started to follow them before any two-word combinations at all had been observed. First combinations occurred at 19 and 20 months. Brown and Fraser's subject Evie was considerably more advanced. She was 25½ months old and her MLU was 2.6. Miller and Ervin's subjects (ages 21–24 months and 24–27 months) were probably also more advanced than Braine's, since they were already producing occasional five-morpheme strings such as 'Miller take off shoe sock', 'Liz her hat back on', and 'Susan blue one sweater on'. In Braine's data from the first months of word combination, two-thirds to three-fourths of the total number of combination types observed were pivot constructions. Not nearly as large a proportion of Miller and Ervin's subjects' combinations could be described as pivotal, although estimates exactly comparable to Braine's cannot be made. Miller and Ervin give figures for construction tokens rather than types (see 2.5 for the distinction), and do not mention the total number of combinations in the samples. Only two-word combinations were analyzed, and some of these were excluded for various reasons. Constructions with operators accounted for approximately 101 of 240 two-word combinations in Susan's sample, and about 123 of 210 in Christy's; the rest of the two-word constructions and all the longer sentences should be added to the total number of constructions to arrive at the exact proportions.

Miller and Ervin's and Brown and Fraser's subjects had perhaps entered a 'second phase' of development outlined by Braine. New word combinations in the speech of his three subjects increased rather slowly for four or five months as new pivots were sequentially put to use. At the fifth or sixth month, the rate of producing new combinations accelerated, due, Braine noted, to the increased tendency to combine open class words. The majority of constructions produced by Brown and Fraser's and Miller and Ervin's subjects were non-pivotal when the studies began, but perhaps pivot constructions had predominated earlier.

Evidently, then, the children studied by Braine, by Miller and Ervin, and by Brown and Fraser were at different developmental stages, since the subjects of the latter two pairs of investigators were producing more non-pivotal constructions and more three-, four-, and five-word strings than were Braine's. Any two-word construction which is not P+O or O+P can be classified as O+O within the framework of the pivot grammar, but when these utterances begin to outnumber pivot constructions, such a classification becomes increasingly inadequate. A more rigorous analysis reveals differentiation of the O class and regularities in O+O strings which a representation of children's syntactic knowledge should account for. Even if a pivot grammar could generate most utterances at the very beginning of word combination, it is not a very revealing model for later developments which take place while average utterance length is still under two morphemes.

3.3   Evidence from other English-speaking children

The foregoing analysis of the original literature from which the concept of the pivot grammar was derived indicates that oversimplification and overgeneralization has led to a model of early child speech which is a poor fit with the data from most of the individual children studied. However, many of these children were probably more advanced linguistically than has been thought. Only the children in Braine's study were observed from the very beginning of word combination. The pivot grammar – or at least a modified version of it – seems to account somewhat better for Braine's data than for the data from the more advanced children. Perhaps, then, the pivot–open model is applicable only to children who are in the very earliest stages of grammatical development, when mean utterance length is only slightly over 1.00. The achievement of a mean utterance length of, let us say, 1.40 or 1.50 entails an increase in grammatical complexity which the pivot grammar is no longer adequate to represent.

Some data which will help us explore this possibility are now available. Speech samples from four American children with mean utterance lengths of under 1.50 will be considered: the investigator's subject, Kendall, and Bloom's (1970) three subjects, Kathryn, Gia, and Eric.

3.3.1 Kendall. Kendall was observed in an effort to obtain a speech sample from a child who was just beginning to make constructions. At the time she was first observed, at age 22 months, 3 weeks, her parents were uncertain whether she was yet combining words in a meaningful, nonaccidental way. Careful attention revealed that such combinations occurred but were still infrequent. Mean utterance length was 1.10. Kendall's speech was followed almost continuously for over two full days from morning until bedtime. Notes were taken by hand because of the extremely low output of constructions. Many single-word utterances were recorded, but notes were mainly restricted to constructions after vocabulary had been well sampled. Her speech was very clear and slow, which facilitated accurate note-taking. A sample of 102 nonimitated construction types (136 tokens) was compiled in this way. These are listed with glosses or notes on the nonlinguistic context in Appendix B.

Since it is impossible to tell whether a word has fixed position unless it occurs in at least several different construction types, and since pivots by definition should occur more often than individual open class words, we will look for pivots among the words Kendall used most often in construction. These were 'Kendall', 'Mommy', 'Daddy', 'house', 'doggie', 'no', 'Kimmy', and 'walk'. Constructions in which these occurred (excluding vocative uses) are presented in Table 3 where a summary of their distribution in first and last position is also given.

TABLE 3. *Kendall, MLU 1.10: high frequency words in construction*

Initial position	Final position
Kendall sit	
Kendall read	
Kendall walk	
Kendall bounce	
Kendall B.M.	
Kendall leave (from 'leaves', noun)	
Kendall chair	
Kendall house	
Kendall foot	
Kendall hurt	
Daddy sit	in Daddy
Daddy hide	
Daddy write	
Daddy walk	
Daddy teeth	
Dad sock	
Daddy here	
Daddy book	
Daddy pat	
Mommy read	find Mommy
Mommy tie-it[a]	inna Mommy
Mommy spider	
Mommy curly	
Mommy bathroom	
Mommy in	
no, Mommy..hand[b]	
	pig house
	go house
	Kendall house
	Melissa house
	Bill house
	Kimmy house
	animal house
	doggie..house
doggie bye	slipper doggie
doggie house	animal dog
doggie slipper	back doggie
doggie..sleepy	
no, self	
no, sit	
no, carry	
no, 'way	
no, cereal	
no, Mommy	
no more	

TABLE 3 *(cont.)*

Initial position	Final position
Kimmy read	
Kimmy bite	
Kimmy B.M.	
Kimmy house	
Kimmy Pam	
Kimmy girl	
walk self	Kendall walk
	Daddy walk
	horse walk
	Melissa walk
	more walk

	Initial	Final	Total
Kendall	10	0	10
Daddy	9	1	10
Mommy	7	2	9
house	0	8	8
doggie	4	3	7
no	7	0	7
Kimmy	6	0	6
walk	1	5	6

[a] 'Tie-it' was probably not analyzed into two morphemes, since 'tie' was always followed by 'it' and never occurred with any other direct object.

[b] Dots indicate a pause without sentence-final intonation contour. (See Glossary for explanation of all notational symbols.)

Most of these words had strong position preferences, but only four occurred exclusively in one position. All of them were among the most frequent of Kendall's single-word utterances, so they cannot be considered pivots according to the definition given by McNeill (1966b). With the exception of 'no' and perhaps 'walk', Kendall's high-frequency words are quite different semantically from most of the pivots described by Brown and Fraser, Braine, and Miller and Ervin, which include 'more', 'off', 'on', 'here', 'there', 'that', 'this', 'allgone', 'want', 'come', 'see', 'fall down', 'all', 'big', 'pretty', 'broken', and a few others. Six of the eight are nouns in adult English, and four of these are the proper names of people important in Kendall's life. Investigators seem to have been reluctant to split nouns of the adult language into pivot and non-pivot classes even when privileges of occurrence warrant it. In the data from Braine's subject Steven, there are three nouns which occurred five or more times, always in final position and with an assortment of complements:

it ball	it doll	it truck
get ball	get doll	there truck
see ball	see doll	there daddy truck
more ball	there doll	there momma truck
there ball	that doll	that truck
	here doll	here truck

These fit the distributional criteria by which Braine identified pivots better than some of the words he called pivots. However, they were considered members of the open class and, like other nouns, could theoretically occur in first position as well as second.

Although 'no' looks semantically rather like some of the pivots described in the original literature, Kendall used it only anaphorically, with the typical adult intonation contour, as in 'no, self' ('Leave me alone, I want to do it myself') and 'no, 'way' (rejecting food which was offered). It was thus not really in construction with the word which followed it and so was grammatically unlike 'no' in constructions like 'no cracker' ('there aren't any crackers' or 'I don't want a cracker') or 'no walk' ('I don't want to walk'), which also occur in the speech of children.

Kendall had a few words which have been identified as pivots for other children, 'that—', 'more—', and '—away', but these were of low frequency in construction and also occurred as single-word utterances.

The position preferences of Kendall's high frequency words seem to be related to certain semantic regularities in her speech. Animate nouns such as 'Kendall', 'Mommy', and 'Daddy' were used mainly as names for possessors ('Daddy book') and as subjects ('Kendall read'). Nouns in these roles were almost always sentence-initial. Inanimate nouns such as 'house' were used to name objects possessed ('Bill house'), locations ('go house'), and direct objects ('close door'), and were usually sentence-final. Verbs occurred mainly with subjects or direct objects. Since combinations with subjects were much more frequent than those with direct objects, verbs occurred most often in final position ('Kendall walk').

Kendall's fairly consistent use of appropriate word orders suggests that she had learned something about the syntactic expression of possession and location and the relationships of subjects and direct objects to verbs.[1] An adequate grammar should be able to represent this knowledge. A pivot grammar cannot. The pivot approach is also inappropriate for Kendall because writing such a grammar would involve classifying nouns like 'Kendall', 'Mommy', 'Daddy', and 'Kimmy' as pivots and those like 'Bill' and 'lady' as open class words, even though these all seem to have played identical syntactic roles and probably had the same privileges of occurrence. This is because the former occurred in many more constructions than the latter and we can therefore detect their strong preference for initial position. If all words with the same privileges of occurrence as 'Kendall', 'Mommy', and so on, were put into the same class, this would cease to be a pivot class which would also include the first-position pivot 'no', and would simply become a collection of all the animate nouns in Kendall's vocabulary. The pivot–open model simply cannot be stretched to fit. The interesting aspects of Kendall's early syntax lie elsewhere. Here, then, is a child who from the very earliest stage of syntactic development did not employ a pivot grammar.

3.3.2 Bloom's subjects. Bloom (1970) investigated the speech of three children, Kathryn, Gia, and Eric, all of whom had mean utterance lengths well below 1.50. She considered the grammars she wrote for Eric pivotal because they were essentially linear and did not provide for hierarchical relationships of sentence constituents. However, they are not pivot grammars in the sense we have been discussing, since the syntactic classes were not determined on the basis of distributional analyses of privileges of occurrence and the rules do not conform to the two-class pivot–open model. The rules (slightly simplified) are

$$S \rightarrow \begin{Bmatrix} P \\ V \end{Bmatrix} N \text{ at MLU 1.19 and } S_1 \rightarrow (P) \begin{Bmatrix} NP \\ V\ (N) \end{Bmatrix}$$

$$S_2 \rightarrow (N)\ (V) \text{ at MLU 1.42.}$$

There is no undifferentiated open class all the members of which enter into construction with pivots. Only nouns follow pivots at the earlier stage, and neither nouns nor verbs have freedom of word order when combining with each other. Thus, Eric's non-pivot words cannot be identified with the open class as it is described in the literature.

Bloom based a compelling argument against the adequacy of pivot grammars on the characteristics of Kathryn's and Gia's speech. The

---

[1] An alternative interpretation of the grammatical functions of subject and direct object as semantic concepts like 'agent' and 'object acted upon' will be considered in Chapter 6.

girls used some words in fixed position with a variety of complements, but these appeared in a relatively small proportion of the total number of constructions. For example, Kathryn's six pivot-like words, 'this', 'that(s)', 'more', ''nother', 'hi', and 'no' occurred in only 69 of 397 construction tokens, or 17 per cent. Gia had a few pivot-like constructions with words like 'more' and 'hi', but her most frequent patterns involved the juxtaposition of nouns and verbs. In the speech of both children, certain words like 'Mommy', 'baby', 'Kathryn', 'raisin', and 'make' occurred even more often than 'pivots' like 'more' and ''nother', and some of these had relatively fixed positions (for example, 'Mommy' occurred initially 29 out of 32 times in Kathryn's sample). Bloom did not consider these to be pivots, however, because the constructions they entered into seemed to express a large number of different grammatical relationships. For example, the children's numerous noun–noun combinations could be interpreted as manifesting such diverse relationships as possessor–object possessed, object located–location, modifier–object modified, subject–object, and conjunction. The kind of analysis on which a pivot grammar is based does not take into account the grammatical or semantic meanings of words in utterances, and the grammar cannot represent the hierarchical organization of sentence constituents or the different syntactic relationships holding between these constituents. All noun–noun strings would most likely be represented as O + O, a linear sequence with no internal structure or restrictions on word order. Bloom felt that 'describing sentences in terms of relative frequencies and patterns of co-occurrence of constituents provides an account of language acquisition which is too closely tied to the surface of sentences to allow a meaningful analysis of the development of grammatical structure' (1968, p. 395). Unlike the pivot–open model, the transformational generative approach to grammar writing adopted by Bloom allows sentential elements to be derived from several different sets of underlying constituents by reference to which the correct syntactic and semantic interpretation can be assigned.

Bloom also objected to the pivot grammar because it has no relationship to the grammar of the language as it is spoken by adults, and it is difficult to account for a child's transition from one to the other. 'The acquisition model that results is fragmented – a mosaic view which consists of a composite of *surface descriptions* which are not interrelated' (Bloom, 1968, p. 396).

Bloom observed that Eric's approach to language learning was different from that of Kathryn and Gia. She offered an interpretation of this difference based on two structurally and functionally distinct aspects of language. Nouns and verbs, she noted, can have different grammatical meanings in different utterances. For example, 'Mommy' is the subject of the sentence in 'Mommy hit' and the direct object of the verb in 'hit Mommy'. Forms like 'no', 'more', ''nother', and 'hi', in contrast, have relatively constant semantic meanings and syntactic functions when combined with other words. Bloom called these 'syntactic operators' or 'syntactic markers'. All three children studied by Bloom had a small number of high frequency words of both types. However, most of Kathryn's and Gia's high frequency words were nouns and verbs belonging to the first category, and their most productive construction patterns involved the juxtaposition of these in utterances expressing a variety of grammatical relationships. In contrast, Eric initially combined these forms only in constructions expressing the verb–object relationship, and his most frequent construction patterns involved rotating different nouns and verbs through fixed frames in which they were operated on in a fairly constant way by syntactic markers like 'no more'. Bloom suggested that children may use different strategies in learning language, some mainly searching out frames in which a syntactic marker applies a constant semantic intent to the forms with which it occurs, and others learning the different syntactic and semantic effects of juxtaposing words in various orders and combinations. She cautioned that these should not be considered mutually exclusive approaches, however, since most children's grammars probably incorporate elements of both.

Brown (1970, in press), drawing upon both Bloom (1970) and Schlesinger (1971), has elaborated somewhat upon the functional and semantic differences between sentences which involve syntactic markers like 'no' or 'more' and those which combine forms like nouns and verbs in variable grammatical relationships. He calls the former 'operations of reference' and the latter 'relations'. Operations of reference are utterance sets such that each is defined by a constant term appearing in conjunction with a variety of other words. Brown summarizes the common semantic functions of operations of reference among the English-speaking children who have been studied as:

1. *Nomination:* 'that', 'this', 'it', 'there', 'here', and 'see', plus nouns, verbs, adjectives, etc. Used deictically as the child points to or otherwise singles out something for attention.

2. *Notice:* 'hi' plus nouns. Not used as a greeting so much as simply a 'taking notice' of the presence of an object.

3. *Recurrence:* 'more' or ''nother' plus nouns, verbs, adjectives, etc. Used to request an additional serving or to remark on the recurrence or repetition of objects and events.

4. *Nonexistence:* 'allgone', 'no', or 'no more' plus nouns, verbs, adjectives, etc. A previously existing or somehow expected referent does not appear.

Brown suggests that constructions with syntactic operators in fixed frames may predominate early in grammatical development, with relational constructions gradually increasing in frequency. This could account, he notes, for the 'pivot look' of some early speech samples. Kendall's early speech demonstrates that grammatical development does not always follow this sequence, however, since syntactic operators were much less frequent in her earliest constructions than nouns, verbs, and other words which played variable grammatical roles.

In the speech of several of the children in the studies upon which the pivot–open model was based, most of the high frequency words with fixed position were syntactic operators like 'on', 'off', 'more', 'allgone', and 'there'. This seems to have led to both the expectation and the desire that pivots operate in a constant way on the words with which they combine. It is easy to accept the idea that the first division a child makes in classifying the words in his vocabulary is between syntactic operators with constant function and the set of lexical items upon which they can operate. The desire that pivots be functionally as well as distributionally different from open class words has perhaps caused semantic considerations to influence the identification of pivots even when the analysis is said to be based strictly on the superficial form and arrangement of words in sentences. Braine, as we saw, classified three nouns in Steven's speech as open class words even though they fit the distributional criteria by which he identified pivots better than some of the words classified as pivots. Probably this was because these nouns, unlike the other high frequency words with fixed position, had variable grammatical functions in sentences.

The pivot–open model, as it is formally defined, ignores the distinction between words which function as syntactic operators and words which combine with each other in a variety of grammatical relationships. Distributional analysis is not supposed to take syntactic or semantic meaning into account. The set of words in a child's vocabulary which can be isolated as 'pivots' because they have fixed position and occur with a large number of complements is thus not necessarily composed only of words which have constant syntactic functions. Syntactic operators and words which play a variety of grammatical roles can both become members of either the pivot or the open class, since the classificational criteria used to separate pivot words from open class words do not distinguish between them. The majority of Kendall's, Kathryn's, and Gia's most frequent words, even those with relatively fixed position, were not syntactic operators. It is hard to imagine what might lead a child to put animate nouns like 'Kendall' and 'Mommy' into the same class as a syntactic operator like 'no', while placing other animate nouns like 'Bill' and 'Pam' into another class, along with other syntactic operators like 'more'. This forces us to realize that the kind of distributional analysis done to discover a child's pivot and open classes cannot be counted on to divide words into categories which are not only distributionally but also functionally distinct.

Even when semantic and syntactic meaning is taken into consideration, the distinction between syntactic operators and other words in a child's vocabulary is not always clear-cut. Words which are operators in some contexts, like Braine's subject Steven's 'more' in 'more ball', function like nouns in others: 'want more'. Verbs often occur in utterances expressing different grammatical relations, like Kendall's 'sit' and 'walk' in 'Kendall sit', 'sit lap', 'Mommy walk', and 'walk self', but sometimes they seem more like operators, like Steven's 'get' and 'want', which always preceded words functioning as direct objects.

Identifying a child's first syntactic classes is extremely difficult. The members of a class should share privileges of occurrence which are different from those of words in other classes, but so far, distributional analysis of privileges of occurrence has not enabled us to distinguish between children's classes in a way which is either accurate or functionally meaningful.

3.4 Evidence from other languages

An analysis of the applicability of the pivot–open model of early child speech to English-speaking children has revealed that the model does not adequately represent the data either from the children on whose speech it was based or from other children. The children's most common construction patterns were similar in many respects, however, and some of these characteristics may be universal in early linguistic development even if the pivot grammar is not. Let us turn now to data from children learning other languages to see how closely their speech conforms to the pivot–open model, and, if the fit is poor, to determine whether deviations from the model are similar across children. In particular, we will consider whether the distinction between 'operations of reference' and 'relational' sentences is useful in describing the speech of non-English-speaking children, and whether the syntactic operators performing 'operations of reference' have similar semantic functions across languages.

3.4.1 Diary studies. An examination of diary studies led Slobin (1966a, 1966c) to suggest that Russian, German, Bulgarian, French, Japanese, and Polish-speaking children make an early division between pivot and open classes. However, diaries are selective in unknown ways, and it is difficult or impossible to investigate with them questions of word frequency, the extent to which the position of given words was fixed, and what types of sequences never or rarely occurred. They therefore cannot be relied on to help us make the distinction we are concerned with between the mere presence of pivot-like constructions and the applicability of a pivot grammar, the rules of which should exhaustively or almost exhaustively account for a child's utterances. Tape-recorded speech samples are a more dependable source of data because they are not selectively responsive to the investigator's interests and include long sequences of consecutive utterances which can be used in frequency counts.

Despite their drawbacks, however, diary studies can give us an idea of the kinds of utterances common in the speech of non-English-speaking children. Slobin (1966c) has identified certain utterances from English, German, and Russian-speaking children as pivotal and classified them according to their semantic characteristics. He outlines the following categories of pivot function:

1. *Modify, qualify:* Words like 'pretty—', 'my—', 'allgone—', 'all—', 'good—', and their translation equivalents.
2. *Locate, name:* 'here—', 'there—', 'see—', 'it—', 'that—', etc.
3. *Describe act:* '—away', '—on', '—off', '—it', '—do', '—walk', '—sleep', etc.
4. *Demand, desire:* 'more—', 'give—', 'want—', 'please—'.
5. *Negate:* 'no—', 'not—', 'don't—'.
6. *Call, salute:* 'hi—', 'bye-bye—', 'night-night—'.

Some of these functions are similar to those of the 'operations of reference' identified by Brown (1970, in press). The *locate, name* category seems identical to Brown's 'nomination'. *Negate* is similar to Brown's 'nonexistence', although Brown would also include 'allgone' and possibly 'away' in this category. *Call, salute* is similar to 'notice'. Other pivots mentioned by Slobin would be classified by Brown as 'relational' terms rather than as operations of reference: for example, 'want', 'walk', 'sleep', and 'do'. In the speech of some children, these may function more like syntactic operators than like relational terms because the grammatical relationship that holds between them and the words with which they are combined is always the same.

The kinds of constructions which are common in the early speech of German, Russian, and American children seem remarkably similar, so we may find them among children learning still other languages.

3.4.2　Finnish. Data from Seppo and Rina will help us decide whether the pivot–open model provides an appropriate representation of the early syntactic knowledge of children acquiring Finnish. The first and second Seppo samples (MLUs 1.42 and 1.81), data from the tapes between these, and the Rina sample (MLU 1.83) are used in this analysis. Unfortunately, no data are available from the very earliest stage of word combination, but we should be able to get an idea of whether pivot grammars were operating or had ever operated and to determine the characteristics of words which occurred especially frequently.

3.4.2.1　Seppo, MLU 1.42. In the earliest Seppo sample, there are 110 different nonimitated constructions (excluding some utterances consisting of a single repeated word). Let us look at two-word combinations to see if pivot and open classes can be distinguished. There are 87 utterance types of these. In analyzing Kendall's sample, we noted that it is appropriate to look for pivots among words which occur in the most different construction types, since pivots are supposed to occur with high frequency relative to other words and since it is impossible to tell if a word has fixed position unless it appears in several utterances. In Seppo's sample, there are seven words which occurred in five or more different constructions. Table 4 lists the constructions containing them and summarizes their distribution in first and last position.

4

TABLE 4. *Seppo, MLU 1.42: high frequency words in construction*

Initial position		Final position	
pois api⟨na⟩	'away monkey'[a]	*takki pois*	'coat off'
pois talli	'away garage'	*mamma pois*	'"food" away'
pois..pamma	'away.."closed"'[a]	*hauva pois*	'doggie away'
		kissa pois	'cat away'
		kirja..pois	'book..away'
		tipu pois	'chick away'
		nöf pois	'"pig" away'
		lauta⟨nen⟩..pois	'plate..away'[a]
		ammu pois	'moo-cow away'
		tuossa pois	'there away'
tipu..lentää	'chick..flies'	*laulaa tipu*	'sings chick'
tipu katsoo	'chick watches'		
tipu..ui	'chick..swims'		
tipu kuti⟨ttaa⟩	'chick tickles'[a]		
tipu mamma	'chick "food"'		
tipu kenkä	'chick shoe'		
tipu pois	'chick away'		
tipu..tuossa	'chick..there'		
bmbm kovaa	'"car" fast'	*pamma bmbm*	'"closed" "car"'
bmbm..käy	'"car"..goes'	*rikki..bmbm*	'broken.."car"'
		ajaa bmbm	'drives "car"'
		laittaa..bmbm	'puts.."car"'
		talli..bmbm	'garage.."car"'
		kovaa kovaa kovaa kovaa..bmbm	'fast fast fast fast.. "car"'
tuossa ammu	'there moo-cow'	*pipi tuossa*	'sore there'
tuossa..tuf tuf	'there.."train"'	*tipu..tuossa*	'chick..there'
tuossa pois	'there away'		
tuossa kenkä	'there shoe'		
täti..vauva	'lady..baby'	*hauva..tadi(n)*	'doggie..lady('s)'[a]
täti auto	'aunt car'	*on tädi*	'is aunt'
täti kahvi	'aunt coffee'		
täti mamma	'lady "food"'		
pamma rikki rikki	'"closed" broken broken'	*kovaa..pam*	'fast.."closed"'
pamma bmbm	'"closed" "car"'	*ajaa..pamma.. pamma*	'drives.."closed" .."closed"'
pamma..ajaa	'"closed"..drives'	*pois..pamma*	'away.."closed"'
äiti..avaa	'mother..opens'	*kuorii äiti*	'peels mother'
äiti lukee	'mother reads'		
äiti, pulla	'mother, coffee cake'		
äiti..tuf tuf	'mother.."train"'		
äiti, taas taas	'mother, again again'		

[a] See Glossary for explanation of notational symbols.

TABLE 4 (*cont.*)

	Initial	Final	Total
pois, 'away, off'	3	10	13
tipu, 'chick'	8	1	9
bmbm, "car"	2	6	8
tuossa, 'there'	4	2	6
täti, 'aunt, lady'	4	2	6
pamma, "closed"	3	3	6
äiti, 'mother'	5	1	6

These words appeared in 49 per cent of all nonimitated construction types. None had absolutely fixed position, although some had strong position preferences. All but three, *pois*, 'away', *tuossa*, 'there', and *pamma*, 'closed', are nouns. Two of these three, *tuossa* and *pois*, are semantically similar to syntactic operators found common among children learning German, English, and Russian. Each occurred with a variety of other words, mostly nouns, with one or two fairly constant functions. The Noun + *pois*, 'away', construction was usually produced in one of two situations:

    1. When Seppo was looking at an animal in a picture and evidently anticipated that it was about to go away in some story about the picture he had in his mind; for example, 'cat away' and 'chick away';

    2. Less frequently, when he was tired of looking at or playing with something and wanted to get rid of it, for example, 'book away' and 'food away'.

Pois, 'away', thus functioned rather like words in Brown's 'non-existence' category of operators, like 'allgone', and 'no more', although Seppo usually used it to express the anticipated or desired disappearance of objects rather than actual disappearance. Similarly, many American children use 'more' to request the recurrence of an object or event as well as to comment upon the actual fact of recurrence. *Pois* was also used once in the sense of 'off' in the utterance *takki pois*, 'coat off', as Seppo tried to get his mother to take her sweater off. This corresponds to correct adult usage.

    Tuossa, 'there', + Noun and Noun + *tuossa* were used deictically, either when Seppo spontaneously pointed out an object or picture or in response to 'where's the Noun?' and 'what's there?' questions. *Tuossa*, 'there', thus resembled operators like 'that—', 'this—', 'there —', 'see—', and 'it—', which are commonly used by English-speaking children under the same circumstances. Brown (1970) classified these as 'nominative' in function. The mothers of both Seppo and Rina typically asked 'what's there (here)?' in situations which elicit 'what's that (this)?' from American mothers (the latter type of question did occur occasionally). The form in which mothers pose questions asking for the names of objects may condition the form of the reply received. Both Seppo and Rina used 'here' and 'there' as operators in pointing out and naming objects far more often than 'this' and 'that'. Seppo, in fact, did not acquire the latter words until months past the first sample. The 'here (there)' + Noun construction was also elicited by 'where's the Noun?', another popular question among the Finnish mothers. When 'where' and 'what' are asked in the presence of a referent which the child is expected to point to and name, they seem to be variants of the same 'naming' game. This game is popular among both American and Finnish parents and their children (especially when a tape recorder is on, since it is an easy way to stimulate conversation), and perhaps accounts for the prevalence of 'nomination' constructions in many samples of early speech.

Seppo's constructions with *pamma* were often difficult to interpret. It was his baby word for a variable meaning glossed here as "closed". It was often used as an exclamation, perhaps in imitation of the sound of something closing. Most of Seppo's uses of it in construction had to do with cars. According to his mother, he understood that a car's doors should be closed before the car moves. Such sentences as '"closed" drives', '"closed" car', '"closed" broken', and 'fast.. "closed"' all were uttered while Seppo played with toy cars which he often pretended were broken. The doors were not movable and were always closed. These utterances were perhaps not rule-governed constructions, but associations of some sort. Thus *pamma* was probably not an operator in the same sense as *pois*, 'away', and *tuossa*, 'there'.

Unlike *pamma*, "closed", both *tuossa*, 'there', and *pois*, 'away', had position preferences. *Tuossa* at first occurred somewhat more often in initial position. During the next four weeks it was more frequent in second position (see Table 5), and then switched back to first position. The semantic functions of the two variations seemed identical. When Seppo's mother asked *missä on* Noun?, 'where is Noun?' Seppo was somewhat more likely to answer *tuossa* + Noun than Noun + *tuossa*, matching the position of his answering 'there' to that of the questioning 'where', but this was not consistent.

In his flexible positioning of *tuossa*, 'there', Seppo was in accord with adult usage, as modeled by his mother. Finnish has many one-word prolocatives (the pronouns 'this', 'that', and 'it' inflected with various locative case endings) which correspond roughly in meaning to 'here', 'there', 'right there', 'over there', 'to right here', 'from there', etc., in English. Let us consider the placement privileges in adult speech only of nondirectional prolocatives, since Seppo did not use directional prolocatives ('to here', 'from there', etc.) until later. Seppo's and Rina's mothers both used about five or six different nondirectional prolocatives in contexts in which the children at first used only one or two, and they sometimes alternated between several forms such as 'here', 'right here', and 'over here' while the nonlinguistic situation remained the same. Oddly, Seppo's mother rarely used *tuossa*, Seppo's only prolocative form at the time of the first sample, but perhaps she had used it more earlier. These different nondirectional prolocatives seem to have virtually identical privileges of occurrence in each mother's speech sample, and so are grouped together for analysis. Seppo's mother produced 41 tokens of Prolocative (+copula)+NP and 14 of NP (+copula) +Prolocative. Choice between the two orders seemed to be stylistic, possibly having something to do with the prominence of the noun phrase's referent in the linguistic or nonlinguistic context. Seppo's variation between *tuossa*, 'there', +Noun and Noun+*tuossa* and his preference for the former order were both consistent with the speech he heard.

The mothers of Seppo and Rina often omitted the copula in constructions with prolocatives, especially when the prolocative followed the noun phrase, as in *pallo siinä*, 'ball there'. According to one adult speaker of Finnish, this omission is characteristic of the speech of adults talking to very young children, but does not occur or would sound strange under other circumstances. Seppo's omission of the copula thus had a model – American children also omit it without the same precedent, however.

Seppo's positioning of *pois*, 'away', like *tuossa*, 'there', was in accord with the speech he heard. In his mother's speech, *pois* had a stronger position preference than *tuossa*. It almost always followed the noun, usually with an intervening verb, as in *tipu meni pois*, '(the) chick went away'. Other orders are grammatically acceptable – for example, *pois meni tipu*, 'away went (the) chick' – but they occurred very infrequently. It is significant, then, that Seppo's second-position preference for *pois* was much stronger than his first-position preference for *tuossa*. When *pois* occurred in initial position, it tended to be more ambiguous semantically than when it occurred in final position. Of three first-position uses of *pois* in this sample, only one referred to the going away of the referent: *pois api⟨na⟩*, 'away monkey', was a response to 'where's the monkey?' and meant something like *apina meni pois*, 'monkey went away'. *Pois talli*, 'away garage', produced while Seppo was pushing a toy car toward an imaginary garage, did not mean that the garage had gone away. Rather, it seemed to be based on the Finnish phrase *pois talliin*, 'away garage-into' ('away into the garage'). With this meaning, *pois* occurs both before and after nouns in adult Finnish. The final use of *pois* in initial position, *pois..pamma*, 'away.. "closed"', produced as Seppo pushed a toy car along, was ambiguous and was perhaps some sort of association rather than a true construction, as noted above.

Later on, Seppo briefly used *pois* more often before nouns than after, with the 'Noun is going (went) away' meaning (Time 3, Table 5). However, most of these constructions occurred in a single tape, within a few moments of each other, and so do not constitute a significant exception to the finding that Seppo's position preferences for both *pois*, 'away', and *tuossa*, 'there', matched those of his mother fairly closely.

Seppo's flexible positioning of *tuossa*, 'there', and *pois*, 'away', should not be surprising. Although words with equivalent semantic functions (which we have identified as 'nomination' and 'nonexistence' following Brown's (1970) classification) often have fixed position in the constructions of English-speaking children, counterexamples occur:

airplane allgone	mess here
Calico allgone	pillow here
allgone juice	here mess
allgone outside	there cow
allgone pacifier	
(Braine's (1963) subject,	(Kendall, MLU 1.48;
Andrew)	see Appendix G)

Fixed word order of children's syntactic operators seems to be associated with fixed word order in the adult model. For example, there are no reports of American children alternating freely between sentences like 'that ball' and 'ball that', nor does English provide a precedent for this. Exceptions occur, of course – 'allgone juice' is not likely to have been modeled – but children mainly seem to take advantage of alternate word orders when these are permissible in the adult language, as for 'here' and 'there' in both English and Finnish.

In discussing the functions of pivots, investigators have noted that some children seem to 'practice' word substitutions by sequentially rotating a variety of words through fixed syntactic frames. Weir's son, for example, produced the following sequences (1962):

what color blanket	there is the light
what color mop	here is the light
what color glass	where is the light

Such substitution patterns did not occur in Seppo's speech samples. As he matured somewhat beyond the stage we are considering (but with MLU still under 2.00), he began to engage in another form of 'practice' – trying out various order arrangements of the same words in an unchanging nonlinguistic context:

> *poika tuossa* 'boy there'
> *poika tuossa*.. 'boy there'
> *tuossa poika* 'there boy'
>
> *isi ajaa siinä* 'daddy drives there'
> *isi siinä ajaa* 'daddy there drives'
>
> *Immi tuossa ajaa*.. 'Immi (= Seppo) there drives'
> *Immi ajaa tuossa*.. 'Immi drives there'
> *tuossa Immi ajaa*.. 'there Immi drives'
> *Immi ajaa tuossa* 'Immi drives there'

(Dots indicate intervening utterances. All the orders are acceptable in adult Finnish.)

This might be viewed as a complementary form of practice to that of word substitution. Such behavior is possibly encouraged by exposure to a language which has more flexible word order than does English. It does not necessarily occur, however: Rina never rearranged word orders within a short period of time in this way.

In addition to *tuossa*, 'there', *pois*, 'away', and *pamma*, "closed", four nouns were singled out on the basis of frequency as possible pivots in Seppo's early speech: 'mother', 'chick', 'lady (aunt)', and "car". These look much like the high-frequency words of Kendall and of one of Bloom's subjects, Kathryn. A name for the mother is common to all three, and the rest are names either for other important people in the child's life or for familiar objects and favorite playthings. Seppo's constructions involving these words seem to express a variety of grammatical relations, a phenomenon which led Bloom to reject the pivot grammar as an adequate representation of sentential structure for her subjects. 'Chick' occurred with verbs as sentence-subject ('chick flies', 'chick swims', etc.), with nouns which might name the direct object of an unspecified action initiated by 'chick' ('chick "food"', which perhaps meant something like 'chick is eating "food"'), and as the object located ('chick shoe', 'chick there'). "Car" functioned as sentence-subject ('"car" goes'), direct object ('drives "car"'), modified noun ('broken "car"'), and located object ('garage "car"'). 'Mother' occurred as sentence-subject in both initial and final position ('mother opens', 'peels mother') and as a vocative, when Seppo was calling his mother's attention to something ('mother, coffee cake', 'mother.. "train"').

The position preferences of these nouns can be explained by reference to the same syntactic or semantic regularities we found in Kendall's speech. Nouns in the roles of sentence-subject, possessor, and object located were almost exclusively names for animate beings, and were most often in initial position. Direct objects, objects possessed, and location names, in contrast, were always inanimate nouns and usually occurred in final position. Words for cars (*bmbm* and *auto*) shared properties of both animate and inanimate nouns and occurred in both initial and final position as sentence-subjects, direct objects, objects located, and objects possessed. Other animate nouns in Seppo's speech performed the same grammatical and semantic functions as the high frequency nouns we have been considering. It would be difficult to justify classifying 'mother' and 'chick' as first-position pivots, thereby separating them from nouns like 'horse' and 'father' which occurred only once or twice in the sample but which probably had the same potential syntactic uses and privileges of occurrence.

Most of Seppo's high frequency words, both nouns and syntactic operators, did not have fixed position and so could not qualify as pivots. They also violated other privileges of occurrence attributed to pivots. They were among the most frequent of single-word utterances. *Pois*, 'away', occurred independently 20 times, *tuossa*, 'there', 10 times, *pamma*, "closed", 15 times, *tipu*, 'chick', 20 times, and *äiti*, 'mother', 8 times. In addition, they occurred in combination with each other in the utterances *tuossa pois*, 'there away', *pois. .pamma*, 'away.."closed"', *pamma bmbm*, '"closed" "car"', *tipu pois*, 'chick away', and *tipu..tuossa*, 'chick..there'.

Had Seppo perhaps once used a pivot grammar, but by this stage had developed beyond it? This is doubtful. Of the two words considered seriously as possible pivots – *tuossa*, 'there', and *pois*, 'away' – only the latter was relatively common in constructions from the earliest observations. *Tuossa* occurred as a single-word utterance from the beginning, but did not enter into construction until the third weekly tape, and of six total combinations, five were in the fourth weekly tape. Its absence in tapes 1, 2, and 5 suggests that it was not yet a deeply rooted construction type, although it became very productive later. Unless Seppo had abandoned words once used as pivots, *pois*, 'away', is the only candidate for a pivot which may have originated much before the start of taping. Even if *pois* was one of the first words to be combined with other words, it is unlikely that it occurred in every early construction. A plausible hypothesis is that Seppo also began very early to make noun–verb combinations which expressed the subject–verb relationship. These strings were far more common from the very earliest tapes than strings of any other description. Kendall demonstrates that there are children who develop like this. From virtually the very beginning of word combination (MLU 1.10), she produced more constructions expressing the subject-verb relationship than any other kind, and used even fewer 'pivotal' constructions than Seppo.

3.4.2.2 Seppo, MLU 1.81. Although a pivot grammar would be an inaccurate representation of Seppo's early linguistic competence, his constructions resembled those of the American children. Like Kendall and like Bloom's subjects Gia and Kathryn, he used a small number of words in a large proportion of constructions. These included both syntactic operators like 'there' and 'away' and nouns naming important people and objects. The constructions involving syntactic operators were much less frequent than those in which nouns and verbs were juxtaposed in a variety of grammatical relationships.

It is possible that constructions which look pivotal because they contain syntactic operators become progressively more frequent rather than less frequent in the early speech of some children. Such constructions could probably not be represented by a pivot grammar, since the child's grammatical system would already have been developing along other lines for some time. Let us follow Seppo's progress through Stage I and then look at Rina to see whether pivot-like constructions flourish later in the acquisition of Finnish, and whether such constructions are semantically similar to those in the speech of children learning other languages.

Seppo's development can be summarized briefly. Tapes have been collapsed into four groups of four tapes each: 2–5, 6–9, 10–13, and 14–17. The last group constitutes the sample at MLU 1.81, used in the analysis of late Stage I speech (Chapter 5). Words which occurred with high frequency in two-word utterances in any one of these four time periods were charted for frequency and position preference in each period (Table 5).

The progress of *pois*, 'away', and *tuossa*, 'there', has already been discussed. *Kovaa*, 'fast' (an adverb in adult Finnish), rose in frequency in the third time period but was important nowhere else. *Rikki*, 'broken', is included even though it was never very frequent because 'broken' was identified as a final-position operator in the speech of one of Brown and Fraser's (1964) subjects, Evie, and it may be common in the speech of children learning other languages as well. Like Evie, Seppo used it with a variety of nouns, all inanimate. Its position was variable. He produced the following within a short period of time, for example:

rikki bmbm	'broken "car"'	*bmbm rikki*	'"car" broken'
rikki auto	'broken car'	*auto rikki*	'car broken'
rikki kynä	'broken pencil'	*palo rikki*	'fire ⟨engine⟩ broken'[1]

In adult Finnish, *rikki* is an adverb (there are other forms for the adjective and the past participle of the verb 'break'). Unlike adjectives, it cannot immediately precede nouns in a modifying relationship, but it can follow them in the construction Noun *on rikki*, 'Noun is broken', superficially identical to constructions involving true adjectives like Noun *on iso*, 'Noun is big'. In Seppo's mother's speech, *rikki* occurred most often after *meni*, 'went', in constructions like *auto meni rikki*, '(the) car went broken'. Seppo's use of *rikki* in second position was probably modeled after this. In first position, it could have been modeled after constructions like *rikki meni auto*, 'broken went (the) car', but this order seems to be rare in adult speech. Seppo's mother

---

[1] Angle brackets indicate that the word enclosed was not actually produced.

TABLE 5. *The position of high frequency words at times 1 through 4*[a]

	Time 1 tapes 2–5 MLU 1.42		Time 2 tapes 6–9 MLU 1.57		Time 3 tapes 10–13 MLU 1.48		Time 4 tapes 14–17 MLU 1.81		Total	
	Initial	Final	Initial	Final	Initial	Final	Initial	Final	Initial	Final
pois, 'away'	3	10	0	3	6	1	2	8	11	22
tipu, 'chick'	8	1	3	0	3	1	1	0	15	2
bmbm, "car"	2	6	3	2	1	1	0	0	6	9
tuossa, 'there'	4	2	6	8	9	2	11	6	30	18
täti, 'aunt'	4	2	1	1	1	1	4	1	10	45
pamma, "closed"	3	3	0	0	0	0	0	1	3	4
äiti, 'mother'	4	1	4	0	2	1	11	0	21	2
auto, 'car'	3	1	2	4	2	4	5	4	12	13
ajaa, 'drives'	2	2	6	4	3	4	0	7	11	17
vetää, 'pulls'	0	1	2	3	2	5	6	8	10	17
kovaa, 'fast'	2	1	0	1	2	8	0	0	4	10
rikki, 'broken'	2	2	2	4	1	1	2	1	7	8
siinä, 'there'	0	0	0	0	1	0	3	11	4	11
missä, 'where'	0	0	0	0	2	1	13	1	15	2
enää, 'any more'	0	0	0	2	0	0	6	0	6	2

[a] Numbers refer to utterance types (as distinct from tokens).

used it only occasionally, when expanding Seppo's constructions with this order. Seppo may have identified *rikki* with his 'true' adjectives because of the similarity between utterances like 'Noun is broken' and 'Noun is big' in adult Finnish. Seppo's adjectives had variable order, as was consistent with the speech he heard.

In the last time period, *äiti*, 'mother', suddenly rose in frequency, with eleven occurrences in first position and none in second. This fixedness of position can be attributed to the continuing tendency for animate nouns to occur in initial position in roles like sentence–subject and possessor.

The only new words with the characteristics of syntactic operators are *siinä*, 'there', *missä*, 'where', and *enää*, 'any more', which occurred in many constructions at Time 4. Constructions with these words are listed in Table 6. *Siinä*, 'there', was used deictically to point out individual instances of an object or action. It was thus similar to Seppo's earlier operator, *tuossa*, 'there'. Unlike *tuossa*, however, it was never used in answer to 'where's the Noun?' or 'what's there?' questions, although this is acceptable. *Siinä* also occurred with verbs, as did

TABLE 6. *Seppo, MLU 1.81: Constructions with* siinä,
'there', missä, *'where', and* enää, *'any more'*

Initial position		Final position	
siinä Batman	'there Batman'	*Ari siinä*	'Ari there'
siinä lintu	'there bird'	*Laila siinä*	'Laila there'
siinä koti	'there home'	*palo siinä*	'fire ⟨engine⟩ there'
		hillo siinä	'jam there'
		Batman siinä	'Batman there'
		fantti siinä	'elephant there'
		api⟨na⟩ siinä	'monkey there'
		vettä siinä	'water there'
		putoo siinä	'falls there'
		tulee..siinä	'comes..there'
		kaatuu siinä	'falls-down there'
missä avain?	'where key?'	*auto missä?*	'car where?'
missä keksi?	'where cracker?'		
missä lintu?	'where bird?'		
missä purkki?	'where can?'		
missä kassi?	'where bag?'		
missä loikka?	'where "Volkswagen"?'		
missä auto?	'where car?'		
missä kuti⟨ttaa⟩?	'where tickles?'		
missä vetää?	'where pulls?'		
missä tuossa?	'where there?'		
missä missä kaikki kirja?	'where where all book?'		
hei hei, missä auto?	'hey hey, where car?'		
missä ui?	'where swims?'		
enää pelaa	'any more plays'		
enää vetää	'any more pulls'		
enää satu	'any more happen'		
enää palo	'any more fire ⟨engine⟩'		
enää pipi	'any more sore'		
setä nyt korjaa enää rikki	'man now fixes any more broken'		

tuossa by this time. In adult speech, *siinä* can either precede or follow
nouns, so Seppo's use of it in either position had a model. Its preference
for second position, however, is not matched in Seppo's mother's
speech sample, in which *siinä* appeared 13 times before nouns and
3 times after nouns.

Missä, 'where', was Seppo's first question-form, used with both
verbs and nouns to request information about the location of pictured or
real objects and actions. Two of the three children in Brown's study had
simple 'where' forms at an equivalent stage of development (MLU about

1.75) (Brown, in press). One of Kernan's (1969) two Samoan subjects used 'where'+Noun at MLU 1.60, and Slobin (1970) reports 'where'+Noun in the early speech of Russian and German children, so the relatively early use of location-asking operators seems to be common.

Seppo used *enää*, 'any more', in construction with nouns, verbs, and adjectives. The meaning of constructions with *enää* was often ambiguous (see 5.7.1 and Table 13). Those which could be interpreted referred to the cessation or nonrecurrence of an activity or a condition: *enää vetää*, 'any more pulls', *setä nyt korjaa enää rikki*, 'man now fixes any more broken'. (This 'sentence' probably consists of two separate sentences which were run together under one intonation contour.) *Enää* thus corresponds to 'no more', the negative operator used by some American children to signal nonrecurrence. Seppo's constructions with *enää* did not emerge until late in Stage I. In almost every tape until the 14th, negative meanings were expressed simply by words for 'no' in isolation: the Finnish *ei* and English 'no'. Constructions with *enää* were anomalous from the standpoint of adult Finnish. When used in constructions with negative meanings, *enää* requires the presence of a form of the negative verb, such as *ei* (third person singular). This negative verb directly precedes the verb to be negated or the copula 'be' (in colloquial speech, the sentence-subject may intervene), and *enää* may follow either the negated word or a subsequent direct object or predicate noun or adjective. Less frequently, *enää* directly follows the negative verb and precedes the word to be negated. The verb or copula which is negated must appear in a 'neutral' present or past form, since person and number are marked in the negative verb. Seppo did not observe this requirement, and his negated verbs, like verbs in other utterances, were usually in the third person singular present tense form. Seppo's *enää vetää*, 'any more pulls', would be rendered by an adult as *ei vedä enää* or *ei enää vedä*, (it) doesn't pull any more', and *enää rikki*, 'any more broken', as *ei ole rikki enää*, *ei ole enää rikki*, or *ei enää ole rikki*, '(it) isn't broken any more'.

Seppo's grammar in late Stage I cannot be described as pivotal any more than it could earlier. The great majority of constructions involve the juxtaposition of nouns, verbs, and adjectives in combinations expressing a variety of grammatical relations. However, Seppo continued to use the syntactic operators he had employed earlier, and added some new ones which resemble those found in the speech of children learning other languages.

3.4.2.3 Rina, MLU 1.83. The earliest sample available for Rina, compiled from tapes 1–5, contains a total of 196 different nonimitated constructions. Of these 126 consist of two words only. To these we can add 23 longer utterances with a repeated word, a vocative, a noun phrase, or a copula. This gives us 149 simple constructions among which to look for pivots. Three words are strikingly frequent. *Tässä*, 'here', appears in 39 different constructions, *Rina* in 29, and *täällä*, 'here', in 20. The next most frequent words are *äiti*, 'mother', in 14, and *ei*, 'no', in 11. We will discount *äiti* as a possible pivot, since all but 5 of its occurrences were vocative. Table 7 gives a complete listing of combinations with *tässä*, *täällä*, *Rina*, and *ei*. Their distribution in initial and final position is presented at the end of the table. Fifty per cent of the total number of nonimitated construction types contains one of these four words. In comparison, the seven most frequent words in the first Seppo sample appear in only 49 per cent of nonimitated construction types.

The word *Rina*, like the high frequency nouns of Seppo, Kendall, and Bloom's subjects Gia and Kathryn, was used in constructions which can be interpreted as expressing a variety of grammatical relations, such as subject–verb ('Rina eats'), object located–location ('Rina floor'), word modified–modifier ('Rina dirty'), verb–indirect object ('give Rina', 'Rina give'), and possessor–object possessed ('Rina girl' – an indignant response to 'whose girl is Rina?'). The occurrence of *Rina* mainly in initial position can be explained, as was the case for the other children's animate nouns, by reference to Rina's apparent knowledge that in Finnish, possessors and sentence-subjects typically precede objects possessed, verbs, and direct objects.

Tässä, 'here', *täällä*, 'here', and *ei*, 'no', are better candidates for pivots. They occurred with a variety of other words in constructions performing the 'operations of reference' called 'nomination' and 'nonexistence' by Brown (1970, in press). *Tässä* and *täällä* were used deictically, like Seppo's *tuossa*, 'there', and *siinä*, 'there', to point out individual instances of a referent and to answer 'Where is Noun?' and 'What is here?' questions. *Ei* was used to deny that someone's name for a referent was correct and to negate verbs and locatives, as in 'no Donald Duck', 'no get', and 'no here'. (See 5.7.1 and Table 13 for a more complete account of the functions of Rina's negatives.)

Tässä, 'here', had a stronger preference for first position than was

TABLE 7. *Rina, MLU 1.83: high frequency words in construction*

Initial position		Final position	
tässä lentokone	'here airplane'	*Mikki-Hiiri tässä*	'Mickey Mouse
tässä setä	'here man'		here'
tässä kirja	'here book'	*brrä tässä*	'"car" here'
tässä lehti	'here magazine'	*ei tässä*	'not here'
tässä brrä	'here "car"'		
tässä keksi	'here cracker'		
tässä aave	'here ghost'		
tässä täti	'here lady'		
tässä Aku-Ankka	'here Donald Duck'		
tässä lintu	'here bird'		
tässä kala	'here fish'		
tässä hauva	'here doggie'		
tässä kukka	'here flower'		
tässä bussi	'here bus'		
tässä ikkuna	'here window'		
tässä heppa	'here horsie'		
tässä..possu	'here..piggie'		
tässä kana	'here chicken'		
tässä pipi	'here sore-place'		
tässä (koira)	'here (dog)'		
tässä elukka	'here creature'		
tässä Rami	'here Rami'		
tässä juna	'here train'		
tässä pää pipi	'here head sore-place'		
tässä täti käsi	'here aunt hand'		
tässä kalalento	'here fish flying' (reversal of 'flying fish')		
tässä tässä lintu	'here here bird'		
tässä susi tää susi	'here wolf this wolf'		
tässä on susi	'here is wolf'		
tässä (oli) heppa	'here (was) horsie'		
tässä..lisää kakku	'here..more cake'		
tässä on	'here is'		
äiti, tässä Aku-Ankka	'mother, here Donald Duck'		
äiti, tässä on Aku-Ankka	'mother, here is Donald Duck'		
tässä Batman	'here Batman'		
auto, tässä auto	'car, here car'		
täällä tyttö	'here girl'	*suu täällä*	'mouth here'
täällä nappi	'here button'	*ovi täällä*	'door here'
täällä varvas	'here toe'	*ikkuna täällä*	'window here'
täällä hauva	'here doggie'	*Aku-Ankka täällä*	'Donald Duck here'
täällä setä	'here man'	*pupu täällä*	'bunny here'
täällä täti	'here lady'	*hattu täällä*	'hat here'
täällä heppa	'here horsie'	*ei täällä*	'no here'
täällä lentokala	'here flying fish'		
täällä Aku-Ankka	'here Donald Duck'		
täällä Mikki-Hiiri	'here Mickey Mouse'		
täällä Rina tukka	'here Rina hair'		

TABLE 7 *(cont.)*

Initial position			Final position
täällä Rina käsi	'here Rina hand'		
täällä on heppa	'here is horsie'		
Rina itse	'Rina (her)self'	*tuossa Rina*	'there Rina'
Rina saa	'Rina gets'	*anna Rinalle*	'give Rina-to'
Rina pelleilee	'Rina clowns'	*otti Rina*	'took Rina' (*Rina* is
Rina repii	'Rina tears'		the subject)
Rina avaa	'Rina opens'		
Rina siivoo	'Rina cleans'		
Rina istuu	'Rina sits'		
Rina putoo	'Rina falls'		
Rina syö	'Rina eats'		
Rina piirtää	'Rina draws'		
Rina laittaa	'Rina makes, fixes'		
Rina ottaa	'Rina takes'		
Rina (katsoo)	'Rina (watches)'		
Rina leikkii	'Rina plays'		
Rina hauva	'Rina dog'		
Rina..Rami	'Rina..Rami'		
Rina tyttö	'Rina girl' ('Rina's girl')		
Rina lattia	'Rina floor' ('Rina is on the floor')		
Rina lika⟨inen⟩	'Rina dirty'		
Rina paperi	'Rina paper'		
Rina kynä	'Rina pencil'		
Rina näitä näitä	'Rina these these'		
Rina tänne	'Rina to-here'		
Rina anna	'Rina give' ('give' is in imperative form, should be *Rinalle anna*, 'Rina-to give'		
Rina lisää kakku	'Rina more cake'		
äiti, Rina iso (kynä)	'aunt, Rina big (pencil)'		
ei susi	'no wolf'		
ei täti	'no aunt'		
ei Pluto	'no Pluto'		
ei Aku-Ankka	'no Donald Duck'		
ei tyy	'no like' (should be *ei tykännyt*, 'didn't like')		
ei saa	'no get' (grammatical)		
ei oo tyttö	'no is girl' ('(it) isn't (a) girl') (grammatical)		
ei Aku-Ankka o(n)	'no Donald Duck is' (should be *ei Aku-Ankka ole*)		
ei tässä	'no here'		
ei täällä	'no here'		
ei (nämä)	'no (these)'		

	Initial	Final	Total
tässä, 'here'	36	3	39
Rina, 'Rina'	26	3	29
täällä, 'here'	13	7	20
ei, 'no', 'not'	11	0	11

modeled in the speech of Rina's mother. In the mother's sample, there are 46 instances of nouns or noun phrases with nondirectional prolocatives in simple sentences. The order is Prolocative (+ Copula) + NP 31 times and NP(+Copula)+Prolocative 15 times. Rina's more consistent placement of *tässä* in first position than Seppo's of his equivalent, *tuossa*, 'there', cannot be ascribed to differences in the input, since her mother placed prolocatives *after* nouns slightly more often than did Seppo's mother. Rina did vary the placement of *täällä*, 'here', in accordance with the modeled frequencies of the two orders.

The pivot–open model is somewhat more applicable to Rina's speech than to Seppo's, since a larger proportion of her utterances involved a small number of words with fairly strong position preferences. Even on strictly distributional grounds, however, we must reject the pivot grammar as an adequate representation of her knowledge. According to the pivot grammar, P in isolation and P+P are ungrammatical. But Rina's *tässä*, 'here', *täällä*, 'here', *ei*, 'no', and *Rina* were among the most frequent of single-word utterances, just as were Seppo's *pois*, 'away', and *tuossa*, 'there'. *Tässä*, *täällä*, and *ei* combined with each other in the utterances *ei tässä*, 'no here', and *ei täällä*, 'no here'. The clearly non-pivotal words in her vocabulary were not an undifferentiated class which could occur with any pivot. With a very few exceptions, only nouns and noun phrases entered into construction with *tässä*, 'here', and *täällä*, 'here'. Rina knew much more at this time than could be accounted for by a pivot grammar. A simple description of non-pivotal constructions as unordered O + O would fail to represent such regularities as the consistent use of subject–verb–object order in subject–verb, verb–object, and subject–verb–object constructions, and the differing privileges of occurrence of animate and inanimate nouns.

3.4.3 Luo and Samoan. In two recently completed studies of child language, explicit attempts were made to determine the applicability of the pivot–open model. Blount (1969), studying Luo, was unable to obtain many utterances from an early stage of development and was forced to rely heavily on parental reports. The speech samples from each child were so small that distributional analysis was impossible. Blount concluded that even if the children passed through a pivot grammar stage, pivotal constructions did not play as important a role in their linguistic development as in that of American children. However,

5

construction patterns which were common in the Luo data resemble those of children learning English, German, Russian, and Finnish, since they involve such words as 'this', 'it (he, she)', 'see', and 'give-me'. Translated utterances include 'it clock', 'this visitor', and 'give-me candy'. These perform such functions as 'nomination' and 'demand, desire'.

Kernan (1969) discussed the pivotal characteristics of the speech of one child acquiring Samoan. A distributional analysis of Sipili's constructions at MLU 1.52 revealed five high frequency words with fixed position. These are translated as 'the', 'sign of the nominative', 'and (for, with)', 'mine (I, me, my)', and 'yours (you, your)'. Kernan noted that although a pivot grammar could be written to generate constructions with these words, it would be unable to distinguish formally between constructions with different structural meanings. For example, 'spank me' and 'my candy', which both use the word *au* ('mine, I, me, my') in second position, would receive the same structural interpretation: O + P. Kernan agreed with Bloom (1970) that meaning should be taken into account in writing grammars for children, although the kind of grammar he adopted was different from hers.

Even on strictly distributional grounds, however, a pivot grammar cannot account well for Sipili's high-frequency construction types. First, the 'open' class (all non-pivot words) was not undifferentiated. Only nouns were used with the forms for 'the' and 'sign of the nominative'. Nouns, moreover, were subdivided, since only common nouns appeared with 'the' while proper nouns and pronouns occurred with 'sign of the nominative'. This follows correct adult usage. 'And (for, with)' also occurred only with nouns and pronouns. Only the pronouns 'mine (I, me, my)' and 'yours (you, your)' occurred with both noun and non-noun forms. Privileges of occurrence, then, were more complex than a simple pivot–open class split could account for. As for the characteristics of the 'pivots', both 'yours (you, yours)' and 'mine (I, me, my)' occurred as single-word utterances, and there were four construction types in which 'pivots' occurred together: '"sign of the nominative" you', '"sign of the nominative" I', 'and me', 'and you'. Since these are all acceptable, intelligible constructions, used appropriately, we would be unjustified in considering them 'mistakes' from Sipili's point of view, but a pivot grammar written for his speech would be unable to generate them since they are P + P. In short, a pivot grammar would be a poor way to represent Sipili's linguistic knowledge not only because, as Kernan argued, it would be unable to represent important structural distinctions, but also because a simple division of vocabulary items into pivot and open classes, with their characteristic privileges of occurrence, would not provide an accurate description of the utterances in Sipili's sample.

Some of Sipili's high frequency words with fixed position functioned like the syntactic operators of the Finnish, American, and Luo children. 'The' and 'sign of the nominative' can both be interpreted as signaling 'nomination' (Kernan called this function 'labeling'). Almost all constructions with these words occurred in response to questions about the identity of objects and people. In 3.4.2.1, we noted that the way in which mothers ask for names seems to influence the form of the child's reply. American mothers usually ask 'what's this (that)?' and elicit 'this (that) Noun'. Finnish mothers ask 'what's here (there)?' and receive 'here (there) Noun'. The typical Samoan version of the 'what' question, 'what (the name of) the thing there?' could suggest either 'the Noun' or 'Noun there' in response. Sipili chose the former, evidently a correct Samoan reply:

> *Leā le mea lea?*   *le lole*
> 'What the thing there?'   'the candy'
>
> *Leā le igoa o le mea lea?*   *le ili*
> 'What the name of the thing there?'   'the fan'

Similarly, questions about the identity of people suggest 'sign of the nominative' + Name as a response:

> *'O ai lou tāmā?*   *'O So'o*
> '"sign of nominative" who your father?'   '"sign of nominative" So'o'

For both of Sipili's 'nomination' constructions, then, the syntactic operator is modeled in the question and appears to condition the form of the reply.

Constructions with the words for 'mine (I, me, my)' and 'yours (you, your)' also have counterparts in the speech of children learning other languages, although at first, proper nouns like the child's name and 'Mommy' are probably more common than pronouns as sentence-subjects, direct objects, and possessives. Sipili's constructions with 'and (for, with)' do not correspond in semantic function to any of the 'operations of reference' or 'pivots' discussed by Brown (1970, in press) and Slobin (1966c).

3.5   Summary of the case against the pivot grammar

The pivot–open model does not accurately represent the data from early speech samples of American, Finnish, and Samoan children. Words in the children's utterances do not conform to the distributional privileges of occurrence specified by the rules of a pivot grammar. All of the children used a small number of words in a relatively large proportion of constructions, but these words rarely incorporate simultaneously all the properties attributed to pivots: fixed position, potential combination with all non-pivot words, not occurring alone, and not occurring in combination with each other. Moreover, none of the children had an undifferentiated open class. The clearly non-pivot words in virtually every sample can be subdivided on distributional grounds. For example, many 'pivots' occur only with nouns of the adult language. Constructions which are definitely not pivotal show enough regularities to preclude considering them unordered combinations of two words from the same class, as they are represented in the pivot grammar formula O + O.

The similarities in the speech of the children studied were striking, even though they cannot be formally represented by the rules of a pivot grammar. Many of the high frequency words of children speaking different languages resembled each other. Some of these, called 'syntactic operators' by Bloom (1970), 'operated' on all the words with which they were combined in a constant fashion, although they did not necessarily have fixed position. The semantic functions of such operators were similar. The function encountered in the most different speech samples was 'nomination' (Brown's term, 1970), in which the child names and may point to objects or people in the immediate context, often in response to a 'what' question. The name word is preceded or followed by a word like 'this', 'that', 'here', 'there', 'it', or 'see'. Nomination was signaled by Seppo's *tuossa*, 'there', and *siinä*, 'there', by Rina's *tässä*, 'here', and *täällä*, 'here', and apparently by the Luo children's 'this' and 'it' and the Samoan child's 'the' and 'sign of the nominative'. Aspects of the semantic category 'nonexistence' or 'negation' were marked by Seppo's *pois*, 'away', and *enää*, 'any more', by Rina's *ei*, 'no', and by 'no', 'allgone', 'no more', and 'away' in the speech of American, Russian, and German children.

Brown identified 'recurrence' and 'notice' as common 'operations of reference' among English-speaking children. Operators signaling these meanings were absent from the Finnish children's speech. Seppo occasionally used *taas*, 'again', in isolation to signal recurrence (although not to ask for a second helping) but this was rare. Rina often used *lisää*, 'more', but this did not seem to be a productive operator since it occurred in combination only with *kakku*, 'cake', and may have been a learned routine.

With further cross-linguistic data, we should be able to make a more complete listing of the semantic functions performed by children's early operators. This list would include such functions outlined by Brown (1970) and Slobin (1966 c) as 'nomination', 'recurrence', 'non-existence' or 'negation', and 'demand, desire', and probably others we have not yet encountered or recognized. Which operators are actually selected by given children would depend both upon individual differences in cognitive makeup and experience and upon the ease and frequency with which particular semantic notions are expressed in different languages and by different parents speaking the same language.

Syntactic operators performing operations of reference were among the most frequent of single-word utterances, and thus lacked one of the properties McNeill (1966 b) considers characteristic of pivots. In Bloom's data, for example, operators like 'more', 'no', ''nother', and 'hi' all occurred frequently as independent utterances, as did Kendall's 'more' and 'that' and the Finnish children's 'here', 'there', 'away', and 'no'. Such words may be practiced singly before they are ever used in construction. We do not have data from the holophrastic stage for Bloom's subjects or the Finnish children, but Kendall used both 'more' and 'that' as single-word utterances before word combination began.

In addition to syntactic operators, names for particular animate beings were frequent in the constructions of the children for whom relatively complete data are available. Names for the self, the mother, and other important family members were especially common. In the Finnish and American children's speech, animate and inanimate nouns tended to have different privileges of occurrence. This can be explained by reference to certain semantic and syntactic regularities. Animate nouns played the roles of sentence-subject and possessor, while in-animate nouns functioned as direct objects, objects possessed, and location names. Since the children fairly consistently used the dominant subject–verb–object, possessor–possessed, and object located–location orders of both Finnish and English, most animate nouns appeared in initial position and most inanimate nouns in final position in two-word utterances. The knowledge of sentence structure suggested by these regularities of word choice and positioning cannot be represented in a pivot grammar.

3.6   Justification for an approach through meaning

The failure of the pivot–open model to represent children's early linguistic knowledge either accurately or in enough depth forces us to look elsewhere for a satisfactory approach to writing grammars for children. Throughout this chapter, we have suggested that many of the characteristics of the speech of the children studied can be adequately accounted for only when semantic and syntactic meaning is taken into consideration. An approach to writing grammars for children which takes meaning into account cannot be undertaken without some justification, or at least recognition that a problem of justification exists. Grammars which do not stay close to the linguistic data, as does the pivot grammar, but which rely heavily on the listener's semantic interpretation of the child's intentions risk attributing more knowledge to the child than he actually possesses. What can we gain by trying to understand what a child means, and how can we minimize the danger of overinterpretation?

As noted in 3.3.2, Bloom (1970) argued that a grammar based on the superficial form and arrangement of words in utterances does not allow analysis of a child's developing grammatical structure. For example, if syntactic structure is assigned strictly on the basis of superficial characteristics of utterances, two different productions of the 'same' utterance would necessarily be assigned the same structure even if the child's intentions were different. Bloom illustrated this problem with Kathryn's construction 'Mommy sock', uttered once as the child picked up a sock belonging to Mommy and once as Mommy put Kathryn's sock on Kathryn. In the first instance, a genitive intention seems likely (as in 'this is *Mommy's sock*') and in the second, the expression of an interaction between an agent, 'Mommy', and an object, 'sock' ('*Mommy* is putting my *sock* on'). If Kathryn's two productions of 'Mommy sock' were motivated by different semantic intentions, the utterance taken out of context is ambiguous, since it can be interpreted in two different ways. It is thus conceptually equivalent to sentences of adult English like 'visiting relatives can be a nuisance' and 'the shooting of the hunters was terrible', which can also be interpreted in more than one way. Linguists use such structural homonyms to illustrate that identical surface structures can result from the realization of quite different underlying structures, in which the sentential elements play different syntactic roles. When an adult says something like 'visiting relatives can be a nuisance', we assume that he has one particular semantic interpretation (corresponding to one underlying structure) in mind, although if he had intended the other interpretation, the same sentence might have resulted. Similarly, it is conceivable that children can produce the 'same' utterance at different times with different semantic intentions. This hypothesis assumes that the cognitive distinctions that children are able to make at an early stage of development are more advanced than the linguistic devices available to them for expressing these distinctions, since the kinds of structural homonyms children may produce are not typically homonyms in adult speech. As the child's linguistic competence develops, 'Mommy sock' would be resolved into two or more superficially distinct utterances. In contrast, structural homonyms produced by adults do not result from greater cognitive than linguistic development but are due to the structural characteristics of the language itself. They can be paraphrased and thus disambiguated by the speaker if necessary.

There is some evidence that children do produce noun–noun constructions like 'Mommy sock' with a variety of semantic intentions. This suggests that they control certain syntactic distinctions which should be represented in grammars written to represent their linguistic knowledge. When we consider the linguistic and nonlinguistic conditions under which different noun–noun strings were produced by Kendall, Bloom's subjects, and the Finnish children, and assign each construction a 'most likely' interpretation, we find that they seem to express such diverse relationships as possessor–object possessed, subject–direct object, object located–location, and modifier–object modified. In most cases the order of the nouns is consistent with that of the adult language: possessors, subjects, objects located, and modifying nouns first, objects possessed, direct objects, location names, and modified nouns second. This may indicate that the children knew something about the syntactic expression of these relations. However, an alternative explanation should be considered. Children could produce many noun–noun combinations which seem semantically and syntactically appropriate simply by naming two salient objects and following the rule 'animate noun precedes inanimate noun'. In adult English and Finnish, at least as modeled by the mothers of Brown's three subjects and of Seppo and Rina, a very high proportion of names for possessors, sentence-subjects, and objects located are animate, and those for objects possessed, direct objects, and locations are inanimate. Adults do not order these appropriately by following an 'animate precedes inanimate' rule but according to the syntactic relations holding between the elements. The tendency for the first noun to be animate and the second inanimate is coincidental. But if children followed such a rule, they would give the false impression of having a more abstract knowledge of the expression of syntactic relations than they really do. For Brown's three subjects at MLUs of about 1.75, 75 per cent of noun–noun combinations followed the animate–inanimate pattern (Brown, in press). For Bloom's subject, Kathryn, at MLU 1.32, the proportion was about 78 per cent. The proportion was lower for the Finnish children and for Kendall: 62 per cent in both samples for Seppo, 47 per cent for Rina, and 54 per cent for Kendall in a sample with an MLU of 1.48. Perhaps all that many children really know about the structure of noun–noun constructions is that an animate noun precedes an inanimate noun.

However, those sentences which violate the rule are usually semantically and syntactically appropriate. Subjects, possessors, and objects located precede direct objects, objects possessed, and location names even when the former are inanimate or the latter animate. Examples include Kendall's 'lotion tummy' when a bottle of lotion was on her tummy, and Rina's *isi tyttö*, 'daddy girl', in response to her mother's question 'whose girl is Rina?' Even though children's exceptions to the animate–inanimate rule may be a small proportion of all noun–noun combinations, the appropriate ordering of the nouns indicates that children do know something about the expression of certain syntactic or semantic relationships. For Kendall, there was additional evidence in the form of the utterances themselves. In 17 noun–noun combinations judged to express a subject–object relation, the stress fell on the final noun 14 times. In 12 interpreted as possessor–object possessed, the stress was on the initial noun 10 times. For other combinations interpreted as object located–location or noun–*is*–noun there was no consistent stress pattern. The distinct stress patterns for subject–object and possessor–object possessed strongly suggest that at least these two structures were cognitively distinguished, even though both took the superficial form of noun–noun. Noun–noun strings in the speech of other children are superficially indistinguishable, however. Brown's subject Eve, for example, used no consistent stress or intonation differences to mark possible grammatical differences in her numerous noun–noun constructions (Brown, in press).

Additional evidence that children have linguistic knowledge that cannot be represented structurally unless meaning is taken into account is the fact that most of the children studied consistently placed subjects before verbs and objects after verbs in subject–verb, verb–object, and subject–verb–object strings.

These facts about children's speech indicate that much information about early linguistic competence cannot be discovered unless we consider the semantic intentions underlying the production of utterances. But we must not do exactly what parents do in interpreting what children mean. When parents expand their children's utterances, they fill in all the articles, inflections, and other functors needed for a grammatical sentence. There is little reason to believe that children intend these elements but simply cannot yet produce them. As Bloom (1970) points out, the student of language acquisition should credit the child with intending only the sentential elements he actually produces, but can give these a syntactic and semantic interpretation.

Justifying our interpretations of particular sentences is often difficult. When we stick closely to the linguistic characteristics of children's utterances and ignore such factors as the context in which they were produced, interpretation is often impossible but at least we are dealing with empirical data which can be examined by anyone. The kinds of nonlinguistic data which we can use in distinguishing between superficially similar sentences and in making more adequate judgments about intentions are also empirical, but at present we do not know how to use them in a very systematic way and must rely largely on our intuitions. Closer study, probably involving the analysis of video tapes of children's nonverbal behavior at the time utterances are produced, should eventually enable us to be more objective. The development of more precise ways of isolating and describing important behavioral sequences will be an important first step towards the more productive use of nonlinguistic data as an aid to interpreting linguistic behavior.

We do not yet know the best way to formalize information about sentence structure gained from taking meaning into account. In the next four chapters we will investigate the advantages and disadvantages of two approaches to grammar writing which allow the representation of such information: transformational generative grammar as formulated by Chomsky (1965) and applied to child speech by Bloom (1970) and case grammar as proposed by Fillmore (1968). Let us turn now to an analysis of early Stage I speech within the framework of transformational generative grammar.

4 Early Stage I speech

In the last chapter, we concluded that the pivot grammar is an inadequate representation of children's early linguistic knowledge and that a grammar which does justice to this knowledge must take into account the meaning of utterances as well as the superficial form and arrangement of the words in them. Transformational generative grammar is one approach to grammar writing which provides for the representation of information about meaning. In the next two chapters, the characteristics of child speech at two stages of development are explored within this theoretical framework. In this chapter a transformational generative grammar based on Seppo's sample at MLU 1.42 (early Stage I) is presented and discussed. His speech is then compared with that of American, Luo, and Samoan children at an equivalent stage of development.

4.1 Transformational generative grammar

Those aspects of transformational generative grammar which are necessary for an understanding of the grammars written for the Finnish children are described briefly below. A more detailed account can be found in Chomsky's *Aspects of the Theory of Syntax* (1965).

In a transformational generative grammar, a sentence receives two representations, a surface structure and an underlying or deep structure. These are related to each other by transformational rules. The surface structure represents the structural and physical characteristics of the sentence as it is spoken. The underlying structure is an abstract representation of the essential syntactic characteristics of the sentence and is never realized directly in speech.

The grammar consists of three components, the *syntactic*, the *phonological*, and the *semantic*. The syntactic component, which specifies both underlying and surface structure, is central in that the other two components operate on its output. The phonological component operates on surface structures to indicate the acoustical properties of sentences, while the semantic component operates on the abstract accounts of sentences provided by underlying structures to produce semantic interpretations. We shall be concerned here only with the syntactic component of children's grammars.

The syntactic component has two parts, a base component and a transformational component. Rules of the base component generate underlying structures of sentences and indicate how particular lexical items are inserted into these structures. Underlying structures are partially generated by phrase structure rules which specify the constituent structure, or the hierarchical organization of elements in a sentence, the grammatical relations holding between the constituents, and the abstract, underlying order of elements. Phrase structure rules are a sequence of branching rewriting rules of the form $X \rightarrow Y$, which is read 'X is rewritten as Y'. Only one element is rewritten at a time. Phrase structure rewriting rules are illustrated in the following fragment of English grammar:

$$1. \ S \rightarrow NP + VP$$
$$2. \ VP \rightarrow V \ (NP)$$
$$3. \ NP \rightarrow Det + N$$
$$4. \ Det \rightarrow \begin{Bmatrix} a \\ the \end{Bmatrix}$$

S stands for Sentence, NP is the major category symbol Noun Phrase, VP is the major category symbol Verb Phrase, V is the lexical category symbol Verb, and N is the lexical category symbol Noun. Det stands for Determiner. The rules specify that a sentence is to be rewritten as a noun phrase plus a verb phrase. The verb phrase is rewritten as a verb plus an optional noun phrase. Noun phrases are rewritten one at a time as a determiner plus a noun. The determiner is rewritten as either 'a' or 'the'. Parentheses indicate optionality. All symbols not enclosed in parentheses are obligatory. Braces indicate that a choice of the enclosed elements is to be made, but that one or the other must be chosen. Concatenation of symbols is indicated by $+$ or $-$, but these can be omitted when parentheses or braces are used.

The constituent structure imposed on sentential elements by phrase structure rules can be represented by a tree-diagram called a phrase-marker. The phrase-marker of a string generated by the above rules looks like the tree diagram on p. 77. A symbol is said to be dominated by the node from which it is immediately derived, working down from the top of a tree-diagram or from the beginning of a set of phrase structure rules. Symbols dominated by the same node are immediate constituents. For example, the V and NP dominated by the VP node are immediate constituents.

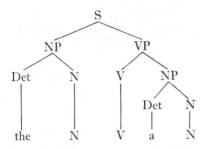

Grammatical functions such as 'subject of the sentence', 'direct object of the verb', and 'predicate of the sentence' are not labeled as category constituents, like NP or VP, but are implicitly indicated by the configurational relationships between the categories in the sentence. The subject is defined as the NP which is directly dominated by S, the predicate as the VP dominated by S, and the direct object as the NP dominated by VP.

Successive application of phrase structure rewriting rules results in the derivation of deep structure strings which consist of grammatical formatives like 'the' and lexical category symbols like N, V, and Adj. Lexical formatives (particular lexical items like 'boy' and 'hit') are ultimately substituted for lexical category symbols in the derivation of terminal strings. Chomsky outlines two methods of accomplishing this substitution. According to one, the base component of the grammar contains two kinds of rewriting rules and a lexicon. The rewriting rules discussed above are called *branching rules* because they analyze a category into a sequence of one or more categories, such as NP → Det + N. Rewriting rules which introduce lexical items are called *subcategorization rules*. These rules rewrite lexical category symbols like N and V as complex symbols (CS), which are sets of specified syntactic features. These syntactic features include:

1. A feature representing the lexical category that dominates the CS, such as +N or +V.

2. A context-sensitive feature specifying the local category frame of the CS to the limits of the node that dominates it, such as, for a noun, [+ Det——] (occurs after a Determiner), or, for a verb, [+——NP] (takes a direct object). This is called strict subcategorization.

3. For noun CSs only, context-free inherent syntactic features such as [+ animate] or [− animate], [+ human] or [− human].

4. For verb and adjective CSs, context-sensitive feature frames, called selection restrictions, which specify the inherent features of nouns with which the CS can occur in construction, such as [+——NP, + animate] (takes as direct object a noun phrase containing a noun marked positively for animacy).

Nouns are selectionally dominant, since verbs and adjectives are chosen in accordance with the features of nouns rather than the other way around. Chomsky offers good reasons for the selectional dominance of nouns and suggests that this may be a universal feature of language.

The lexicon is an unordered list of lexical entries. Each entry consists of the phonological representation of a lexical item and a set of syntactic features of the kind described above. A general rule of grammar allows a lexical item to be substituted for a complex symbol in a preterminal string if the set of syntactic features of the lexical item match those of the CS.

In the second method of lexical substitution outlined by Chomsky, subcategorization rules are eliminated from the system of rewriting rules and assigned to the lexicon. The base is thus divided into two parts, a categorial component and a lexicon. The categorial component consists entirely of branching rewriting rules, and its job is to represent constituent structure and to define the basic grammatical relations that function in the deep structure of the language. In the categorial component, a lexical category symbol is rewritten not as a CS but as a fixed dummy symbol, △, for which a particular lexical item is substituted. The information needed to match CSs and lexical items in the method of lexical substitution discussed above is still used, but in a different way. Lexical items are assigned inherent features, strict subcategorization frames, and selection restrictions, and are substitutable for dummy symbols of preterminal strings provided that these symbols do not occur in contexts which violate the restrictions specified by the syntactic features of the lexical items. Instead of the single, context-free lexical substitution rule used to match CSs and lexical items in the above method, several context-sensitive rules assigned to the lexicon now provide for lexical substitution.

The transformational component of the syntactic component operates upon the underlying structures of sentences to produce surface structures through the application of sequences of ordered rules, some of which are obligatory and others optional. The transformational component is thus the link between underlying and surface structures insofar as they differ. While the phrase structure rules directly rewrite symbols, the transformational rules rewrite indefinitely numerous specific strings, as long as they satisfy a given structural description (S.D.), into strings with given other structural descriptions. The operation(s) to be performed on a string with a given structural description are indicated by a rule which specifies a particular structural change (S.C.), such as reordering, deletion, or addition of elements.

The transformational grammars written for Seppo and Rina are composed of the three kinds of rules needed in the syntactic component: *phrase structure rules*, which give the underlying order of the elements in a sentence, their hierarchical organization, and the grammatical relations holding between them; *lexicon feature rules*, which provide for the substitution of lexical items into preterminal strings; and *transformational rules*, which specify operations to be performed on underlying strings of certain descriptions.

The method of lexical substitution used in the grammars does not correspond exactly to either method discussed by Chomsky. It is a modified version of the second method, in which subcategorization rules are eliminated from the system of rewriting rules and assigned to the lexicon, leaving a categorial component composed entirely of branching rewriting rules. The syntactic features of lexical items are given as redundancy rules which add and specify features whenever these can be predicted by general rules. In the first Seppo grammar, for example, the rule [+animate] → [−V——, −N——] specifies that if an item has the inherent feature [+animate], it also has the context-sensitive category frame features [−V——] and [−N——].

Lexical category symbols of preterminal strings are not rewritten as the fixed dummy symbol △. Fewer and less complicated rules are needed in the children's grammars if a lexical item is simply allowed to substitute for a lexical category symbol in a preterminal string provided that the item has a syntactic feature which corresponds to the lexical category of the symbol, such as +N, +V, or +Adj, and the symbol does not occur in a context which violates the context-sensitive features of the item. If an item is given no context-sensitive category frame features or selection restrictions, like the adjectives in all the grammars or like words with the features [+N, −animate, +vehicle] in the first Seppo grammar, it can substitute in any context for a corresponding lexical category symbol. Category frames in some instances are not local, since they extend beyond the limits of the node dominating the lexical category symbol to be replaced. This seemed to be a necessary alteration of Chomsky's proposals if all the co-occurrence restrictions of lexical items in the children's grammars were to be specified.

Chomsky (1965, p. 111) notes that the context-sensitive features of a lexical item can correspond only to frames in which the item *can* appear, or only to frames in which it *cannot* appear, or strict sub-categorization features can be marked one way and selection restrictions the other. Specifying only the contexts in which lexical items cannot appear allows the most concise formulation of lexicon feature rules in the grammars for Seppo and Rina. A lexical item can be substituted for an appropriate lexical category symbol in any context unless the context is explicitly forbidden by a negatively marked category frame. For example, animate nouns in the first Seppo grammar cannot follow verbs or nouns because they have the category frame features $[-V\text{———}]$ and $[-N\text{———}]$, but they can replace a lexical category symbol N in any other context in a preterminal string. When lexical items are sub-divided with respect to a category frame feature – for example, in the second grammar for Seppo,

$$[+\text{pronoun}] \rightarrow \left[\pm\text{———}\begin{Bmatrix}V\\N\end{Bmatrix}\right]$$

– items marked negatively cannot occur in the specified context while items marked positively can, and both can replace appropriate category symbols in any other context not explicitly forbidden to them.

4.2   Determination of grammatical categories

The rules of the base component of a grammar must have grammatical categories with which to work. Distributional analysis of privileges of occurrence is effective in revealing the grammatical classes of a language as it is spoken by adults. The presence of inflectional clues usually aids the analysis. In English, for example, count nouns can be identified as a class of words which can occur before the plural morpheme -*s*. In Finnish, nouns and adjectives can be distinguished from other words because they can precede certain inflections called case endings. The grammatical development of American and Finnish children is well advanced before inflection begins, so the only distribu-tional criteria upon which judgments about grammatical class membership can be made involve word order and co-occurrence restrictions. Attempts to discover children's grammatical classes with these criteria led to the pivot–open model of early speech. In Chapter 3, we concluded that the model fails to characterize the privileges of occurrence of words in children's early utterances accurately and underrepresents children's knowledge by describing most noun–verb, verb–noun, and noun–noun combinations as concatenations of words from the same class, even though certain regularities suggest that they are not.

It is not yet clear whether a careful distributional analysis of the arrangement of words in one child's constructions can reveal the syntactic classes needed for an adequate representation of the child's linguistic knowledge. It is possible that children sometimes distinguish cognitively between groups of words on the basis of meaning, but that this distinction is not initially reflected in a difference in distributional privileges of occurrence but only in a difference in the semantic or syntactic functions performed by the words. Whether words distinguished in this way should be considered members of different classes before clear-cut distributional differences emerge is uncertain.

The present study does not attempt to resolve these theoretical problems involved in identifying word classes. The method used in classifying Seppo's and Rina's words was designed to allow the grammars to generate the desired strings with categories which looked like reasonable guesses at the word classes the children themselves might have used. However, whether the children actually regarded the words classified together as similar at some level is undetermined.

The classification method is similar to that devised by Bloom (1970) for classifying her subjects' words. It takes into account both privileges of occurrence and grammatical function. Bloom noted that noun forms of the adult language were the most abundant words in the children's lexicons, and that the children's developing ideas of syntax apparently had to do with an increasing appreciation of possibilities for combining nouns with other nouns and with new and different forms like adjectives, verbs, and prepositions. This seemed to be true also of the Finnish children. Following Bloom, therefore, nouns were considered a 'given' category and [+ N] was assigned to all lexical items which are nouns in adult Finnish. The class membership of other lexical items was then determined by reference to their occurrence with nouns in various syntactic relationships. The principles outlined by Bloom for making these classifications have been roughly followed in classifying the

6

Finnish children's words, but some alterations and additions have been made where necessary.

1. *Verbs* were defined as words which occurred with nouns in constructions in which one or more of the following grammatical relationships held, as judged from linguistic and nonlinguistic context:

(*a*) Predicative: N+V or V+N, with the noun functioning as the sentence-subject and the verb as the sentence-predicate.

(*b*) Directive objective: V+N or N+V, with the noun functioning as the direct object of the verb.

(*c*) Locative: V+N or N+V, with the noun indicating the location of the state or activity identified by the verb. This criterion was needed only twice, in classifying *asuu*, 'lives', and *viedään*, 'take' as verbs in the second Seppo grammar.

Verbs were subdivided into intransitive and transitive classes ([± ——(NP)] according to whether they could occur with nouns in a directive objective relationship. Parentheses (which indicate optionality) enclose the NP in the feature [± ——(NP)] because verbs which were able to take direct objects did not always do so – they occurred both with and without objects. A more refined subdivision might have been made between verbs which always occurred with objects and those which sometimes did. This was not done because the total number of verbs involved was very small and there was a good possibility that those few which always in the samples took objects could also have appeared without them. In adult Finnish, there are many transitive verbs which can optionally occur without direct objects. Most of these have English translations for which the object is not deletable. Finnish direct objects are especially likely to be omitted when they are clearly understood from context and would be represented by 'it' in English. All of the verbs classified in the children's lexicons as able to occur both with and without objects had the same privileges of occurrence in the children's mothers' speech.

2. *Adjectives* were defined as words which occurred before nouns with an attributive relationship. Following Bloom's formulation, some nouns were cross-classified as adjectives if they occurred before other nouns with this function.

3. *Adverbs* were defined as words which occurred either before or after verbs with a modifying relationship of time ('now', 'still', 'soon', 'then') or of manner ('like-that', 'fast'). The category of adverbs was needed only for the second Seppo grammar.

4. *Prolocatives* were defined as lexical items which occurred in a locative relationship with words classed as nouns or verbs, indicating the location of the object, act, or state referred to. Examples are the Finnish words for 'here', 'there', 'to-here', and 'to-there'.

For both children there was a residue of words which occurred in constructions but which could not be classified according to the criteria described. These are listed separately in the lexicons. All words which occurred only in single-word utterances are also listed separately, since there was no criterion available for determining their class membership.

Inherent features, strict subcategorization frames, and selection restrictions were assigned according to the needs of the individual grammars. Animacy or inanimacy of nouns was important for both children. Nouns were marked [+animate] in the lexicons only if they are animate in adult Finnish (nouns referring to dolls, stuffed animals, and pictures of animate beings are considered animate), and if they occurred in contexts in the samples in which nouns which are not animate in adult Finnish did not occur. These contexts are indicated by the context-sensitive category frame features of animate and inanimate nouns. Many nouns which are animate in adult speech did not appear in these contexts in the samples, although they might have in larger samples. Verbs were marked for selection restrictions like [+——N, +animate] (takes an animate object) and [+N, −animate——] (takes an inanimate subject) only if in the sample or in tapes prior to the sample they actually occurred in such contexts.

Most words classified as verbs, adjectives, adverbs, and prolocatives in the children's lexicons are classified similarly in adult Finnish, but there are some exceptions. For example, Seppo's baby word *uffuf*, "naughty, dirty", was classified as a verb, even though it was an adjective for his mother, because unlike his other adjectives it never preceded nouns in his speech but only followed them. Similarly, Seppo's *kovaa*, 'fast', an adverb in adult Finnish, was classified in the lexicon for the first grammar as a verb meaning 'go fast' (his mother always expanded it in this way), because it did not occur in conjunction with verbs but only with nouns.

Seppo's word *pois*, 'away', was given two lexical entries, one as an intransitive verb with the understood meaning *menee pois*, 'goes away', and one as an optionally transitive verb meaning *ota pois*, 'take off, away'. In the first sense it was used with animate noun subjects to refer to the departure of the person or animal in question (*tipu pois*, 'chick (goes) away'), while in the second sense it was used with inanimate noun direct objects to indicate a desire for the object named to be taken off or away (*takki pois*, '(take) coat off', *kirja pois*, '(take) book away'). Like *pois* in the latter sense, *kiinni*, 'closed', was classed as a transitive verb with the understood meaning *pane kiinni*, 'put closed', i.e. 'close'. In adult Finnish, *pois* and *kiinni* in these senses are particles akin to the particles of English separable verbs. Like these, they can be kept together with the verb before the direct object or moved to post-object position. In Seppo's first sample they always follow the object, which is the most frequent order in adult speech, but in other tapes they occasionally precede it, so a transformation for the repositioning of *pois* and *kiinni* is made optional.

Seppo's *rikki*, 'broken', was classified as an adjective although it is an adverb in adult Finnish and cannot occur before a noun with an attributive relationship (see 3.4.2.2). It was not clear whether Seppo distinguished *rikki* from his 'true' adjectives. In the first sample and for a few weeks thereafter, adjectives were rare and occurred only before nouns or in isolation, but as they became more frequent, they occurred both before and after nouns, as did *rikki*. In all the tapes of Seppo's speech up through the second sample, *rikki* occurred in only one phrase used as an adverb: *bmbm rikki meni*, '"car" broken went'. This was probably a memorized routine since it was the only instance of a past tense for many weeks to come, and similar sentences were modeled frequently in parental speech.

4.3   Transformational generative grammar for Seppo at MLU 1.42

The phrase structure rules, lexicon feature rules, and transformational rules of the syntactic component of a grammar for Seppo, based on the nonimitated utterances of the speech sample collected from him when his MLU was 1.42, are presented below. The lexicon is given in Appendix D. Constructions in the sample which can be generated by the grammar are presented in Appendix E, classified according to the grammatical relations holding between the major constituents. Single-word utterances and their frequencies of occurrence are listed in Appendix F. Most of these can also be generated by the grammar. Constructions which cannot be generated are presented in Appendix G.

Phrase Structure Rules

   1. $S_1 \rightarrow (M \lozenge N)^1$

   2. $S_2 \rightarrow (N)$ VP

---

[1] Linking parentheses are used here to indicate that either or both of the elements so linked can be selected, but at least one must be selected. That is, S cannot be rewritten as nothing.

3. $M \rightarrow \begin{Bmatrix} Adj \\ N \end{Bmatrix}$

4. $VP \rightarrow \begin{Bmatrix} V\ (N) \\ Loc \end{Bmatrix}$

5. $Loc \rightarrow \begin{Bmatrix} N \\ Proloc \end{Bmatrix}$

Lexicon Feature Rules

1. $N \rightarrow [+N, \pm\text{animate}]$
2. $[-\text{animate}] \rightarrow [\pm\text{vehicle}]$
3. $[+\text{animate}] \rightarrow [-V\text{——}, -N\text{——}]$
4. $[-\text{animate}, -\text{vehicle}] \rightarrow [\text{——}V, -\text{——}N]$
5. $V \rightarrow [+V, \pm\text{——}(N)]$
6. $Adj \rightarrow [+Adj]$
7. $Proloc \rightarrow [+Proloc]$
8. $[+Proloc] \rightarrow$ *tuossa*, 'there'

Transformational Rules

1. Treordering: optional
   (*a*) Placement of *pois*, 'away', and *kiinni*, 'closed'

   S.D.: $\begin{Bmatrix} pois \\ kiinni \end{Bmatrix} N$

   S.C.: $x_1 - x_2 \Rightarrow x_2 - x_1$
   (*b*) Placement of prolocative

   S.D.: $N + Proloc$

   S.C.: $x_1 - x_2 \Rightarrow x_2 - x_1$

2. Tverb deletion: optional

   S.D.: $N + V + N$

   S.C.: $x_1 - x_2 - x_3 \Rightarrow x_1 - x_3$

The following discussion of the grammar is divided into three parts, corresponding to the three different kinds of rules specified.

4.3.1 Phrase structure rules. The phrase structure rules provide for nouns, verbs, adjectives, and prolocatives in isolation, and for constructions with the following syntactic interpretations:

subject–verb $(N + V)$
verb–object $(V + N)$

subject–verb–object (N+V+N)
noun–locative (N+N, N+Proloc)
modifier–noun (N+N, Adj+N)

Whether Seppo's noun modifiers were productive at this time is uncertain. There are only two instances of Adj+N in the sample: *rikki auto*, 'broken car', and *pikku kala*, 'little fish'. The only adjectives occurring in isolation in the sample are *rikki*, 'broken', and *korkea*, 'high'; the latter was not classifiable as an adjective for Seppo since it never modified a noun. When the modifier constituent in Seppo's grammar is realized as N rather than as Adj, the first noun in the resulting N+N string specifies a possessor and the second an object possessed. There were three such strings in the sample: *täti auto*, 'aunt car', *isä kello*, 'father clock', and *setä kello*, 'uncle clock'. The first two had been modeled by the mother earlier in the taping session and thus may have been delayed imitations. One more genitive construction was observed during this period, although it was not tape recorded: *Laila kenkä*, 'Laila shoe', as Seppo held up his sister Laila's shoe. During the next few weeks, both Adj+Noun and genitive strings became increasingly common. It is probable that they were just beginning to be established as productive construction patterns at the time of Seppo's early Stage I sample.

It is unclear whether adjectives and genitive nouns should be grouped together as realizations of a single constituent, 'modifier', or whether adjective–noun and genitive–noun strings should be generated as two different sentence patterns. In more psychological terms, the question is whether or not Seppo in some sense regarded the two types of modification as equivalent. Support for one solution or the other is almost nonexistent at this early stage. Later on, adjective–noun and genitive–noun strings were both possible realizations of NP, and could occur in identical contexts such as in response to 'what is that?' questions or as sentence-subjects and direct objects. At this time, however, only single nouns were so used. Genitive–noun seemed to emerge before adjective–noun as a possible answer to 'what' questions, while adjective–noun occurred slightly before genitive–noun as subject or object, but this may reflect sampling limitations rather than real differences. Whether adjectives and genitive nouns could precede the same set of nouns, which would support grouping them together as one constituent, is also uncertain. There are too few utterances in the first sample to allow a judgment. Within the next few weeks, most adjectives modified both animate and inanimate nouns, while genitives occurred only with inanimate nouns like 'pencil', 'hat', 'car', and 'nose'. The first genitive–noun construction in which the object possessed was animate was observed several months after the first sample: *Laila hiiri*, 'Laila mouse'. In the mother's speech, objects possessed were also nearly always inanimate, so the characteristics of Seppo's genitive constructions may simply have reflected the characteristics of objects commonly possessed by members of his family rather than a real restriction in underlying competence. A decision was finally made to group adjectives and genitive nouns together as modifiers because they appeared later on in similar contexts at close to the same time.

In transformational grammars for English, genitive–noun and adjective–noun strings are usually derived transformationally from underlying N *has* N and N *is* Adjective strings. A parallel derivation of such strings for either of the Finnish children was rejected, because genitive–noun and adjective–noun strings seem to have been primitive construction patterns in the children's grammars. They did not produce N *has* N or N (*is*) Adjective constructions until after genitive–noun and adjective–noun constructions were well established, and when these strings eventually did begin to appear, they were far less numerous than the earlier forms.

4.3.2 Lexicon feature rules. Nouns are given the inherent feature [+animate] or [−animate]. Inanimate nouns are subdivided into [+vehicle] and [−vehicle]. The lexicon feature rules insure that all nouns which precede verbs and other nouns as sentence-subjects, objects located, or genitives have the feature either [+animate] or [+vehicle], and that all nouns which follow verbs and other nouns as direct objects, location names, and objects possessed have the feature [−animate] (but see 4.3.1 on whether this restriction on objects possessed should be included in the grammar).

In Seppo's speech for many months to come, words for vehicles functioned like animate nouns in roles like 'sentence-subject with a main verb' and 'object located'. Unlike animate nouns and like other inanimate nouns, they also served as direct objects and objects possessed. In the first sample, only two words needed to be classified as [+vehicle]: *auto*, 'car', and *bmbm*, "car". A larger sample might have revealed that *tuf tuf*, "train", *kuorma-auto*, 'truck', *lentokone*, 'airplane', and *kan*, "tractor" (Seppo's baby word) could also function like both animate and inanimate nouns. In the tapes, relatively few verbs were used with [+vehicle] subjects, and these usually named actions which can appropriately be performed by vehicles, such as *käy*, 'goes', *kovaa*, '(goes) fast', and *vetää*, 'pulls'. However, there was evidence that Seppo also considered vehicles capable of performing actions typically associated with animate subjects. The utterances *auto aa-aa*, 'car "sleeps"', and *uffuf linja-auto puree*, '"naughty" bus bites', both occurred a few weeks after the sample being considered. Seppo's parents seemed willing to consider vehicles as animate in some ways, perhaps taking their cue from Seppo. For example, Seppo's father once said, with no prompting from Seppo, *lentokonekin aa-aa tallissa*, '(the) airplane-also "sleeps" garage-in'. Kernan (1969), in analyzing the speech of the Samoan girl Tofi at MLU 1.60, also found that a word for automobile was used in roles which are normally associated with animate nouns, such as agent and possessor. The similarity in children's minds between vehicles and animate beings may be that both are perceived as capable of independent movement, or as capable of initiating a force. It is possible that children initially use these criteria rather than animacy to subclassify names for objects.

In the sample upon which this grammar for Seppo is based, all verbs occurred exclusively with [+animate] or [+vehicle] nouns as subjects, and, when transitive, with [−animate] nouns as objects. This information can be conveyed in different ways. As noted in 4.1, Chomsky argues that there are good reasons for considering nouns selectionally dominant over verbs and adjectives in English, and suggests that this may be a universal feature of language. If, in accordance with this formulation, particular verbs are to be inserted into preterminal strings only after particular nouns are selected, we would need to assign to every verb in Seppo's lexicon the selection restrictions either [−[−animate]——] or [+[+animate]——] and [+[+vehicle]——], and, for transitive verbs, either [−——[+animate]] or [+——[−animate]]. Sentences with inanimate subjects or animate objects would be blocked when a search through the lexicon would fail to turn up any verbs which could occur in these contexts. Since these features exhaustively characterized Seppo's verbs, the same restrictions can also be conveyed by assigning category frame features to nouns which prevent animate nouns from following verbs and inanimate nouns from preceding verbs. Perhaps one solution corresponds more closely than the other to Seppo's linguistic knowledge at this time, but this could not be determined.

The solution of assigning category frame features to nouns was adopted in the grammar because co-occurrence restrictions between nouns and other nouns also had to be specified, and these restrictions could be indicated economically with essentially the same rules which specified the co-occurrence restrictions between nouns and verbs.

4.3.3 Transformational rules

4.3.3.1 Prolocative placement. In addition to the transformation reordering *pois*, 'away', and *kiinni* 'closed', which is described in 4.2, the grammar specifies optional transformations for prolocative re-ordering and verb deletion. The prolocative reordering transformation derives *tuossa*, 'there', $+N$ strings from $N + tuossa$ strings. This transformation possibly should have been made more general, to reorder any $N + Loc$ string. In the sample, there were four utterance types of $N + N_{loc.}$ and two of $N_{loc.} + N$:

auto talli	'car garage'	*talli..bmbm*	'garage.."car"'
ankka vettä	'duck water'	*ulo⟨s⟩ takki*	'to-outside coat'
ankka puu	'duck tree'		
tipu kenkä	'chick shoe'		

In the nonlinguistic contexts of all these utterances except 'chick shoe', the objects referred to were moving towards the locations specified rather than situated at those locations. For example, the duck in a picture was not in the water but walking towards it. The car was not in the garage but being pushed towards it by Seppo. In adult Finnish, $N + N_{loc.}$ is the dominant order but $N_{loc.} + N$ is a legitimate alternative, both in locative–copula–subject and locative–verb–subject (or locative–subject–verb) strings. Strings with the latter orders are quite rare compared to strings with the dominant order in Seppo's mother's speech sample, however. In Seppo's speech, $N_{loc.} + N$ strings continued to occur occasionally in the tapes following those from which the first sample was taken, but were so infrequent that it is impossible to decide whether the order was productive. The grammar therefore does not generate it. In contrast, strings containing *tuossa* 'there', plus a noun continued to occur with increasing frequency in both word orders (see Table 5).

4.3.3.2 Verb deletion transformation and Bloom's reduction transformation. An optional verb deletion rule in the grammar for Seppo specifies the following operation:

$$\text{S.D.}: N+V+N$$
$$\text{S.C.}: x_1-x_2-x_3 \Rightarrow x_1-x_3$$

This rule provides for the generation of $N+N$ strings in which the first noun functions as sentence-subject and the second noun as direct object. In the sample at MLU 1.42, there were only three constructions judged to be of this type:

(1) (*S* looking at a picture of a
camel eating a flower)   *humma* 'horsie'[1]
                                humma 'horsie'
Syö kukkaa. 'Eats (a) flower'.
                                > *humma kukka* 'horsie flower'

(2) (*S* looking at a picture of a bird
eating cereal out of a bowl) > *tipu mamma*   'chick "food"'
Tipu siinä mammaa syö. 'Chick
there "food" eats'.

(3) (*S* looking at a picture of a lady
serving food to a bear seated at
a table with an empty plate in
front of him)   > *täti mamma*   'lady "food"'

However, this construction pattern continued to appear in the tapes for many months to come, although always infrequently, and was probably productive. Rina also produced such constructions.

Accounting for strings like these is difficult, and the type of solution chosen has certain grammatical and psychological implications. Bloom (1970) found subject–object constructions numerous in data from her subjects Kathryn and Gia. At the time for which she wrote grammars, the children also produced many subject–verb and verb–object strings. Bloom felt that the occurrence of these three types of strings indicated that the children knew about the relationships which hold between subject, verb, and object, and about the appropriate word order for

---

[1] In examples like these, the child's utterances appear on the right side, the interlocutor's on the left. The interlocutor is the mother unless otherwise specified. The symbol > indicates which utterance or utterances in a sequence exemplifies the construction type being discussed. The description of the nonlinguistic context is enclosed in parentheses. *S* stands for Seppo, *R* for Rina, *M* for Mother, and *B* for the investigator.

expressing these relationships. Since the fully developed subject–verb–
object construction almost never occurred, however, it seemed as if
the children were constrained with respect to the maximum sentence
length they could handle and were forced to omit one element if they
produced the other two. Constructions of other sorts were also limited
to two words. To account both for the relatively complex knowledge
of sentence construction indicated by the children's production of
subject–verb, verb–object, and subject–object strings, and for the fact
that this knowledge rarely achieved full expression in any one sentence,
Bloom postulated an underlying structure for sentences which was
richer than the surface structures derived from it. The deep structures
generated by her grammars obligatorily included the grammatical
functions *sentence-subject* and *sentence-predicate*. Subjects were single
nouns or pronouns, and predicates were predicate nominatives (nouns
or modified nouns) or verbs with optional direct objects or particles.
The nonoccurrence in surface structure of strings longer than two
category symbols was accounted for by a *reduction transformation* which
obligatorily deleted one or more elements if more than two were present
in deep structure. Two major types of reduction, *linear* and *hierarchical*,
resulted from the operation of the reduction transformation:

1. In linear reduction, one major category was deleted if another occurred
or was expanded. For example, if the complement of the verb phrase (direct
object or particle) was included, the subject might be deleted. Thus, underlying subject–verb–object became verb–object. If the predicate nominative
was expanded to include an adjective, a demonstrative pronoun subject
might be deleted. Demonstrative–adjective–noun would thus become
adjective–noun.
2. In hierarchical reduction, there was reduction within a major category
when another category was included. For example, if the subject was
included, the verb or the object noun was deleted from the verb phrase, and
underlying subject–verb–object became subject–verb or subject–object.

In the grammars written for the Finnish children, subject–object
strings are derived by deletion of an underlying verb, as in Bloom's
grammars, but the reason for this formulation is different from Bloom's.
Bloom justified the inclusion of elements such as sentence-subject and
verb in deep structure when they are lacking in surface structure by
giving two objections to an alternative representation of the same
distributional facts, that of introducing categories into deep structure
as optional. First, she argued that optionality implies that all options
may potentially be exercised, but for her subjects, only subject–verb,

verb–object, and subject–object could be selected, but not all three at once. Secondly, if elements were made optional,

the semantic interpretation of utterances in which elements that were not immediate constituents were juxtaposed in production (such as subject–object strings...) would postulate intervening constituents which could not be structurally accounted for. The occurrence of the N+N sentences with the structural description *subject–object* implied the designation of a dummy element linking the two categories in an underlying representation. The relational nature of the grammatical function *direct object* depends on the existence of another constituent also dominated by the same syntactic node, VP (1970, pp. 72–3).

Arguments against both of Bloom's objections to the solution of optionality are presented below.

1. *Optionality implies that all options can be exercised*

In Bloom's data there were a very few utterances in which all options for choosing subject, verb, and object simultaneously were exercised, and these could not be generated by the grammars because they violated the reduction transformation. Brown (in press), in discussing a more advanced stage of linguistic development, notes that a constraint on sentence length is still present but with the limit now three rather than two constituents. A very few utterances with four constituents did occur in his data, however. He suggests that apparent limits on sentence length at these two stages of development may be a function of sample size. More examples of sentences ruled beyond the child's competence might well turn up in larger samples, indicating that exercise of all options is possible, although infrequent.

When Seppo's mean length of utterance was only slightly higher than that of Bloom's subjects, he was clearly capable of exercising all options in generating strings with subject, verb, and object constituents, since he produced several subject–verb–object constructions. Why could a grammar for him not generate subject–object strings as an optional choice of two out of three elements? Before answering this question, we must examine Bloom's second objection to the optionality solution.

2. *Optionality does not always provide the elements needed in deep structure for the interpretation of utterances*

Bloom noted that the syntactic and semantic interpretation of subject–object strings requires that the nouns functioning as subject and object be dominated by different nodes in underlying structure, so that their functions can be identified by reference to the major categories from which they are derived. An underlying structure in which both nouns are dominated by the same node, as illustrated in this tree-diagram,

would be adequate for representing N + N strings in which the relationship is one of attribution or conjunction, but would not allow strings of this sort to be distinguished from those which express a subject–object or a noun–locative relationship.

Bloom's method of insuring the appropriate syntactic and semantic interpretation of subject–object strings was to have the second noun be dominated by a VP which also dominated a dummy verb, as in this tree-diagram:

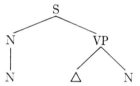

The verb was then deleted by the reduction transformation. Inclusion of the verb in the VP apparently was motivated by Bloom's observation that the relational nature of the grammatical function *direct object* depends on the existence of a verb dominated by the VP which also dominates the direct object (1970, p. 73). In transformational generative grammar, as in traditional analyses of constituent structure, the verb and the direct object of a sentence are regarded as one constituent and the subject as another. The fact that deep structure elements are analyzed in a certain way in the adult language is not in itself sufficient reason for postulating the same constituent structure in children's utterances. As we will discuss in Chapter 6, it is uncertain whether children's linguistic competence includes an understanding of constituent structure as it is represented in a transformational grammar. For example, there is little evidence that the apparent verb phrases in children's speech have any psychological unity as constituents for the children, and that elements functioning as direct objects depend on the presence of a verb any more than elements functioning as subjects do. Bloom perhaps relies too heavily on formulations designed to account for adult speech in arguing that a child's sentence which contains a direct object must also contain a verb in its deep structure representation.

Even if we wish to retain the configuration of deep structure elements postulated by transformational grammar, there is a method of deriving the two nouns of subject–object strings from appropriate different nodes to allow syntactic and semantic interpretation without including an underlying verb. According to Chomsky (1965, p. 69), 'object of' is the relation holding between the NP of a VP and the whole VP, not between the NP and the V of the VP. Thus, we could simply specify that one possible realization of the VP constituent is N alone, as illustrated in this tree-diagram:

The grammatical functions of the nouns could be determined, as in Bloom's grammars, by reference to the domination of the first noun by S and the second by VP.

This solution was not adopted in the grammars for the Finnish children, however. Subject–object strings are derived from underlying subject–verb–object strings, as in Bloom's grammars. The purpose of postulating an underlying verb is to insure that the subject and object nouns in subject–object strings have appropriate syntactic features. In Seppo's speech at the stage represented by the first grammar, subject nouns were always animate or vehicles and object nouns inanimate, whether or not there was an intervening verb. This is provided for when a verb is present in underlying structure by the category frame features of nouns, which indicate which nouns can precede verbs and which can follow verbs:

$$[+\text{animate}] \rightarrow [-\text{V}\underline{\quad}]$$
$$[-\text{animate}, -\text{vehicle}] \rightarrow [\underline{\quad}\text{V}]$$

If no verb is specified in the underlying structures of subject–object strings, we must indicate the syntactic features of the subject and object nouns by reference to their occurrence with each other, with rules such as:

$$[+\text{animate}] \rightarrow [-\text{N}\text{———}]$$
$$[-\text{animate}, -\text{vehicle}] \rightarrow [-\text{———N}]$$

There are two main objections to such a formulation:

1. When animacy of subjects and inanimacy of objects is provided for by two distinct types of rules, depending upon whether a verb is present, a regularity is not accounted for economically and the rules probably have little correspondence to the psychological principles governing the choice of nouns as subjects and objects.

2. There would be no way to differentiate between N+N strings which express such different syntactic relationships as possessor–object possessed, object located–location, and subject–object, in order to specify different restrictions on the syntactic features of the nouns involved. In the sample for Seppo at MLU 1.42, objects located, possessors, and subjects were in fact all animate or vehicles, and location names, objects possessed, and direct objects were inanimate, so such a differentiation was not necessary.

This regularity began to break down slightly later on, however, making it impossible to specify the characteristics of subject and object nouns by reference to their occurrence before or after other nouns. The fact that it would be possible at all at first may have been accidental, so a rule for the correct generation of subject–object strings should not be formulated to depend on it.

In the first grammar for Seppo, all verbs were identical with respect to the features of the nouns with which they could occur, so appropriate lexical items could be introduced into the roles of subject and object simply by reference to the presence of a lexical category symbol V preceding or following the lexical category symbol N to be replaced. Gradually, the co-occurrence restrictions between verbs, subject nouns, and object nouns became more complex, with some verbs still taking only animate subjects and inanimate objects and others taking animate objects or inanimate subjects as well. These restrictions are represented in the second Seppo grammar as selection restrictions for verbs. As noted in 4.3.2, co-occurrence restrictions between nouns and verbs in the first grammar could also have been specified in this way.

When the co-occurrence restrictions between nouns and verbs are such that they cannot be stated by general rules such as 'all nouns following verbs are inanimate', insuring that the restrictions are followed depends upon the substitution of particular lexical items for category symbols in preterminal strings. Specific nouns in the roles of subject and object and specific verbs must be selected and their inherent features and selection restrictions noted before a match can be verified. If our argument that underlying verbs must be generated to account for the features associated with subjects and objects is valid, then we must also postulate that *particular* verbs are selected and then deleted. In the grammars for the Finnish children, then, specific lexical items are considered present in underlying structure but deleted in surface structure in subject–object strings. This is contrary to Bloom's formulation. She asserts that the reduction transformation 'did not operate on particular lexical items but rather on the elements representing the categories in the underlying structure from which lexical items are derived' (1970, p. 166).

The claim that the children had particular verbs in mind which were not expressed in surface structure is rather strong. It is possible, as Bloom suggests, that children are not thinking of specific verbs at all when they produce subject–object strings, but only of very generalized representations of actions. Bloom (1970, p. 166) hypothesizes that some verb deletions in her subjects' speech may have occurred because the children did not know an appropriate lexical item to fill the verb slot. When the Finnish children produced subject–object strings, however, there was often strong evidence that they were thinking of particular verbs associated with certain selection restrictions rather than of unspecified dummy representations of action. Evidence is scanty in the first Seppo sample, since Seppo produced only three subject–object strings. In one of them, as we saw, his mother had modeled the 'missing' verb as well as the direct object:

(1) (*S* looking at a picture of a
     camel eating a flower)   *humma*   'horsie'
                                   humma   'horsie'
     Syö kukkaa. 'Eats (a) flower'.
                      > *humma kukka*   'horsie flower'

In the other two utterances, *tipu mamma*, 'chick "food"' and *täti mamma*, 'lady "food"', 'eats' and 'gives' may have been the respective underlying verbs, judging from the nonlinguistic contexts and the way in which the utterances were expanded by the mother. Although these verbs did not occur in this sample, they appeared almost immediately in subsequent tapes and it is likely that they were already known.

There is better evidence for specific underlying verbs in later tapes. The following examples are taken from the second Seppo sample.

(2) (*B* has been drawing cat faces
     for *S*)

B: *Kuka piirsi kissan?*
'Who drew (a) cat?'

täti 'aunt'

B: *Täti, niin.* 'Aunt, yes'.

pikku (kissa) 'little (cat)'

B: *Mitäs Seppo nyt piirtää?*
'What is Seppo drawing
now?'

kissa (istuu)——— 'cat (sits)———'[1]

B: *Toisella kynällä.* 'With (the)
other pen'.

täti ottaa 'aunt takes'

B: '*Täti ottaa*'. 'Aunt takes'.
(*S* tries to get *B* to draw
again)

> *kissa, täti kissa* 'cat, aunt cat'
> *täti kissa*   'aunt cat'

B: (drawing another cat):
Täti piirtää kissaa.
'Aunt is drawing (a) cat'.

The verb *piirtää*, 'draws', was well known to Seppo at this time and occurred in several utterances in the sample, such as *Laila piirtää*, 'Laila draws', and *poika piirtää tuohon*, 'boy draws to-there'. The next week, under circumstances almost identical to those described above, two utterances occurred which suggest that *piirtää*, 'draws', was indeed the underlying verb in the constructions of example (2): *piirrä kissa* 'draw cat' (imperative form of verb) and *kissa piirtää*, 'cat draws' (object–verb). The most compelling reason for postulating *piirtää*, 'draws' as the underlying verb is that it was one of very few verbs in Seppo's lexicon which could take animate objects at this time. Earlier, for example, Seppo had said *pupu piirtää nalle*, 'bunny draws bear', while looking at a picture of a rabbit painting a portrait of another rabbit. Up to the time of example (2), the only other verbs which had ever taken animate objects were *syö*, 'eats', *hakee*, 'fetches', and *työntää*, 'pushes'. Example (2), therefore, provides support for the argument that the inherent features of nouns functioning as subject and object are related to the selection restrictions of the verbs with which they are associated in utterances. The animacy of the direct object in the utterance 'aunt cat' was closely tied to the presence of a particular underlying verb 'draws', which was one of very few verbs

---

[1] '———' indicates a portion of the utterance which was unclear and could not be transcribed.

which could take animate objects at this time. If an unspecified dummy verb had been deleted rather than a particular lexical item, there would have been no way to account for the relatively unusual syntactic feature of this direct object.

In the following sequence from the second Seppo sample, the 'missing' verb in *hiiri omena*, 'mouse apple', is clearly *syö*, 'eats':

> (3) (*S* has been trying to make a
>   toy mouse 'eat' a cardamom
>   seed by holding the seed up
>   to its mouth)
>
> | | |
> |---|---|
> | *hiiri syö* | 'mouse eats' |
> | *hiiri syö* | 'mouse eats' |
>
> *Kardemummaa.* 'Cardamom'.
>
> | | |
> |---|---|
> | *kardemumma* | 'cardamom' |
>
> *Syöks se?* '(Does) it eat?'
> *Syöks hiiri kardemummaa?*
> '(Does the) mouse eat cardamom?'
> *Mitä se syö?* 'What (does) it
>   eat?'
>
> | | |
> |---|---|
> | *syö kardemumma* | 'eats cardamom' |
>
> ⋮
>
> | | |
> |---|---|
> | *syö..tuota..omena*[1] | eats..that.. |
> | | apple' |
>
> *Omenaa syö.* 'Apple (it) eats'.
>
> > *hiiri omena* 'mouse apple'

Similarly, there is little doubt that 'eats' was the 'intended' verb in the utterance *hiiri tämmö*, 'mouse this-kind-of-thing', in the following sequence:

> (4) (Same circumstance as in (3)
>   above)
>
> | | |
> |---|---|
> | *syö* | 'eats' |
>
> *Haluaa—mitä hiiri—*[2]
> 'wants—what (does the)
>   mouse—'
>
> | | |
> |---|---|
> | *tämmö* | 'this-kind-of-thing' |
>
> *Ei tämmöstä syö.* 'Not this-kind-
>   of-thing (it) eats'.
> *Mitä hiiri syö—*'What (does the)
>   mouse eat—'
>
> | | |
> |---|---|
> | *keksi..keksi..——vettä* | |
> | 'cracker..cracker..——water' | |

---

[1] Vertical dots indicate intervening utterances.
[2] '—' indicates that the utterance was broken off or interrupted.

Keksi. Vettä se syö.
'Cracker. Water it eats'.

> *hiiri tämmö* 'mouse this-kind-of-thing'

Ei tämmöstä. 'Not this-kind-of-thing'.
Juustoa syö. 'Cheese (it) eats'.

juusto syö 'cheese (it) eats'

Joo. Ja—'Yes. And—'

tämmö syö 'this-kind-of-thing (it) eats'

Subject–object strings in Rina's speech also often occurred in speech contexts from which the missing verb could easily be inferred:

(5) (*R* trying to get *M* to give her another piece of cake)

> *Rina lisää kakku* 'Rina more cake'

Et sä jaksaa, kulta, enää. 'You don't have the strength to, dear, any more'.

tässä..lisää kakku 'here..more cake'
saa lisää kakku 'gets more cake'

Kuka saa lisää kakkua?
'Who gets more cake?'

aaa.. 'aaa..'

Joo, Melissa-täti—
'Yes, Aunt Melissa—'

_____ '___'

Rina saa lisää kakku 'Rina gets more cake'
Rina saa lisää kakku 'Rina gets more cake'

(6) (*R* is in next room trying to find a pencil)
B: *Tule tänne, Rina.*
'Come here, Rina'.

> *Rina kynä* 'Rina pencil'
Rina otti kynä 'Rina took pencil'

Subject–object strings sometimes resulted from the child's reduction of a parent's immediately preceding subject–verb–object string:

(7) (*S* and *M* looking at a picture of a fox on a motocycle)

7-2

Kettu ajaa mootori-pyörää.
'(A) fox drives (a) motorcycle'.

> *kettu..mooto*   'fox..motor'

Seppo later produced the full subject–verb–object string himself: *kettu ajaa mooto,* 'fox drives motor'.

(8) (*S* and *M* looking at a picture
     of a car pulling a boat)
     auto vetää venettä.
     '(the) car pulls (the) boat'.

> *auto vene*   'car boat'

Contrary to Bloom's suggestion that verb deletions may take place when appropriate lexical items are unknown, the verbs omitted in these reductions of parental utterances were often among the verbs used most frequently by the child. For example, at the times the above reductions were produced, Seppo used *ajaa,* 'drives', and *vetää,* 'pulls', more often than any other verbs in his vocabulary in verb–object and subject–verb–object constructions. He undoubtedly understood their meanings in his mother's utterances and was probably aware that they linked the two nouns in his own reductions.

In summary, the decision to generate subject–object strings in the grammars for both Seppo and Rina by deletion not of unspecified dummy verbs but of particular lexical items rested upon two sorts of evidence:

1. Evidence that the selection restrictions of the 'missing' verb were closely tied to the inherent features of the subject and object nouns. The best example of this is the utterance *täti kissa,* 'aunt cat'. The presence of the animate object 'cat' is linked to the implicit presence of a verb 'draws', which has the selection restriction [+——[+animate]], as demonstrated in the earlier utterance 'bunny draws bear'.

2. Evidence from linguistic context that the child had specific verbs in mind, which he often expressed in subject–verb, verb–object, or subject–verb–object strings preceding or following the subject–object string.

This sort of evidence for particular underlying lexical items may not be present in the speech of all children. Bloom evidently did not find it, although she does not discuss this in detail. The best method of generating subject–object strings, then, must probably be determined on the basis of the characteristics of the speech of individual children being studied.

Whether a provision for generating such strings should be included in the grammars at all is uncertain. Unless otherwise specified, grammars are intended to represent only information about competence, not about the factors influencing actual sentence production or comprehension. Bloom regarded both subject and predicate, with predicate expanded as V and an optional NP or particle, as part of her subjects' underlying linguistic competence. She formulated the reduction transformation to account for the children's apparent inability, due to unknown cognitive limitations, to program more than two items at the same time from the underlying sequence. Brown (in press) suggests that children's production of reduced strings like subject–object may reflect the operation of performance variables rather than aspects of their linguistic competence. Subject–object strings continue to occur in children's speech long after subject–verb–object strings are also produced, so they cannot always be accounted for by an overall constraint on sentence length. Performance factors cause adults to produce many sentence fragments, but this is regarded as irrelevant to their underlying competence. Similar fragments in children's speech, hypothesizes Brown, may result from an imperfect knowledge of rules of discourse. Children may overgeneralize about what constituents of sentences are optionally omissible in certain contexts from observing many examples of omission in their parents' speech. Even if some subject–object strings result from a general limitation on sentence length, it is not clear that this should be considered a matter of competence. Adults also have finite memories and cannot program sentences beyond a certain length, but this is regarded as an aspect of performance rather than of competence. Grammars for the language as it is spoken by adults are capable of generating infinitely long strings.

In writing grammars for children, it is tempting to undertake two tasks at once, that of representing what children actually know about language and that of specifying what they are able to produce. When the discrepancy between the two is great, as apparently was the case for Bloom's subjects, it is difficult to decide which to emphasize. Bloom's formulation of the reduction transformation seems to be a compromise, and perhaps this is the best solution. However, the distinction between rules designed to represent competence and those designed to represent performance limitations should be made clear. The optional verb deletion transformations of the grammars written for Seppo and Rina are regarded as specifications of performance variables which were important enough to warrant representation in the grammars. Other aspects of performance, such as word repetition, were not considered similarly significant.

4.3.4 Summary of the grammar. The grammar written for Seppo at MLU 1.42 generates constructions with the following syntactic interpretations and frequencies of occurrence in the sample:

Syntactic interpretation	Construction	f: type/token
subject–verb	N + V	30/44
verb–object	V + N	3/4
	N + *pois*, 'away'	3/4
	N + *kiinni*, 'closed'	1/1
subject–object	N + N	3/5
subject–verb–object	N + V + N	6/7
noun–locative	N + N	4/5
	N + Proloc	2/2
	Proloc + N	3/3
modifier–noun	N + N	3/7
	Adj + N	2/2

The syntactic classes needed for Seppo's grammar at this stage were *noun, verb, adjective,* and *prolocative.* Nouns were subdivided into animate and inanimate, with inanimate nouns still further subdivided into vehicle and nonvehicle classes. These distinctions were needed because only animate nouns and words for vehicles occurred with verbs and with other nouns as sentence-subjects, objects located, and possessors, and only inanimate nouns functioned as direct objects, location names, and objects possessed. Nouns modified by adjectives were either animate or inanimate. Verbs were subdivided into those which never took objects and those which optionally took objects.

Alternate orderings were specified only for N + Prolocative, *kiinni,* 'closed', + N, and *pois,* 'away, off', + N strings. Other reorderings did occur, however, and their increasing frequency and correspondence to legitimate alternate orders of adult Finnish suggest that they were not random errors at this time. Subject–verb–object is the dominant, unmarked order pattern of Finnish. Other orders are permissible as stylistic variants emphasizing different sentential elements. Let us compare the frequencies with which various word orders of subject, verb, and object occurred in Seppo's sample at MLU 1.42 and in his mother's 1000 utterance sample:

	Seppo f: tokens	Mother f: tokens	
S + V	44	47	
V + S	4	5	
			(includes both
V + O	4	16	imperative and
O + V	1	3	nonimperative
			utterances)
S + V + O	7	32	
O + S + V	1	—	
O + V + S	—	1	
V + S + O	—	1	
S + O + V	—	1	

(See Appendix E for listings of the S + V, V + O, and S + V + O constructions in Seppo's sample, and Appendix G, 'Constructions not generated by the grammar', for the V + S, O + V, and O + S + V constructions.) Seppo's constructions with the less frequent orders were not produced under unusual extralinguistic circumstances, nor, insofar as could be determined, did they express meanings different from those expressed by the more common orders. Seppo was clearly sensitive to the order patterns of the speech modeled for him and had learned the important characteristics of Finnish dominant word order. The orders Seppo used in the tapes following this early sample indicate that V + S and O + V (but not O + S + V, which never occurred again and did not appear in the mother's sample) became productive as alternates to the dominant orders. At this stage, there were too few V + S and O + V constructions to justify the conclusion that these orders were already productive, so the grammar does not generate them. The significance of Seppo's flexible word order will be considered in more detail in Chapter 5.

Seppo's grammar differed from that of adult Finnish in several major respects. It did not provide for sentence conjoining or recursion through sentence embedding. Strings were thus necessarily finite in length. Also lacking were specifications for inflections of any kind, pronouns (including personal, impersonal, and demonstrative), copulas, catenative verbs (want to, have to, need to, etc.), questions, and negative constructions.

With a very few exceptions, noted in the lexicons, Seppo's verbs had a single, invariant form in both the early and late Stage I samples. This form is identical to the third person singular, present indicative form of adult Finnish, which is often the same as the verb stem, except for a lengthened final vowel. For many verbs, this form is also the same as the infinitive, and differs from the second person singular imperative form only by the lengthening of the final vowel. For other verbs, it is identical to the infinitive but quite different from the imperative. For still other verbs, it is identical to the imperative but different from the infinitive. For a few verbs, the third singular form is quite different from both the infinitive and the imperative. Since Seppo's invariant verb was always in the third person singular form even when this is different from the infinitive or the imperative or both, it is likely that he paid primary attention to this form in adult speech and also based on it his verbs which have identical infinitives or imperatives.

Seppo's noun forms, like those of his verbs, were basically invariant, and did not contrast with related forms in his speech. For many nouns, the form was clearly the nominative singular, which is often identical to the noun stem used with inflections. For nouns ending in -*a*, -*o*, or -*u*, Seppo could have derived his form from either the nominative or the partitive. The two forms are the same except that the partitive has a lengthened final vowel. For example, *hiekka* (nominative), *hiekkaa* (partitive) 'sand'; *auto* (nominative), *autoo* (partitive) 'car'. (In standard Finnish, the partitive of words in -*o* and -*u* is -*a* – for example, *autoa* – but in colloquial speech the partitive is often formed simply by lengthening the final -*o* or -*u*). Seppo often lengthened the final vowels of words in all parts of speech. The lengthening served no grammatical purpose in Seppo's speech, as it did not distinguish between nouns in different syntactic roles. It occurred especially often with words in isolation, and had the character of phonological play. This form of play may have originated in Seppo's observation of long final vowels on some of the words he heard. However, English-speaking children sometimes engage in the same sort of play, even though the lengthening of vowels can have no grammatical significance. Nouns which cannot be changed from nominative to partitive simply by vowel lengthening were never in the partitive in Seppo's speech, with two exceptions. For example, he produced *äiti* (nominative) but not *äitiä* (partitive), 'mother' and *kahvi* (nominative), but not *kahvia* (partitive), 'coffee'. The two exceptions were *vettä*, 'water', and *lunta*, 'snow'. These did not contrast with any other forms in Seppo's speech. The nominatives of these nouns are phonologically quite different (*vesi* and *lumi* respectively), and are much rarer than the partitives in adult speech.

Seppo's failure at this time and for some time to come to use long and short final vowels appropriately to signal different syntactic functions indicates that he did not yet distinguish between nominative and partitive. Further evidence for this conclusion is that he occasionally produced utterances like *kaunis vettä*, 'beautiful water' and *iso vettä*, 'big water', in which a nominative adjective is incorrectly paired with a partitive noun, exactly as a nominative adjective is correctly paired with a nominative noun in other utterances he produced, such as *kaunis tyttö*, 'beautiful girl', and *iso tyttö*, 'big girl'.

Another difference between Seppo's grammar and that of adult Finnish is that his modifier–noun constructions never appeared in a syntactic context, for example, as sentence-subjects or direct objects. All subjects and objects were simple nouns at this stage. They did not expand into noun phrases until the time of the second Seppo grammar.

Although 'no' occurred frequently in isolation at this time, it did not combine with other words. Yes–no interrogation and Wh questions were also missing. In adult Finnish, yes–no questions are not characterized by a special intonation, so this device for marking questions was not available to Seppo as it is to American children. Questions are formed by suffixing a question particle to the word being questioned, which is usually the verb. This word is brought to the front of the sentence. The particle must be also attached to words questioned in isolation. Neither Seppo nor Rina learned the use of the question particle until long after Stage I.

4.4 Comparison with English-speaking children

The English-speaking children with whom Seppo can be compared at this stage of development are Bloom's (1970) subjects Kathryn, Gia, and Eric at MLUs 1.32, 1.34, and 1.42 respectively, and Kendall at MLU 1.48 (see Appendix C for a listing of constructions in Kendall's sample). These mean utterance lengths are close to Seppo's 1.42.

The children's speech was strikingly similar, both in broad outline and in many fine details. The children were working on an almost identical set of construction patterns, and what differences there were seem to have been no greater between Seppo and the American children than among the American children. Table 8 lists important construction patterns and notes whether they were produced by each of the five children. The patterns most common across all the children involve the expression of subject, verb, and object relationships and the modification of nouns in various ways. Demonstrative pronouns with nouns (e.g. 'that doggie'), negative words in construction with one other element, and nouns and verbs with locatives also occurred, but not in the speech of as many of the children. Let us examine the characteristics of the construction patterns listed in Table 8 more closely.

TABLE 8. *Early Stage I: main construction patterns of Finnish and American children*[a]

Construction pattern	Seppo MLU 1.42	Kathryn MLU 1.32	Gia MLU 1.34	Eric MLU 1.42	Kendall MLU 1.48
subject–verb	×	×	×	×	×
verb–object	×	×	×	×	×
subject–object	×	×	×	—	×
subject–verb–object	×	(×)	—	—	×
adjective–noun	×	×	—	—	×
attributive noun–noun	—	×	×	—	—
genitive noun–noun	×	×	×	—	×
demonstrative pronoun–noun	(×)	×	(×)	—	×
noun–locative	×	(×)	(×)	—	×
verb–locative	(×)	—	—	—	×
negative–noun	—	×	(×)	×	(×)
negative–verb	—	×	—	×	—

[a] Parentheses indicate that although the construction pattern occurred, there were extremely few examples of it and it may not have been productive yet.

4.4.1 Subject–verb–object relationships: frequencies of production and word order. Seppo and Kendall both produced subject–verb, verb–object, subject–object, and subject–verb–object strings. All three of Bloom's subjects produced subject–verb and verb–object strings, two of the three produced subject–object strings, and one was barely beginning to produce subject–verb–object strings. The rank order frequencies with which these occurred varied. All of Bloom's children produced more verb–object than subject–verb combinations, and Bloom hypothesized that subject–verb was a more recent development of their grammars. Seppo, in contrast, produced by far the most subject–verb combinations, with subject–verb–object next and finally verb–object. This difference between some American and Finnish children is also present later in development. Brown's three subjects at MLUs of approximately 1.75 produced more verb–object than subject–verb strings (unpublished materials), while Seppo and Rina at that stage both produced many more subject–verb strings. Kendall's speech indicates that English- and Finnish-speaking children do not necessarily differ in this respect, however, since at MLUs of both 1.10 and 1.48 she produced many more subject–verb than verb–object combinations and thus was more similar to Seppo and Rina than to Bloom's and Brown's subjects.

It is possible that structural differences between Finnish and English tend to cause children learning the two languages to stress subject–verb and verb–object relationships differentially. As noted in 4.2, many English verbs which require direct objects have Finnish translations which appear both with and without objects. Just as the English verbs 'read', 'eat', and 'drink' occur with and without objects, the Finnish verbs 'give', 'hold onto', 'pull', 'tow', 'serve', 'fix', and others appeared both with and without objects in Seppo's mother's speech. Perhaps Finnish children are more likely than American children to regard objects as dispensable if they are obvious from context because they are exposed to more verbs of this type. However, this hypothesis is weak, since if it had been the case that the children had produced more verb–object than subject–verb strings, this could also have been 'explained' by reference to another aspect of the linguistic input to the children: that the Finnish mothers, unlike American mothers, often omitted sentence-subjects, providing models of nonimperative verb–object strings from which their children might have concluded that subjects are dispensable.

Possibly children's differing preferences for subject–verb and verb–object constructions are related to the relative frequencies with which their parents model these constructions. Brown and his associates have examined mother–child frequencies of production of various constructions, from major sentence patterns to the several allomorphs of 'be', and have found that 'frequencies in child speech, within the limits of the child's competence, tend to match adult frequencies, with mother-child correlations ranging from .65 to .90' (Brown, Cazden, Bellugi-Klima, 1968, p. 64). The rank order frequencies with which Seppo and his mother produced constructions expressing subject, verb, and object relationships also match:

	Seppo f: tokens	Mother f: tokens
$\begin{cases} S+V \\ V+S \end{cases}$	48	52
$\begin{cases} S+V+O \\ \text{and other orders} \end{cases}$	8	35
$\begin{cases} V+O \\ O+V \end{cases}$	5	19

The match between Rina and her mother is somewhat poorer, since in the mother's sample there are almost equal numbers of subject–verb, verb–object, and subject–verb–object strings, while in Rina's sample at MLU 1.83 there are almost equal numbers of subject–verb and subject–verb–object but far fewer of verb–object. Unfortunately, the same analysis is not available for the mothers of the American children, so we cannot tell whether verb–object is more frequently modeled for them than is subject–verb, thus accounting in some as yet unknown way for their preference (with the exception of Kendall) for verb–object over subject–verb strings.

The American children and Seppo had all learned the appropriate order in which to arrange words to express subject–verb–object relationships. The American children made occasional mistakes, usually involving the placement of the object before the verb in two-word utterances, but these were relatively rare. Seppo had evidently learned some of the alternate order patterns of Finnish but had a clear preference at this stage for the dominant order.

4.4.2 Animacy. Animacy or inanimacy of nouns was important in the grammars of all the children except Eric. Almost all sentence-subjects before main verbs were animate in the speech of Kathryn, Gia, Kendall, and Seppo. Seppo's direct objects were always inanimate, and Kathryn's and Gia's usually were. Nouns naming locations were inanimate for all the children. All Kathryn's modified nouns were inanimate, while Gia's, Kendall's, and Seppo's were both animate and inanimate. Thus, although animacy or lack of it was generally significant, exact details of distribution varied. Animacy of subjects, and, to a slightly lesser extent, inanimacy of objects was common. At a higher MLU of approximately 1.75, both of the Finnish children and Brown's three subjects also showed strong preferences for animate subjects and inanimate objects.

4.4.3 Locatives. All the children except Eric produced N + N strings which expressed a locative relationship. These were relatively infrequent, but evidently productive, at least for Kendall and Seppo. None of the children used obligatory prepositions or case suffixes with the locative nouns. The second nouns in most of Seppo's N + N$_{loc.}$ strings named a location towards which the referent of the first noun was moving. Locative nouns never named a location away from which the referent was moving. Most of the $N + N_{loc.}$ strings of the American children, in contrast, seemed to indicate position-at rather than movement. In adult Finnish, directional movement is more precisely marked than in English. For example, the Finnish equivalents of 'where are you going?', 'put that on the table', and 'get off the bus', are '*to* where are you going?', 'put that on*to* the table', and 'get off *from* the bus'. If Seppo noticed locative inflections, his attention may have been drawn to directional aspects of location more than an American child's is. It would be interesting to know whether different languages or cultures emphasize the various kinds of locative relationships objects may have to each other differentially, and whether children are sensitive to such emphases and formulate their early locative constructions accordingly.

No provision for $V + N_{loc.}$ constructions was made in the grammars written for either Seppo or Bloom's subjects. This construction pattern began to emerge in the next month for Seppo and already occurred in Kendall's sample. Since Kendall's MLU was slightly higher than those of Seppo and Bloom's children, and her grammar was more advanced in certain ways (she produced subject–verb–locative strings, for example, which the others did not), it is possible that $N + N_{loc.}$ constructions precede $V + N_{loc.}$ constructions in the linguistic development of many or most children.

4.4.4 Noun modification. All the children produced some modified nouns. Kathryn used adjectives, attributive nouns, and genitive nouns as modifiers. Gia used attributive and genitive nouns but not adjectives, except for 'more'. Kendall and Seppo used genitive nouns and adjectives. Eric used only 'more'. Adjective–noun was by far the most common order. There were only a few noun–adjective constructions, which were probably primitive forms of the copular sentence pattern 'Noun *is* Adjective'. Noun modification developed first in isolation, and modifiers and nouns were probably not initially organized together as a single noun phrase constituent. Only later were modified nouns embedded into longer sentences.

4.4.5 Pronouns. None of the children used personal pronouns often. Kathryn and Gia had a few constructions with 'I', 'me', and 'my'. For Eric, 'I' as sentence-subject seemed to be just emerging from a preverbal schwa vowel, but was marginal at this time. Seppo and Kendall used no personal pronouns at all. Unlike American children, however, Seppo still did not use them at MLU 1.81 nor did Rina at MLU 1.83. Kathryn, Gia, and Kendall often used their own names to refer to themselves, but Eric and Seppo never did. Some of the American children used 'it' occasionally, usually in the role of direct object, but Seppo did not.

The demonstrative pronouns 'this' and 'that' were used extensively only by Bloom's subject Kathryn, in 'this (that)' + N constructions. Kendall produced this construction pattern occasionally, Gia only twice, and Eric not at all. Seppo produced only *tää kello*, 'this clock', which may have been a phonetic accident (see Appendix G). He used *tuossa*, 'there', with nouns in some of the same contexts in which American children use 'this' or 'that', such as in answer to 'what' questions. As noted in 3.4.2.1 and 3.4.3, the form of children's replies to these questions seems to be conditioned by the form of the question.

4.4.6 Negatives and interrogatives. Bloom's subject Kathryn used 'no' productively in combination with both nouns and verbs. A few instances of 'no' in construction occurred in Gia's sample, but these did not appear to contrast with non-negative forms. Eric used the constructions 'no more' + N and 'no' + V. Kendall produced a few 'no' + N constructions. Negatives in construction did not appear in Seppo's sample at all, although he used 'no' in isolation abundantly. Negative constructions did not emerge in Seppo's grammar until the time of the second sample at MLU 1.81.

Kendall, and probably Bloom's subjects, used rising intonation to mark yes–no questions. Seppo had not learned the use of the Finnish question inflection, and Finnish did not offer him any special questioning intonation. Some of the American children produced a few Wh questions, but most of these had the character of memorized routines. For the most part, productive construction patterns involving Wh words did not appear to have emerged yet. Seppo asked no Wh questions of any kind.

4.4.7 Some differences from the adult languages. There was no need for grammars for either the American children or Seppo to generate noun or verb inflections, articles (not present in adult Finnish, either), sentence adverbials, copulas, verbal auxiliaries, catenative verbs, or conjoined or embedded sentences. Most utterances could be generated directly by the base components of the grammars. Transformational components were rudimentary, containing only reduction (or verb deletion) transformations (which perhaps have more to do with performance than with underlying competence) and reordering rules.

4.5 Comparison with Luo children

Blount (1969) had great difficulty collecting utterances from Luo children at an early stage of development, due both to the children's fear of strangers and to the training they had received not to talk extensively with visitors. Since data from individual children were meager, Blount grouped together utterances from different children which seemed to have been produced at equivalent stages of development, and wrote grammars for these stages. The grammar for the first stage was based on only 9 utterance types, 2 from one child and 7 from another. All but 4 of these were imperative verb–object strings. The grammar for the second stage was based on 49 utterance types from 5 children. Blount was unable to determine mean utterance lengths. Close examination of the characteristics of the Luo children's constructions indicates that the utterances from Blount's stage II sample are very similar to those produced by Kendall at MLU 1.48 and slightly more advanced than those of Bloom's subjects and Seppo at slightly lower mean utterance lengths.

To facilitate comparison, the Luo utterances of Blount's stage II (translated into English) have been roughly grouped according to grammatical relations. Table 9 presents this classification. Since all the constructions from Blount's stage I have structurally identical counterparts in stage II, they are also included to provide a larger sample.

The kinds of grammatical relationships expressed by constructions of the Luo, Finnish, and American children at this stage of development are very similar. Subjects, verbs, direct objects, modifiers (both adjectival and genitive), locatives, and pronominal introducers are all present and combined in similar ways. Since the total number of Luo utterances is small and not all the children produced utterances of each kind, it is difficult to know what to make of the relative frequencies of construction types. The most productive patterns may have been subject–verb, verb–object, subject–verb–object, demonstrative pronoun–noun, and noun–possessive adjective. Noun–locative adverb and subject–verb–locative strings also occurred. These correspond rather

TABLE 9. *Constructions in Luo sample (translated), grouped according to grammatical relationships*

1. *Subject–Verb*	5. *Noun–Locative*
he-brought[a]	she here
car runs	she there
I-know	cigarette down
I-not-know[b]	6. *Demonstrative pronoun–Noun*
I-refuse	it European
I-sick	it clock
you-eat?	it thing-this
European comes	this one
it-has-hole[b]	this one European[d]
2. *Verb–Object*	this visitor
eat medicine	that-there it chicken[c]
drink porridge	7. *Subject–Verb–Object*
see candy	I-see-them
see that-there[c]	I-burned-him
cover-me	I-see European
hand (over)-it	I-want food
give-me potato[c]	I-want water
give-me water	hunger bites-me
give-me milk	he-brought this one
give-me banana	I-drink water
give-me porridge	8. *Subject–Verb–Locative*
give-me candy	he-went Ulanda
food give-me	he-goes river
3. *Noun–Genitive*	here it-has-hole[b]
this one his[d]	9. *Demonstrative pronoun–Noun–*
hand-mine	*Genitive*
head-mine	that-there box ours[c]
shoes-mine	10. *Not classified*
leg-mine	father cigarette
4. *Noun–Adjective*	I-want to-go to-sleep
pepper hot	Mamma goes to-wash
thing-that good	absent/without

[a] Hyphens preceding or following pronouns indicate the presence of pronominal inflections of the verb.

[b] 'not-know' and 'has-hole' are single verbs; 'not-know' does not involve syntactic negation.

[c] 'give-me' and 'that-there' were probably learned as single units, since they did not contrast with similar forms to indicate that the component morphemes were controlled separately.

[d] Blount suggests that 'this' and 'this one' may have been free variants of the same form.

closely to the construction patterns produced most frequently by the American children and Seppo at this stage:

subject–verb
verb–object
subject–object
subject–verb–object
noun–locative (including both locative adverbs and locative nouns)
demonstrative pronoun–noun
modifier–noun (including genitive nouns, attributive nouns, and adjectives as modifiers)

All the combinations of subject, verb, and object which Seppo and the American children produced occurred in the Luo sample, with the possible exception of subject–object. The Luo utterance 'father cigarette' may have been either a subject–object string ('father smokes a cigarette') or a genitive–noun string ('father's cigarette'). The Luo sample lacked the construction $N + N_{loc.}$; only $N +$ locative adverb occurred, corresponding to Seppo's $N +$ 'there' and equivalent constructions of the English-speaking children. The Luo sample contained two subject–verb–locative constructions, which were not found at this time in the speech of Seppo or Bloom's subjects. However, this construction emerged for Seppo almost immediately after the grammar at MLU 1.42, and was productive in Kendall's speech at MLU 1.48. Unlike Seppo, Bloom's children, and Kendall, the Luo children did not produce genitive noun–noun constructions (unless 'father cigarette' had such a meaning). Genitive constructions in the Luo sample were a few combinations of noun–possessive adjective, mostly from one child. The adjective–noun constructions of Seppo and the American children had counterparts in two Luo constructions. As in the American and Finnish samples, modified nouns in the Luo sample occurred only as independent utterances rather than as constituents of longer sentences, with one exception ('that–there box ours'). The lack of genitive noun–noun, noun–noun$_{loc.}$, and subject–object constructions in the Luo sample meant that there were virtually no combinations of two nouns. Demonstrative pronoun–noun constructions, which were popular with Kathryn although rare for Gia and almost nonexistent for Seppo and Eric, had counterparts in Luo utterances such as 'it' $+ N$ and 'this (this one)' $+ N$.

According to Blount, the word order of adult Luo is highly constrained, despite the rich inflectional system. Like the Finnish and

8

American children at this stage, the Luo children had already learned the dominant orders and made few mistakes.

Negation was still undeveloped for the Luo children at this time, as it was for Seppo and Gia. The equivalents of 'no' and 'don't' appeared in isolation, but were not yet combined in constructions. Eric and especially Kathryn, in contrast, used 'no' with both nouns and verbs.

The only major difference between the speech of the Luo children and that of the Finnish and American children was that only the Luos used certain inflections productively at this time. These inflections, affixed to verbs, mark personal pronouns and 'it' in the roles of subject and direct object. Since pronominal subjects and objects can be expressed without inflection in Finnish and English, the Luo children used inflections only to supply syntactic information which the other children could provide without functors. However, personal pronouns were absent in the Finnish sample and very rare and probably not yet productive in the English samples. The Luo children did not express other meanings which are marked inflectionally in all three languages, such as pluralization and past tense. The implications of differences among children in the early use of inflections and other functors will be considered in the next section, which compares the Finnish, American, and Luo children with a Samoan child.

4.6   Comparison with a Samoan child

Speech samples from two Samoan children, Sipili (MLU 1.52) and Tofi (MLU 1.60), are available (Kernan, 1969). Only data from the former will be considered here. The latter's speech seems more comparable to that of Seppo, Rina, and Brown's subjects at MLUs of close to 1.75, and will be discussed in Chapter 5.

In the grammars Kernan wrote for his subjects, constructions are not analyzed according to the grammatical relationships they express but strictly according to their semantic characteristics. For comparison with data from the other children, Sipili's utterances have been reclassified by grammatical relationships. This is perhaps risky for some construction patterns, since Kernan does not tell us whether, for example, an *agent–action* string would be represented in a more traditional grammar as *subject–verb* or in some other way. Table 10 lists the utterances in English translation, with original word order preserved.

TABLE 10. *Constructions in Samoan sample (translated):*
Sipili, MLU 1.52

1. *Verb–Subject*
   brought Keith
   brought Tasi
   goes Va
2. *Verb–Object*
   spank me
   take me
   hit you ⎱ (two utterance types)
   hit you ⎰
   do work
   nurse girl
3. *Noun–Genitive*
   boat mine
   candy mine
   balloon mine
   thing mine
   lessons mine
   ball mine
   bicycle mine
   swing mine
   candy yours
   ball yours
   this yours ⎱ (two utterance types)
   this yours ⎰
   pie Tafale
   our thing
   house Sina
   balloon mama
   balloon of mine
   ball of mine
   thing of mine
   tricycle of mine
   candy of mine
   Joshua, ball of mine
   the nose of mine
4. *Noun–Adjective*
   children older
5. *Noun–Indirect object*
   balloon for Fai

6. *Noun–Locative*
   ball there
7. *Verb–Locative*
   go home
8. *'the'–Noun*
   the fan
   the head
   the nose
   ⋮
   (total of 10 utterance types)
9. *'sign of nominative'–Noun (or Pronoun)*
   'sign of nom.' So'o
   'sign of nom.' Tasi
   'sign of nom.' you
   ⋮
   (total of 17 utterance types)
10. *'and (for, with)'–Noun (or Pronoun)*
    and So'o
    and Claudia
    and Sua
    ⋮
    (total of 12 utterance types)
11. *Noun–Genitive–Locative*
    candy yours there
    candy mine there
12. *Negatives*
    not eat
    not eat Upia
    not eat you
    not eat candy
    yes, not eat
    not fit
    whine word-no
13. *Wh question*
    car whose that?
14. *Not classified*
    want to defecate
    in (the) shirt
    we children

Like the American and Finnish children, Sipili produced the following construction patterns (ordered appropriately for Samoan):

subject–verb
verb–object
genitive–noun
adjective–noun
noun–locative

Of these, perhaps only the first three were really productive patterns, since there was only one token each of the last two. Sipili also produced one verb–locative string, 'go home'. We noted that this construction pattern was productive for Kendall at MLU 1.48 and soon became so for Seppo. In two other constructions in Sipili's sample, elaborated noun phrases appeared as constituents of longer sentences: 'candy yours there', 'candy mine there'. This was rare among the other children at this early stage, the only examples being Kendall's 'that Kimmy ball' and the Luo·'that-there box ours'. Kendall's and Sipili's MLUs at 1.48 and 1.52 respectively were higher than those of Bloom's children and Seppo, so the embedding of modified nouns into longer constructions perhaps begins between MLUs of approximately 1.40 and 1.50. Sipili also produced a few simple negatives and one Wh question. He used intonation to mark yes–no questions. These patterns were found among some of the other children studied. Sipili's sample contained one noun–indirect object construction: 'balloon for Fai'. Indirect objects did not occur in the samples from Seppo, Bloom's subjects, or the Luo children. Kendall produced two ambiguous utterances, 'Kendall read Daddy', and 'Daddy read Kendall', which may have meant either 'Kendall read to Daddy', or 'Kendall read with Daddy', and vice versa. Indirect objects, then, are uncommon at this early stage of development. They apparently just begin to emerge at the stage considered in Chapter 5, when MLU is close to two morphemes.

Sipili produced three types of constructions which had no syntactic counterparts in the other children's samples:

'the'+N[1]
'sign of the nominative'+N
'and (for, with)'+N

'The'+N and 'sign of the nominative'+N functioned semantically like the American children's 'this (that)'+N and Seppo's 'there'+N as responses to questions about the identity of objects and people (see 3.4.3 for examples). The grammatical functors 'the' and 'sign of the nominative' were evidently closely tied to their roles as introducers for noun responses, since they were almost never used to mark nouns

---

[1] Bloom's subjects, although not Kendall, often produced a schwa vowel before nouns and in other contexts; this may have been an early attempt at words such as 'a', 'the', and 'I'.

in other roles, such as direct object ('nurse *the* girl') or sentence-subject ('*the* ball there').

The construction pattern 'and (for, with)' + N cannot be accounted for as a version of a semantic or syntactic function which appears in the speech of the children learning other languages. It is perhaps atypical, since it does not occur in the sample of the other Samoan child.

Except for 'the', 'sign of the nominative', and 'and (for, with)', Sipili's speech largely lacked functors. 'Of' occasionally appeared in the context 'N——mine', but was more often missing. It is difficult to assess the overall significance of Sipili's omission of functors without knowing how many and what functors are obligatory in Samoan, but it is consistent with the linguistic behavior of the American and Finnish children at this stage.

The Luo and Samoan data reviewed here and in the preceding section indicate that the acquisition of inflections and other functors is not as delayed in the speech of all children as it is in that of typical American and Finnish children. However, the data suggest that when children in Stage I do use functors, these functors generally mark only semantic or syntactic meanings which are expressed – more usually without the use of functors – in the early speech of all children. The evidence on this matter is not yet clear, however. Counter-evidence for the hypothesis comes from Burling's (1959) son. Burling believes that the child learned Garo, a Tibeto-Burman language, like a Garo child. The boy began to produce morphological and syntactic combinations almost simultaneously. At the same time that his first productive two-word constructions appeared (subject–verb strings), he began adding suffixes to verbs both in isolation and in combination with subjects to mark such meanings as 'future', 'past', 'present or habitual', and 'imperative'. Numerous other inflections, with meanings like 'continuous', 'causative', 'progression towards speaker', 'neutral interrogation', and 'interrogation anticipating agreement', were added as more kinds of combinations of one noun with one verb emerged. Some of these meanings seem rather difficult, and none were formally expressed in the constructions of the Finnish, American, Samoan, or Luo children at this early stage of development. Data from other languages are needed before we can come to firm conclusions about the syntactic and semantic role of inflections and other grammatical morphemes in early child speech.

4.7   Summary of early Stage I speech

A comparison of Seppo's speech at MLU 1.42 to that of American, Luo, and Samoan children at an equivalent stage of development reveals many similarities. All the children were working on the expression of subject–verb–object relationships. Words in these roles were combined in subject–verb, verb–object, and, less commonly, subject–object strings. Some children also produced subject–verb–object strings; this was probably a later development of their grammars. Other productive patterns for most or all of the children were noun–locative, genitive–noun, adjective–noun, and demonstrative pronoun–noun (with language-appropriate orderings). The embedding of an elaborated noun phrase such as adjective–noun or genitive–noun into a longer sentence was still largely absent. Word order was quite stable and corresponded to the dominant or only adult pattern. A distinction between animate and inanimate nouns was found in the speech of many of the children, commonly manifested as the tendency for subjects to be animate and objects to be inanimate. Personal pronouns were rare or absent in the speech of the children with the lower MLUs (Seppo and Bloom's subjects) but present in that of some with higher MLUs or otherwise more complex speech (Sipili and the Luo children, but not Kendall). Elementary negative constructions occurred in the samples of three American children and the Samoan child but not in those of another American child, the Finnish child, and the Luo children. Yes–no questions were posed only by children whose languages offer a questioning intonation which can be superimposed upon declarative utterances. Wh questions were rudimentary or absent in all the samples.

None of the grammars written for the children provided for the embedding or conjoining of sentences. Almost all constructions were simple and could not be broken down into more elementary components. In addition, the grammars lacked provisions for copulas, articles (except before nouns in isolation for the Samoan child), verbal auxiliaries, catenative verbs, prepositions, and postpositions. Inflections were also absent except for verbal affixes marking pronominal subjects and objects in subject–verb, verb–object, and subject–verb–object strings in the Luo sample. The English, Finnish, and Samoan equivalents of these do not involve inflection.

The vast majority of the children's utterances consisted of no more than two morphemes. Some three-morpheme sentences occur in all the samples, but most three-term construction patterns are represented by so few utterances in any individual sample that it is impossible to determine whether they were productive yet. In contrast, three-term strings are frequent in all the late Stage I samples. In an analysis based in part on data from the Finnish, Luo, and Samoan children investigated here, Slobin (1970) observes that a two-word stage of development appears to be universal, suggesting the 'maturation of a language acquisition device with a fairly fixed programming span for utterances at the start'. The present data also indicate that the initial constraint which holds sentence length to no more than two morphemes begins to relax at about the same point in development for all children: when the proportion of two- to one-word utterances rises above a certain critical level marked by a mean utterance length of about 1.30 to 1.50. It is not predictable *a priori* that equivalent MLUs mark the emergence of productive three-term construction patterns in children learning different languages, since it is possible to imagine, for example, a child whose mean length of utterance slowly climbs towards two morphemes simply because an increasing proportion of his utterances become exactly two morphemes long.

To summarize the findings of this chapter briefly, the speech of children in several different linguistic communities during the developmental period marked by MLU boundaries of about 1.30 to 1.50 morphemes was very similar with respect to the kinds of constructions produced, the length and internal complexity of utterances, the omission of obligatory elements, and the absence of certain construction patterns and operations.

5 *Late Stage I Speech*

By about three months after collection of the sample upon which the grammar for Seppo presented in Chapter 4 was based, Seppo's mean length of utterance had risen to 1.81 morphemes and was comparable to that of Rina's in the earliest data available for her: 1.83 morphemes. In this chapter, grammars for Seppo and Rina are presented and compared. Their speech is then compared with that of Brown's three American subjects, Adam, Eve, and Sarah, at similar MLUs and to that of a somewhat less advanced Samoan child. As at the earlier stage of development investigated in the last chapter, the children's utterances were so similar in almost all major respects that the summary of the syntactic characteristics of their speech given in section 5.8 could be reworded as a set of hypotheses about the universal characteristics of child speech at a mean utterance length of about one-and-a-half to two morphemes.

5.1 Transformational generative grammar for Seppo at MLU 1.81

The grammar for Seppo at this stage is more complicated than that for the earlier stage. Seppo now produced two- and three-word constructions more often. Because these expressed many new combinations of grammatical relations, and the reordering of sentence constituents was more common, each different construction pattern in the sample is represented by a smaller proportion of the total number of constructions than in the earlier sample. Construction patterns represented by only one or two utterances were generally not accounted for in the first grammar, and all patterns generated by the grammar did occur (although, of course, not every predicted potential sentence occurred). In the later sample, however, there are many construction patterns which, although represented by only a few utterances each, seem closely related to more frequent patterns. Therefore, determining which constructions resulted from productive rules is more difficult than before. A few structural patterns which do not actually occur or occur very rarely are generated by the grammars, sometimes because they seem to be the 'logical' base strings underlying utterances which do occur. It is assumed that predicted but rare or nonoccurring patterns would have been better represented in a larger sample.

The phrase structure rules, lexicon feature rules, and transformational rules of a grammar for Seppo based on the nonimitated utterances of the sample at MLU 1.81 are presented below. The lexicon is given in Appendix H. Constructions generated by the grammar are listed in Appendix I, classified according to the grammatical relationships holding between the constituents. Single-word utterances and their frequencies of occurrence are given in Appendix J. Constructions not generated by the grammar are presented in Appendix K.

Phrase Structure Rules

1. $S_1 \rightarrow$ Wh–loc $\begin{Bmatrix} NP \\ V \end{Bmatrix}$

2. $S_2 \rightarrow$ Neg $\begin{Bmatrix} N \\ V \\ Adj \end{Bmatrix}$

3. $S_3 \rightarrow (NP \text{ Ȳ } VP)^1$

4. $VP \rightarrow \begin{Bmatrix} \text{Predicate} \\ V \text{ (NP) (Loc) (Adv)} \end{Bmatrix}$

5. Predicate $\rightarrow \begin{Bmatrix} Adj \\ N \\ Loc \end{Bmatrix}$

6. $NP \rightarrow (M) N$

7. $M \rightarrow \begin{Bmatrix} Adj \\ N \end{Bmatrix}$

8. $Loc \rightarrow \begin{Bmatrix} N \\ Proloc \end{Bmatrix}$

Lexicon Feature Rules

1. $N \rightarrow [+N, \pm \text{pronoun}]$

2. $[+\text{pronoun}] \rightarrow \left[\pm \underline{\hspace{1em}} \begin{Bmatrix} V \\ N \end{Bmatrix} \right]$

3. $[-\text{pronoun}] \rightarrow [\pm \text{animate}]$

4. $[-\text{animate}] \rightarrow [\pm \text{vehicle}]$

5. Proloc $\rightarrow [+\text{Proloc}, \pm \text{directional}]$

---

[1] Linking parentheses are used to indicate that either constituent or both may be selected, but at least one *must* be selected.

6. $[+\text{directional}] \rightarrow [-\text{NP}\underline{\hspace{1cm}}]$
7. $V \rightarrow [+V, \pm\underline{\hspace{1cm}}(\text{NP}), \pm[-\text{animate}, -\text{vehicle}]\underline{\hspace{1cm}},$
$$\pm\underline{\hspace{1cm}}[+\text{directional}]]$$
8. $[+\underline{\hspace{1cm}}(\text{NP})] \rightarrow [\pm\underline{\hspace{1cm}}[+\text{animate}]]$
9. $\text{Adj} \rightarrow [+\text{Adj}]$
10. $\text{Adv} \rightarrow [+\text{Adv}]$
11. $\text{Neg} \rightarrow$ *enää*, 'any more'
12. $\text{Wh–loc} \rightarrow$ *missä*, 'where'

Transformational Rules

1. Treordering: optional

   (*a*) Reversal of prolocative and NP
   S.D.: $\text{NP} + \text{Proloc}$
   S.C.: $x_1 - x_2 \Rightarrow x_2 - x_1$

   (*b*) Fronting of adverb or prolocative
   S.D.: $X + V + Y \begin{Bmatrix} \text{Adv} \\ \text{Proloc} \end{Bmatrix}$ Where X and Y may be NP or null, but at least one must not be null
   S.C.: $x_1 - x_2 - x_3 - x_4 \Rightarrow x_4 - x_1 - x_2 - x_3$

   (c) Reversal of verb and direct object, locative, or adverb
   S.D.: $X + V \begin{Bmatrix} \text{N} \\ \text{Loc} \\ \text{Adv} \end{Bmatrix} Y$ Where X may be NP, Adv, or null, and Y may be Adv or null
   S.C.: $x_1 - x_2 - x_3 - x_4 \Rightarrow x_1 - x_3 - x_2 - x_4$

   (*d*) Reversal of subject and verb
   S.D.: $X + \text{NP} + V + Y$ Where X and Y may be Proloc or null
   S.C.: $x_1 - x_2 - x_3 - x_4 \Rightarrow x_1 - x_3 - x_2 - x_4$

2. Tverb deletion: optional

   S.D.: $N + V \begin{Bmatrix} \text{N} \\ \text{Loc} \end{Bmatrix}$
   S.C.: $x_1 - x_2 - x_3 \Rightarrow x_1 - x_3$

5.1.1 The distinction between copular and main verb sentences.

A major problem in formulating the grammar involved deciding whether to distinguish formally between main verb and copular sentences. In the adult grammars of both Finnish and English, such a distinction is essential. Copulas take predicate adjectives, while most main verbs do not. Nouns occurring after a copula usually agree in number with the sentence-subject, whereas nouns occurring after a main verb need not. In both Finnish and English, the complement of a copula can be an adjective ('John is *big*'), a predicate nominative ('this is *a house*'), or a locative phrase ('the ball is *on the table*'). In Finnish, certain adverbs such as *rikki*, 'broken', *kiinni*, 'closed', and *auki*, 'open', may also follow copulas. These are adjectives in English, but they cannot precede a noun as modifier in Finnish.

The copular verb is lacking in Seppo's speech at this stage, but there is nevertheless some evidence for making a distinction between main verb and copular sentences. At MLU 1.42 there was virtually none. In the earlier sample, the only 'missing copula' sentence pattern which seemed to be productive was noun–locative, as in 'chick there' and 'chick shoe'. Two unique utterances, 'dog...aunt's' and 'this clock', may also have been copular sentences. Since there was no way to determine whether Seppo distinguished between possible copular sentences like 'chick there' and 'chick shoe' and other noun–locative combinations in which the missing element appeared from context to be a verb of motion rather than a copula, constructions of both types were generated by the same rules:

$$S \rightarrow (N)\ VP$$
$$VP \rightarrow Loc$$
$$Loc \rightarrow \begin{Bmatrix} N \\ Proloc \end{Bmatrix}$$

Two developments in Seppo's sample at MLU 1.81 suggest that copular and main verb sentence patterns should be distinguished. First, noun–adjective joined noun–locative as a possible 'missing copula' construction pattern. Noun–adjective strings might also be interpreted as transformationally reordered variants of deep structure adjective–noun strings. However, when nouns modified by adjectives occurred as constituents of longer sentences, the adjective–noun order was almost invariably used:

> *kiltti täti. . käve⟨lee⟩*   'nice lady. . walks'
> *iso api⟨na⟩ tulee*   'big monkey comes'
> *nostaa iso kivi*   'lifts big stone'

If noun–adjective had been a variation of adjective–noun rather than organized as a different sentence pattern, utterances like 'monkey big comes' and 'lifts stone big' should also have occurred, but they did not.

A second development was that Seppo at this time began to produce demonstrative pronoun–noun constructions which were probably modeled on adult copular sentences. In the sample at MLU 1.81, there was only one such utterance, the first since the uncertain 'this clock' of several months before:

> (*S* holding up a jigsaw puzzle
> piece shaped like a fish)   *tämä kala*   'this fish'

A copular verb is required before the predicate nominative in the adult equivalent: *tämä on kala*, 'this is (a) fish'. Three weeks after the sample, Seppo said *tää tädi*,[1] 'this aunt', probably meaning 'this is aunt's', as he pointed to the investigator's tape recorder. In the next two weeks the demonstrative pronoun–noun sentence pattern became firmly established. A total of 16 such utterances occurred in two consecutive tapes, involving these pronouns: *tää*, 'this', *tämä*, 'this', and *se*, 'it'. The first copulas were also produced at this time: *on Ford*, 'is Ford', an affirmative response to 'is it a Ford?' and *kissa oli uffuf*, 'cat was "naughty"'.

In summary, the decision to make a formal distinction in the grammar between copular and main verb sentences was based on:

1. The production of noun–adjective strings. These did not occur as constituents of longer sentences, and therefore appeared to be organized as a different type of utterance than adjective–noun strings.

2. The emergence of the demonstrative pronoun–noun construction pattern. Although only one example appeared in the sample on which the grammar is based, this pattern seemed to be on the verge of productivity if it was not already productive.

5.1.2 Prolocatives and pronouns. In the earlier sample, there was only one prolocative: *tuossa*, 'there'. This entered into construction almost exclusively with nouns. By the sample at MLU 1.81, Seppo had acquired many more prolocative forms, and these combined with both nouns and verbs. In the lexicon for the second grammar, prolocatives are marked for whether or not they indicate directional movement:

[– directional]		[+ directional]	
tuossa	'(right) there'	*tuohon*	'to (right) there'
tässä	'(right) here'	*tuonne*	'to (over) there'
siinä	'(right) there'	*siihen*	'to (right) there'
siellä	'(over) there'	*sinne*	'to (over) there'

Directional prolocatives can follow only verbs in the grammar, while nondirectional prolocatives can follow both nouns, as realizations of the copular predicate, and verbs. Noun-directional prolocative con-

---

[1] The consonant gradation which is appropriate for inflection was made (*tädi-* instead of the nominative *täti*), but no genitive *-n* was suffixed.

structions like *avain sinne*, 'key to-there', are derived from underlying noun–verb–directional prolocative strings by application of the optional verb deletion transformation.

Seppo seemed to use the equivalents of 'here' and 'there' interchangeably. Whether he understood the semantic difference between the two types of prolocatives could not be determined. All the locations to which he referred were quite near him, and his mother also used both 'here' and 'there' in such situations.

Nouns are subdivided into [+pronoun] and [−pronoun] classes in the grammar. Seppo used no personal pronouns at this time or for many months to come. He referred to himself, although infrequently, either as 'Immi', a family nickname, or as *poika*, 'boy'. At the time of the earlier sample, he never made self-reference. In both samples, all conversation was conducted in the third person singular, with the interlocutor referred to as 'mother', 'aunt', 'daddy', etc., rather than as 'you'. Seppo's failure to use the third person singular personal pronoun *hän*, 'he, she', can be readily understood, since *se*, 'it', is very often substituted for it in colloquial Finnish. Seppo did begin to use 'it' at about this time. His slowness (compared to American children) to acquire other personal pronouns may be related to the way his mother talked to him. Examples of personal pronouns were extremely rare in her speech in all the tapes up through the second sample. She almost always addressed Seppo in the third person, using his name and 'mother' rather than 'you' and 'I'. There were a few tokens of 'we' and 'our', but almost none of 'they', 'them', or 'their'. Seppo's father also tended to speak to Seppo in the third person, although he used more personal pronouns than the mother. Lack of modeling cannot be the only explanation for Seppo's late acquisition of personal pronouns, however, since Rina also did not use them until long after this stage even though her mother used them quite frequently.

In adult Finnish, nouns and pronouns used as sentence-subjects are usually in the nominative case (the minimal, free-standing, uninflected form). Direct objects in most types of sentences have partitive (-*a/ä*, -*ta/tä*) or genitive/accusative (-*n*) inflections. Seppo at this time incorrectly used the nominative form of nouns for direct objects as well as for subjects. His pronouns were somewhat distinguished with respect to the subject and object roles, however. In the sample at MLU 1.81, the nominative form *tämä*, 'this', occurred only as subject (two utterance types), while the partitive forms *tätä*, 'this', *sitä*, 'it', and *lisää*, 'more', occurred only as direct objects. *Tämmö*, 'this-kind-of-thing', was also used only as direct object. Seppo omitted the final syllable of this pronoun (*-nen* (nominative), *-sen* (genitive/accusative), or *-stä* (partitive)) so it was not marked for case. Two other pronouns occurred in the tapes immediately preceding the sample and in the remainder of the last tape used for the sample. *Se*, 'it' (nominative) was used only as subject, while *kaikki*, 'all, everything, everyone' (nominative) was used as both subject and object: *kaikki ratsastaa*, 'everyone rides', *kaikki leikkii*, 'everyone plays', *laittaa kaikki*, 'fixes everything'.

In adult Finnish, the choice between the partitive and the genitive/accusative inflections for direct objects depends upon the inherent semantic characteristics of the verb, upon whether the action specified is regarded as complete as opposed to incomplete or continuing, and upon whether the entire object or only part of it is involved. Some verbs (e.g. 'love', 'look-at') can take only partitive objects, while others ('eat', 'draw') can take either partitive or genitive/accusative objects according to context. Seppo did not yet produce pronouns with genitive/accusative inflections. He sometimes used pronouns with partitive inflections as direct objects in contexts which called for the genitive/accusative case, as in *isi sitä toi*, 'daddy it brought', and *isi tätä toi*, 'daddy this brought' (action completed, entire object involved).

The distinction Seppo made between pronouns in subject and object roles was only partial. This became increasingly apparent during the weeks following the sample, as pronouns began to be used more often. In general, Seppo did not use partitive pronouns as sentence-subjects (there was only one exception, *tätä kuuluu*, 'this belongs (fits, goes)', produced while Seppo worked a jigsaw puzzle), but he sometimes used nominative pronouns as direct objects:

> *tyttö kaataa toi*   'girl spills that' (*toi* is a colloquial version of *tuo*, 'that')
> *tämä korjasi*   'this fixed' (*tämä* is direct object)
> *kippi-auto vetää tämä*   'dump truck pulls this'
> *tämä vetää kippi-auto*   'this pulls dump truck' (*tämä* is direct object)
> *tuosta..vetää..se pois*   'from-there..pulls..it away'
> *juo tämä*   'drink this' (imperative intent; verb form either second person singular, imperative, or third person singular, present indicative)

In adult Finnish, imperative sentences provide a model for using nominatives as direct objects. When the noun or pronoun functioning as direct object in an affirmative sentence would be in the genitive/accusative case in an equivalent nonimperative sentence, the nominative form is used, as in *ota se*, 'take it'. When the object would be in the partitive case in the nonimperative equivalent, however, it is also partitive in the imperative, as in *katso sitä*, 'look-at it'. Seppo may have noticed that some direct objects are nominative, and, failing to realize that this occurs only under certain semantic and syntactic conditions, may have generalized to the rule that any direct object can be nominative. Children's use of particular pronoun forms as subjects and objects cannot always be explained by reference to modeling, however, since children learning English occasionally use accusative pronouns as subjects (e.g. 'her curl my hair', 'where me sleep?' (Brown, in press)), even though there is no model for this.

Seppo's pronouns are subdivided in the grammar on the basis of whether or not they occurred before nouns and verbs as sentence-subjects:

$$[+\text{pronoun}] \rightarrow \left[\pm\!\!-\!\!\left\{ \begin{matrix} V \\ N \end{matrix} \right\} \right]$$

Only *tämä*, 'this', is marked

$$\left[+\!\!-\!\!\left\{ \begin{matrix} V \\ N \end{matrix} \right\} \right],$$

but *se*, 'it', and *kaikki*, 'all, everything, everyone', would also be so marked in the lexicon for a larger sample. Pronouns which can serve as subjects are not barred from following verbs as direct objects. Pronouns are not prevented from following modifiers, because a very few utterances like *rikki tämä*, 'broken this' and *nyt lisää tämä*, 'now more this' occurred in tapes before and after the sample. These are not grammatical in adult Finnish.

The Finnish equivalent of 'that' did not occur in Seppo's sample. All uses of 'this' seemed appropriate, since the objects referred to were either in Seppo's hand or right in front of him on the floor or table. Seppo used 'it' in situations similar to those in which he used 'this'. For example:

> (*M* has been trying to get *S* to
> tell about a book his father
> gave him)   > *isi sitä toi*   'daddy it brought'
> *Isi sitä toi, niin.*[1]
> 'Daddy it brought, yes'.

[1] Seppo's mother confirmed his utterance even though the pronoun should have been genitive/accusative rather than partitive, and she considered the subject–object–verb order a little odd.

> *Sepolle oman kirjan.*
> 'To-Seppo (his) own book'.
>
> > *isi tätä toi*   'daddy this brought'

Since Seppo referred only to nearby objects, it is impossible to determine whether he understood the semantic difference between 'this' and 'it', or that 'this' cannot be used to refer to objects far from the speaker.

5.1.3   Transformational rules. Transformations were needed in the grammar at this stage, as they were at the earlier stage, to provide for optional reorderings of base strings and for verb deletion. The object, verb, locative, and adverb constituents seem to have been free to occupy almost any position with respect to each other. It is difficult to postulate an underlying order with any certainty for these, or to provide for all possible reorderings. Although the object, locative, and adverb constituents were not mutually exclusive, Seppo was much less likely to combine them than to choose one of them as a complement to a verb or a subject–verb string. Only five combinations of two of the three occurred in the sample:

locative–verb–adverb:	*koti syödään kohta*	'home (we)-eat soon'
adverb–object–verb:	*nyt avain vetää*	'now key pulls'
	kohta ukko pois	'soon old-man away'
	sitten. . ukko pois	'then. . old-man away'
object–verb–adverb:	*auto. . hakee nyt*	'car. . looks-for now'

In all the tapes preceding the sample, there were three utterances in which verb, object, and adverb occurred together and four in which verb, object, and locative occurred together. The order of constituents varied in these constructions. The deep structure order specified by the grammar's phrase structure rules and the rearrangements provided for by the reordering transformations indicate only the most frequent order patterns found in the sample and in the immediately preceding and following tapes.

The verb deletion transformation is needed, as in the earlier sample, to provide for subject–object strings. In addition, it derives noun–locative strings from underlying noun–verb–locative strings. Noun–locative strings in which the locative constituent is realized as a noun or a nondirectional prolocative can be generated as copular sentences or as main verb sentences from which the verb is deleted. In the earlier grammar, there were several noun–noun$_{loc}$. strings in which the 'missing element' appeared to be a verb of motion rather than a copula. Seppo produced no verb–locative or subject–verb–locative strings at that time, so it would have been difficult to argue that he really had an underlying verb in mind when he produced these constructions. Verb–locative and subject–verb–locative strings had become common by the second sample, so it is easier to justify postulating an underlying verb. The verbs deleted in deriving noncopular noun–locative constructions are not restricted to verbs of motion, since there are a few noun–prolocative and noun–noun$_{loc.}$ strings from which verbs such as 'eats' and 'sits' may have been deleted, judging from nonlinguistic context and the immediately preceding and following utterances.

Noun–locative sentences judged to have resulted from deletion of a main verb differ superficially from noun–locative copular sentences only when the locative constituent is a directional prolocative, as in *avain sinne*, 'key to-there'. Directional prolocatives cannot immediately follow nouns in the grammar's phrase structure rules, as can non-directional prolocatives and nouns functioning as locatives, but can only be introduced into deep structure strings in a post-verb position. A construction like 'key to-there' must therefore be derived by deletion of a verb. There were only four verbs marked as able to precede a directional prolocative at this time: *menee (meni)*, 'goes (went)', *piirtää*, 'draws', *putoo*, 'falls', and *istuu*, 'sits (down)'. All of these can take directional prolocatives in adult Finnish. The verb deletion transformation must delete one of these in deriving a noun-directional prolocative string, since if it were to delete only a dummy verb, there would be no way to account for the presence of a directional prolocative in the surface string. As for subject–object constructions, it is almost always possible to guess the missing verb from context or from preceding or following utterances (see 4.3.3.2).

5.1.4 Upper limits on sentence length. The grammar generates several strings with four or more constituents, and the maximum string possible contains seven, with the following syntactic interpretation:

modifier–subject–verb–modifier–object–locative–adverb

However, the longest strings which actually occur in the sample contain only three constituents (often reordered):

subject–verb–object
modifier–subject–verb
modifier–subject–locative

verb–modifier–object
subject–verb–locative
subject–verb–adverb
verb–locative–adverb
verb–object–adverb
Wh–loc–modifier–noun

Should this apparent constraint on sentence length be accounted for in the grammar? As noted in 4.3.3.2, Bloom's (1970) subjects at a lower mean utterance length almost never produced strings longer than two constituents. Since the phrase structure rules Bloom formulated for her subjects' grammars were capable of generating several different types of strings of three or more constituents, she postulated a reduction transformation to delete verbs, subjects, direct objects, adjectives, and particles if the retention of these in addition to other elements would cause surface strings to be longer than two constituents. One justification offered by Bloom for the reduction transformation is that it deletes elements which are necessary in deep structure for the semantic interpretation of utterances. If these elements are not included in deep structure, 'the semantic interpretation of utterances in which elements that were not immediate constituents were juxtaposed in production (such as subject–object strings...) would postulate intervening constituents which could not be structurally accounted for' (Bloom, 1970, p. 72). Verbs were the only 'intervening constituents' which were ever needed for semantic interpretation. Although I disagreed with Bloom (4.3.3.2) that the semantic interpretation of subject–object strings depends on the presence of a verb in deep structure, I concluded that an underlying verb is required to account for the syntactic characteristics of the subject and object nouns. Other constituents deleted by Bloom's reduction transformation, such as subjects, objects, and adjectives, are needed neither for the semantic interpretation of utterances nor to account for the syntactic features of the constituents which do appear in surface structure, so their presence in deep structure when they are absent from surface structure cannot be justified on these grounds.

Bloom's reduction transformation, then, is responsible for two different types of operations:

1. Allowing a constituent (verb) which, according to Bloom, is necessary for the semantic interpretation of the utterance to be present in deep structure but absent from surface structure.

2. Insuring that no surface string is longer than two constituents.

In the grammars for Bloom's children, provisions for carrying out these two operations could be collapsed into a single rule simply because no strings, including those from which verbs had been deleted, were longer than two constituents. The characteristics of Seppo's speech at MLUs of both 1.42 and 1.81 demonstrate that the problem of accounting for an apparent constraint on sentence length is distinct from the problem of accounting for the superficial absence of constituents which are needed in underlying structure. One kind of explanation may be needed but not the other, or the requirements of each may differ. By accounting for both verb deletion and the constraint on sentence length in one operation, Bloom's reduction transformation treats two theoretically distinct problems as if they were one. While a verb deletion transformation is necessary in Seppo's grammars to account for subject–object strings and for subject–locative strings from which a noncopular verb is missing, it cannot be combined with a rule which would prevent surface strings from being no longer than three constituents. An additional transformation to limit sentence length by reduction cannot be justified on the grounds that the deleted elements, such as modifiers, locatives, adverbs, subjects, and objects, are necessary in underlying structure.

If a limitation on sentence length is to be included in the grammar for Seppo, the best solution appears to be one which allows constituents to be optional, with choices limited to a maximum of three (the verb, however, is not optional in noncopular sentences, and if a modifier is chosen, a modified noun must also be included). Once three constituents have been selected, the constraint on sentence length would prohibit further choosing. It is not clear what formal representation a rule like this could be given. This theoretical problem is not dealt with here, however, since it was decided not to limit sentence length in Seppo's grammar. As noted in 4.3.3.2, a constraint on sentence length may be a matter of performance rather than of underlying competence. Moreover, we cannot be certain that the constraint is real rather than a function of sample size. There is evidence that Seppo was in fact able to program utterances longer than three constituents. As early as five weeks before the sample we are considering, the following two utterances were produced:

täti ajaa bmbm kovaa	'aunt drives "car" fast' (subject–verb–object–adverb)

bmbm talli setä. .ajaa bmbm	' "car " garage man. .drives "car" ' (object–locative–subject–verb–object)

In the tape taken one week after the sample, these occurred:

isi joo pestään juna	'daddy already wash[1] train' (subject–adverb–verb–object)
kaksi humma aura vetää	'two horse plow pulls'[2] (modifier–subject–verb–object)

If four constituents were possible at a time when even three were infrequent, utterances of five or more constituents may have occurred occasionally by the time three constituents became common. For this reason, no constraint on sentence length is included in the grammar.

5.2   Comparison of the grammars for Seppo at MLUs 1.42 and 1.81

Provisions of the early grammar for Seppo remain the backbone of the later grammar. Most changes in Seppo's speech were combinations and elaborations of existing patterns. Most utterances in the earlier sample were no longer than two constituents, with the exception of subject–verb–object strings. Two major types of elaboration now resulted in several different three-term construction patterns:

1. Modifier–noun strings, which occurred earlier only as independent utterances, could now be embedded into longer utterances as expansions of either subject or object nouns.
2. In the earlier grammar, there was a mutually exclusive choice between the locative constituent and a verb with an optional direct object. Now the locative constituent could be chosen in addition to the verb, resulting in subject–verb–locative strings.

The second grammar provides for the generation of a few constructions which are qualitatively new, not just elaborations of pre-existing patterns. A new constituent, the adverb, began to occur in verb–adverb, subject–verb–adverb, and verb–object–adverb constructions. Other new construction patterns were the copular sentence types pronoun–noun and noun–adjective, questions with *missä*, 'where', plus a noun phrase or a verb, and negative constructions with Seppo's negative word *enää*, 'any more', plus a noun, verb, or adjective (see

---

[1] The verb form is incorrect: *pestään* is the impersonal form of the verb, while the third person singular form *pesi*, 'washed', is required by context.
[2] The verb is in the third person singular form, which adults often use with plural subjects in colloquial speech.

3.4.2.2 and 5.5 for discussions of this word). Seppo still lacked a way of asking for the name of an object with some kind of 'what' question and of posing yes–no questions. He understood 'what' questions and gave appropriate responses, but apparently did not yet understand yes–no questions, since he almost never answered appropriately. As in the earlier grammar, utterances with imperative intent were not formally distinguished from declarative utterances. Seppo did not use the imperative form of verbs (where these differ distinctly from the third person singular form), and he sometimes omitted subjects both from sentences which had imperative intent and from those which did not.

Between the first and second samples, Seppo began to use impersonal pronouns as both sentence-subjects and direct objects. Many new prolocatives came into use. Seppo also began to relax restrictions on the semantic characteristics of nouns in the roles of subject and direct object. Earlier, all sentence-subjects with main verbs had been either animate or words for cars, and all direct objects had been inanimate. In the second sample, two verbs, *hakee*, 'looks-for', and *työntää*, 'pushes', occurred with animate objects, as had *syö*, 'eats', and *piirtää*, 'draws', slightly earlier. The class of [+ vehicle] words used as subjects now included not only words for cars but also 'helicopter', 'tow truck', 'trailer truck', 'boat', 'fire engine', and 'train'. Other words for vehicles, such as 'tractor' and 'bicycle', probably also belonged in this class, but they did not occur as sentence-subjects in the sample. Nonvehicle inanimate nouns were just beginning to appear as subjects with main verbs:

torni kaatuu	'tower falls-down'
lanka menee	'spool goes'
lanka menee tuohon	'spool goes to-there'
sinne meni (avain)	'to-there went (key)'
menee nappi tuohon tuohon	'goes button to-there to-there'

In the following few weeks, the number of verbs used with nonvehicle inanimate subjects or with animate objects continued to increase slowly. For example, nouns and pronouns with inanimate referents appeared as subjects with 'comes', 'is-lost', 'got broken', 'pulls', 'revolves', and 'belongs', and animate nouns occurred as direct objects with 'hurts', 'pulls', 'takes', 'seeks', 'takes-care-of', and 'puts'.

The transformational components of the two grammars for Seppo are identical in principle. Both contain only optional reordering rules and an optional verb deletion rule. The reordering rules of the second grammar are much more elaborate than those of the first because there were more different kinds of constructions, each with its own reordering possibilities. There are still no transformations to provide for sentence conjoining and embedding, inflections, copulas, postpositions, or tense markers. Seppo produced simple negative constructions and 'where' questions in the second sample, but he still lacked the transformational machinery for negating or asking 'where' of any affirmative sentence he was able to produce. His negative word and 'where' were attached only to simple nouns, verbs, and adjectives, with a very few exceptions.

In the next section, a grammar for Rina is presented and discussed. The addition of this material to that from Seppo will help us to get a more general idea of the speech of Finnish children at this stage of development, so that we can better compare it to that of children learning other languages.

5.3   Transformational generative grammar for Rina at MLU 1.83

The phrase structure rules, lexicon feature rules, and transformational rules of a grammar for Rina based on nonimitated utterances in the sample at MLU 1.83 are presented below. The lexicon is given in Appendix L. Constructions generated by the grammar are listed in Appendix M, classified according to the grammatical relationships holding between the constituents. Single-word utterances and their frequencies of occurrence are given in Appendix N. Constructions not generated by the grammar are presented in Appendix O.

Phrase Structure Rules

1. $S_1 \rightarrow \text{Wh-loc} + \text{N}$

2. $S_2 \rightarrow \text{Neg} \begin{Bmatrix} \text{N} \\ \text{V} \\ \text{Proloc} \end{Bmatrix}$

3. $S_3 \rightarrow \text{(Dem) (Cop) NP}$

4. $S_4 \rightarrow \text{(N) VP}$

5. $\text{VP} \rightarrow \text{V (NP) (N) (Loc)}$

6. $\text{Dem} \rightarrow \begin{Bmatrix} \textit{tää}, \text{ 'this'} \\ \text{Proloc} \end{Bmatrix}$

7. $\text{NP} \rightarrow \text{(M) N}$

8. $\text{M} \rightarrow \begin{Bmatrix} \text{Adj} \\ \text{N} \end{Bmatrix}$

9. $\text{Loc} \rightarrow \begin{Bmatrix} \text{N} \\ \text{Proloc} \end{Bmatrix}$

Lexicon Feature Rules

1. $\text{N} \rightarrow [+\text{N}, \pm\text{pronoun}]$
2. $[+\text{pronoun}] \rightarrow [-\!\!-\!\!-\text{V}, -\begin{Bmatrix} \text{N} \\ \text{Adj} \end{Bmatrix}\!\!-\!\!-]$
3. $[-\text{pronoun}] \rightarrow [\pm\text{animate}]$
4. $[-\text{animate}] \rightarrow [-\!\!-\!\!-\text{N}]$
5. $\text{Proloc} \rightarrow [+\text{Proloc}, \pm\text{directional}]$
6. $[+\text{directional}] \rightarrow [-\!\!-\!\!-(\text{Cop}) \text{ NP}]$
7. $\text{V} \rightarrow [+\text{V}, \pm\!\!-\!\!-(\text{NP}), -[-\text{animate}]\!\!-\!\!-, \pm\!\!-\!\!-[+\text{directional}]]$
8. $[+\!\!-\!\!-(\text{NP})] \rightarrow [-\!\!-\!\!-[\text{NP}, +\text{animate}], \pm\!\!-\!\!-(\text{NP}) [+\text{N}, +\text{ani-}$
   $\text{mate}]]$
9. $\text{Adj} \rightarrow [+\text{Adj}]$
10. $\text{Cop} \rightarrow on,$ 'is'
11. $\text{Neg} \rightarrow ei,$ 'no, not'
12. $\text{Wh--loc} \rightarrow miss\ddot{a},$ 'where'

Transformational Rules

1. Tindirect object inflection: optional

   $\text{S.D.: X} \begin{Bmatrix} antaa, \text{ 'gives'} \\ anna, \text{ 'give'} \end{Bmatrix} \text{Y} + [+\text{N}, +\text{animate}]$

   Where X may be N or null and Y may be NP or null
   $\text{S.C.: } x_1 - x_2 - x_3 - x_4 \Rightarrow x_1 - x_2 - x_3 - x_4 - lle,$ 'to'

2. Treordering: optional
   (*a*) Reversal of direct and indirect objects

   $\text{S.D.: } \begin{Bmatrix} antaa, \text{ 'gives'} \\ anna, \text{ 'give'} \end{Bmatrix} \text{NP} + [+\text{N}, +\text{animate}]$

   $\text{S.C.: } x_1 - x_2 - x_3 \Rightarrow x_1 - x_3 - x_2$

   (*b*) Reversal of verb and indirect object

   $\text{S.D.: } \begin{Bmatrix} antaa, \text{ 'gives'} \\ anna, \text{ 'give'} \end{Bmatrix} [+\text{N}, +\text{animate}]$

   $\text{S.C.: } x_1 - x_2 \Rightarrow x_2 - x_1$

   (*c*) Reversal of *pois*, 'away', and direct object
   $\text{S.D.: } pois, +\text{NP}$
   $\text{S.C.: } x_1 - x_2 \Rightarrow x_2 - x_1$

   (*d*) Reversal of prolocative and NP
   $\text{S.D.: Proloc} + \text{NP}$
   $\text{S.C.: } x_1 - x_2 \Rightarrow x_2 - x_1$

3. T verb deletion: optional

$$\text{S.D.: } X + V \begin{Bmatrix} NP \\ Loc \end{Bmatrix} Y \qquad \text{Where X and Y may be N or null,}$$
$$\text{but at least one must not be null}$$
$$\text{S.C.: } x_1 - x_2 - x_3 - x_4 \Rightarrow x_1 - x_3 - x_4$$

5.3.1 Phrase structure rules. Most of Rina's constructions, like Seppo's, follow either a main verb or a copular sentence pattern. The children did not observe the distinction in quite the same way, however, and rules for generating sentences of the two types differ in the grammars. In Finnish, the predicate of a copular sentence can be a locative, predicate nominative, adjective, or adverb of a certain type. Rina's copular predicates consisted only of prolocatives and predicate nominatives. Unlike Seppo, she never used adjectives or locative nouns as predicates except in two partially imitated utterances:

> (*R* has food on her leg)
> *Kuka on likainen?*
> 'Who is dirty?'
>
> > *Rina lika⟨inen⟩*   'Rina dirty'
>
> (*R* is sitting on the floor)
> *Kuka on lattialla?*
>   'Who is on (the) floor?'
>
> > *Rina lattia*   'Rina floor'

In Seppo's grammar, copular sentences can be partially derived by following two rules which also generate main verb utterances:

$$S \rightarrow (NP) \, VP$$
$$VP \rightarrow \begin{Bmatrix} \text{Predicate} \\ V \, (NP) \, (Loc) \, (Adv) \end{Bmatrix}$$

When VP is rewritten as Predicate rather than as V (NP) (Loc) (Adv), a copular sentence results. These rules indicate that the subjects of Seppo's copular and main verb sentences are similar. Simple nouns, modified nouns, and demonstrative pronouns occur as subjects in utterances of both types:

Copular sentences		*Main verb sentences*	
possu tuossa	'piggie there'	*possu ajaa*	'piggie drives'
tässä pikku traktori	'here little tractor'	*kiltti täti..käve⟨lee⟩*	'nice lady.. walks'
tämä kala	'this fish'	*tämä tuli*	'this came'

This is not the case in Rina's speech. Her main verb sentences have only simple nouns as subjects, while her copular sentences have nouns (*tässä setä*, 'here man'), modified nouns (*täällä Rina nenä*, 'here Rina nose'), and pronouns (*tää setä*, 'this man'). Copular sentences must therefore be generated separately from main verb sentences so that the permissible subjects of the two sentence types can be specified. In the grammar, predicate prolocatives (*tässä*, 'here', *täällä*, 'here', etc.) and subject demonstrative pronouns (*tää*, 'this') are grouped together as realizations of a single constituent, Dem (demonstrative), which precedes simple or modified nouns. There are two reasons for deriving copular sentences in this way:

1. Utterances involving both predicate prolocatives and demonstrative pronouns had a deictic function, and were usually accompanied by a point to the object referred to. They often occurred in response to 'what is that?' or 'what is there?' questions.

2. The demonstrative word, whether prolocative or pronoun, almost always preceded the name of the object pointed out. If, as in Seppo's grammar, predicate prolocatives were generated as realizations of VP after a subject NP, almost every NP+Proloc string would be subjected to a reordering transformation. It seems a more accurate representation of Rina's linguistic knowledge to generate them directly in their most common order pattern. The few NP+Proloc strings in the sample are derived by following a re-ordering transformation which applies only to prolocatives and not to demonstrative pronouns preceding noun phrases.

Unlike Seppo, Rina occasionally used the copula *on*, 'is'. This occurred both after a demonstrative prolocative, as in *tässä on susi*, 'here is wolf', and without a demonstrative, as in *on lintu*, 'is bird'. The latter type of utterance was Rina's rejoinder to her mother's questions about identity, such as *onko tämä lintu?*, 'is this (a) bird?' and *onko tässä lintu?*, 'is here (a) bird?' Although a pronoun or pro-locative is technically needed in reply, as in *tämä on lintu*, 'this is (a) bird' and *tässä on lintu*, 'here is (a) bird', Rina had a model for omitting them, since her mother sometimes omitted them in answering her own questions. Rina did not produce any full demonstrative pronoun–copula–noun strings in the sample, although her two tokens of *tää on*, 'this is', suggest that she may have had the competence to do so.

Rina used the copula in a few other kinds of utterances:

ei oo tyttö	'no is girl'	('(it's) not a girl')
ei Aku-Ankka o(n)	'no Donald Duck is'	('(it's) not Donald Duck')
Ramilla on Aku-Ankka	'Rami-at is Donald Duck'	('Rami has Donald Duck')
tytöllä on	'girl-at is'	('girl has')

In the first two of these, the copula is used in conjunction with a negative verb, *ei*, which requires a special form of the copula, *ole*, or, colloquially, *oo*. Because Rina's pronunciation was unclear, it could not be determined whether she distinguished between *on* in affirmative sentences and *oo* in negative sentences. In utterances of both types, the word was pronounced something like [o:] or [ol]. Rina's placement of the copula either before or after the noun was acceptable. A pronoun subject would be correct, but is often omitted by adults. In the second two utterances above, Rina demonstrates an incipient control over the Finnish method of expressing 'have' (Finnish lacks a verb 'to have'). She produced more utterances of this kind in subsequent tapes, although she did not always include the copula nor the obligatory inflection on the noun naming the possessor:

lintulla[1] *on pipi*	'bird-at is sore'	('bird has sore')
tätillä[1]..*pipi*	'aunt-at..sore'	('aunt (has) sore')
Rina pipi	'Rina sore'	('Rina (has) sore')

Rina produced many main verb sentences. The majority of these are subject–verb and subject–verb–object strings. Somewhat less frequent are subject–verb–locative, verb–object, and subject–object strings. The verb phrase of main verb sentences contains several optional constituents in the grammar:

$$VP \rightarrow V \ (NP) \ (N) \ (Loc)$$

NP functions as direct object. N functions as indirect object. Only one verb in the lexicon is marked as able to take an indirect object: *antaa*, 'gives', and its variant *anna*, 'give'.[2] There is one example of a subject–verb–object–indirect object string in the sample, and several of verb–indirect object and direct object–indirect object.

All subjects of main verb sentences are simple nouns, while direct objects are nouns, pronouns, and, in a very few instances, modified nouns. The grammar's specification that direct objects can be rewritten as M+N as well as N alone may be slightly premature. Modified direct objects occur in only five utterances:

---

[1] Rina usually failed to observe consonant gradation at this stage, and added inflections directly to nominative singular noun forms. *Lintu-lla* and *täti-llä* should have been *linnu-lla* and *tädi-llä* in these utterances.

[2] *Antaa* is the third person singular form and the infinitive of 'give', and *anna* is the second person singular imperative form. Rina seemed to use these forms appropriately in this sample, but she sometimes interchanged them in subsequent tapes. This suggests that she did not yet fully distinguish between them, so they have been considered free variants of the same form in the grammar.

Rina saa lisää kakku	'Rina gets more cake'
Rina lisää kakku	'Rina more cake' (see example (5) in 4.3.3.2 for context)
tätille (tuo) keksi[1]	'to-aunt (that) cracker'
tätille tätä keksi[1]	'to-aunt this cracker'
repii. . Aku Rami	'tears. . Donald Rami' (means 'tears Rami's Donald', produced as Rina tore her brother's Donald Duck comic book)

In addition, there is the following sequence:

(*R* trying to get *B* to give her the
larger of two pens which belonged
to *B*)

> *iso kynä*   'big pen'
> *anna*   'give'
> *täti, Rina iso (kynä)*   'aunt, Rina big (pen)'
> *iso anna*   'big give'

Judging from the preceding and following utterances, the verb *anna*, 'give', was present in underlying structure in 'aunt, Rina big pen', but it is uncertain whether the last word in this utterance was really *kynä*, 'pen', or, in fact, *anna*, 'give'. There are no more instances of modified object nouns in subsequent tapes until six weeks after the sample. Although the modification of objects appeared earlier than the modification of subjects in Rina's grammar, it was still relatively undeveloped at the time we are considering.

Rina's main use of modified nouns as constituents of longer utterances was in the copular sentence pattern Dem + NP. *Lisää kakku*, 'more cake', *pää pipi*, 'head sore', and several genitive–noun combinations occurred in utterances of this type in the sample, and there are many examples of modified nouns following demonstratives in subsequent tapes.

The maximum string which can be generated by the grammar consists of six constituents, with the following syntactic interpretation:

subject–verb–modifier–object–indirect object–locative

Such a string never actually occurred. The longest strings in the sample which can be generated by the grammar are two four-term utterances:

---

[1] In these utterances, the verb *anna* or *antaa*, 'give', is considered present in underlying structure and deleted in surface structure.

subject–verb–object–indirect object: *äiti antaa paperi Rina* 'mother gives paper Rina'

subject–verb–modifier–object: *Rina saa lisää kakku* 'Rina gets more cake'

In immediately subsequent tapes, there are also a few subject–verb–object–locative strings such as *Rinä syö kättä. .tuossa,* 'Rina eats hand . .there'. Most strings at this time consisted of a selection of two or three of the six possible constituents, sometimes reordered. For example:

subject–verb:	*Rina syö*	'Rina eats'
verb–object:	*piirtää tätä*	'draws this'
subject–object:	*Rina kynä*	'Rina pencil' (see example (6) in 4.3.3.2 for context)
verb–locative:	*tässä anna tässä*	'here give here'
subject–locative:	*Rina paperi*	'Rina paper' (means 'Rina draws onto paper')
verb–indirect object:	*anna Rina*	'give Rina'
subject–verb–object:	*Rina syö. .keksi*	'Rina eats. .cracker'
subject–verb–locative:	*Rina piirtää tässä*	'Rina draws here'
verb–object–locative:	*(tuossa) anna. .näitä*	'(there) give. .these'
modifier–object–indirect object:	*tätille tätä keksi*	'to-aunt this cracker'
subject–modifier–object:	*Rina lisää kakku*	'Rina more cake' (see example (5) in 4.3.3.2 for context)
verb–modifier–object:	*repii. .Aku. .Rami*	'tears Donald Rami' (means 'tears Rami's Donald')

Should the absence of five- and six-term strings be accounted for in the grammar? For reasons discussed in connection with Seppo's grammar, it was decided to provide for the absence of verbs in some surface structures by an optional verb deletion transformation and to simply note the absence of strings of longer than four constituents without making a formal provision for a constraint on sentence length.

5.3.2 Lexicon feature rules. Only animate nouns occurred as sentence–subjects with main verbs in Rina's speech at this time. All of these referred to humans, with one exception: *nalle. .katsoo,* 'teddy bear . .watches'. Most direct objects were inanimate, but there were five which would be considered animate in adult Finnish:

Rina kissa. .(haluu)	'Rina cat. .(wants)'
Rina katsoo Aku-Ankka	'Rina looks-at Donald Duck'
Rina laittaa hevonen	'Rina makes horse'
Rina piirtää Mataami-Mimmi	'Rina draws Madam-Mimmi'
	(a name)
hauva pois	'doggie (take) away'

In the sample, none of these nouns played grammatical roles which were restricted to animate nouns in Rina's speech, like sentence-subject or genitive. It was therefore impossible to determine if they were animate in the terms of Rina's grammar, so they could not be marked [+animate] in the lexicon. All transitive verbs consequently are given the selection restriction [———[+animate]]. A larger sample, however, might have revealed that the verbs 'wants', 'looks-at', 'makes', 'draws', and '(take) away' could take both animate and inanimate direct objects and should also have received the selection restriction [+———[+animate]].

Rina's nouns were subdivided into [+pronoun] and [−pronoun] classes. Pronouns did not appear as subjects with main verbs, nor were they modified. *Tää*, 'this' (nominative), was used as subject in demonstrative copular sentences, while *tätä*, 'this', *näitä*, 'these', and *lisää*, 'more', functioned only as direct objects. These three have partitive inflections and so are appropriate as objects. In subsequent tapes, nominative pronouns also were used, incorrectly, as direct objects, as in:

haluu tää	'wants this'
äiti, Rina tää avaa	'mother, Rina this opens'
toi tässä maalaa	'that here paints' (produced while Rina was painting a shoe in a picture, to which she pointed while saying 'that')

Partitive pronouns did not appear as subjects of either main verb or copular sentences. This distribution of nominative and partitive pronouns in subject and object roles is identical to that in Seppo's sample (see 5.1.2). Like Seppo, Rina used no pronouns with the genitive/accusative inflection -*n* at this time, but the contexts in which she used pronouns did not call for them.

As was also the case with Seppo, it was impossible to tell if Rina distinguished between 'this' and 'that' and between 'here' and 'there'. She used only demonstrative pronouns translated as 'this' at this stage.

Since she used them only to refer to objects or drawings right in front of her or in her hand, no obvious errors were made. The demonstrative adjectives *tuo*, 'that' (nominative) and *tätä*, 'this' (partitive) occurred in the same speech context, as Rina gave a cracker to the investigator:

tätille (tuo) keksi	'to-aunt (that) cracker'
tätille tätä keksi	'to-aunt this cracker'

They did not appear to contrast, but either one was appropriate in the situation. Similarly, constructions with 'here' and 'there' did not contrast, since both were used to refer only to nearby locations. Rina's mother also used both 'here' and 'there' in these situations.

5.3.3 Transformational rules. The transformational rules of Rina's grammar are all optional. They specify the addition, reordering, and deletion of elements. Nouns serving as indirect objects may receive the allative case inflection, *-lle*, 'to', in the grammar. Rina had also begun to mark the possessor in the Finnish equivalent of Noun *has* Noun sentences, but these constructions were still rare and are not provided for. In adult Finnish, the adessive case, *-lla/llä*, is used in Noun *has* Noun constructions. In Rina's speech at this time, the inflections marking indirect objects and possessors were phonetically indistinguishable, always being realized as [li]. It is therefore unclear whether Rina distinguished cognitively between the allative and the adessive cases.

Slobin (1966a) noted that when new grammatical cases entered the speech of the Russian child Zhenya, they immediately began to perform several syntactic functions. For example, the first datives were used to indicate both the indirect object of action and motion directed towards an individual. This was not true of Rina's earliest inflections. In Finnish, the allative case *-lle* is used to mark both indirect objects and directed motion. Rina at first used it only for indirect objects, although she often accompanied it with a motion towards the person to whom she gave something. Although she occasionally produced utterances which required an inflection to mark directed motion, she did not use *-lle* or any other inflection for this purpose for months to come. For example, in the sample at MLU 1.83, the utterance *Rina laittaa paperi*, 'Rina puts (makes) paper', produced while Rina was drawing on a paper, should have been either *Rina laittaa paperille* or *Rina laittaa paperiin*, 'Rina puts (makes) onto-paper'. The adessive case *-lla/llä* is used in adult Finnish to mark the possessor in Noun *has* Noun sentences, to indicate location on, at, or near, and for instrumentals. Rina at first used it only to mark possessors. Several weeks later, she began to use it occasionally to mark instruments, as in *isi tuli autolla*, 'daddy came by-car'. It was not used to indicate a locative relationship until several months later.

Slobin (1966*a*) also noted that morphological classes with clearly concrete referents emerge first in the speech of Russian children. For example, the first prepositions are used only to mark concrete meanings which can be understood by the child from visual perception, such as spatial relationships. Certain case endings in Finnish (the allative, the adessive, and others), are equivalent to certain English and Russian prepositions in that they are used to mark locative relationships. In Rina's speech, as we have seen, these were first used to mark non-locative meanings which cannot be understood from visual perception alone, such as indirect object and possessor. In contrast, when Seppo began to acquire some of these inflections (a few weeks past the stage we are considering), he used them exclusively to mark locative relationships. The semantic characteristics of children's earliest inflections clearly need further investigation, as noted also in 4.6.

In addition to indirect object inflection, transformations in Rina's grammar specify several optional reordering transformations and the optional deletion of the verb from (subject)–verb–(object)–(indirect object) and subject–verb–locative strings. The justification for the verb deletion transformation is the same as that given for a similar rule in Seppo's grammar (see 4.3.3.2 and 5.1.3). Two of the reordering transformations are similar to those for Seppo. These specify the derivation of noun–prolocative strings from prolocative–noun strings (the transformation for Seppo indicates the reverse operation), and the optional placement of the verb *pois*, 'away', with the understood meaning *ota pois*, 'take away', after the direct object. The two other reordering transformations deal with the order of direct and indirect objects in relation to each other and to the verb. Although Rina's word order was not fixed, it was not as flexible as Seppo's. At the time of this sample, only the reordering of prolocative–noun, *pois*, 'away'–direct object, verb–indirect object, and direct object–indirect object appeared to be productive, as judged from the frequencies of various orders both in the sample and in immediately subsequent tapes. In addition to strings with the dominant orders, subject–locative–verb and verb–subject strings occurred in the sample, but these did not continue as productive reorderings. Other orders which occurred in or just past the sample, however, such as object–verb, locative–subject–verb, locative–verb–subject, subject–object–verb, and object–subject–verb, continued on as infrequent, but evidently nonaccidental, alternatives to the dominant orders. Word order as a variable of the Finnish children's speech is considered in greater detail in 5.6.

5.4   Comparison of the grammars for Seppo and Rina

The speech of the two Finnish children was very similar with respect both to the construction patterns present and the elements and operations lacking. Both children produced main verb and copular sentences, and combined negative markers and the interrogative 'where' with one other element like a noun or a verb. Constructions were rarely longer than two or three constituents. Most obligatory functors were still omitted. Rina, unlike Seppo, however, had begun to use case endings occasionally to mark possessors in the Finnish equivalent of Noun *has* Noun sentences and for indirect objects, and sometimes supplied the copular verb where required. Neither child used inflections to mark direct objects and locatives (except on pronouns and prolocatives, words which were probably learned as units), genitives, and plurals. The children both used the nominative singular form of nouns for all syntactic roles. Verbs were in the third person singular present indicative form, except for one or two examples each of imperatives (Rina only), past tense, and the impersonal form, which is used colloquially in adult Finnish with *me*, 'we', as the first person plural verb form. Neither child had productive rules yet for deriving these forms from his unmarked verbs. The transformational components of the children's grammars are of relatively minor importance. Most utterances can be generated directly with phrase structure rules, with the occasional application of optional reordering or verb deletion transformations. There is no transformational mechanism in either grammar for generating strings of infinite length through operations of sentence embedding or conjoining.

The frequencies with which the children's main construction patterns occurred in the samples are presented in Table 11. The frequency of each pattern in Seppo's earlier sample is also included to allow a comparison of his early and late Stage I constructions.

Both children were working on very nearly the same set of sentence

TABLE 11. *Seppo's and Rina's main construction patterns:*[a]
early and late Stage I frequencies

	Seppo MLU 1.42	Seppo MLU 1.81	Rina MLU 1.83
Two-term utterances			
Main verb patterns			
subject–verb	34	69	21
verb–object	8	9	6
subject–object	3	3	3
verb–locative[b]	1	12	1
subject–locative[b,c]	6	4	2
verb–indirect object	—	—	3
verb–adverb	—	7	—
adjective–noun	4	10	3
genitive–noun	4	10	4
attributive noun–noun	—	4	1
Copular patterns			
demonstrative prolocative–noun	5	24	54
noun–locative noun[c]	1	3	1
noun–adjective	—	5	1
demonstrative pronoun–noun	1	1	6
Other			
negative–noun	—	2	7
negative–verb	—	4	2
negative–prolocative	—	—	2
where–noun	—	8	2
where–verb	—	3	—
Three-term utterances			
Main verb patterns			
subject–verb–object	7	8	21
subject–verb–locative	—	21	8
subject–verb–adverb	—	4	—
verb–object–locative	—	—	2
verb–object–adverb	1	4	—
verb–locative–adverb	—	1	—
modifier–subject–verb	—	5	—
verb–modifier–object	—	2	2
subject–modifier–object	—	—	1
modifier–object–indirect object	—	—	3
modifier–subject–locative	—	1	—
Copular pattern			
prolocative–modifier–noun	—	1	7
Other			
where–modifier–noun	—	1	—

TABLE II. (*cont.*)

	Seppo MLU 1.42	Seppo MLU 1.81	Rina MLU 1.83
Four-term utterances			
Main verb patterns			
subject–verb–object–indirect object	—	—	1
subject–verb–modifier–object	—	—	1

[a] Utterance types only. All word orders of each pattern counted, except that adjective–noun and noun–adjective are distinguished. Utterances with copulas or repeated words are included, as are some constructions which are not generated by the grammars (see Appendices G, K and O).

[b] Locatives include both nouns and prolocatives.

[c] Judgment from context involved in deciding whether a noun–locative string is a copular or a main verb sentence.

patterns. Although the absolute and relative frequencies with which they produced utterances of various patterns differ somewhat, the differences seem relatively minor and probably in some cases reflect limited sample size. The children showed many of the same 'preferences', as judged by frequency of production, for constituents in certain syntactic roles. They expressed more subjects than direct objects, and produced more sentences with both subject and verb, and, optionally, another constituent than those with any other two constituents. Seppo used locatives more than Rina, however, while Rina produced more sentences with direct objects than Seppo.

In Seppo's first sample, the only three-term constructions, with one exception, were subject–verb–object strings. In his second sample, there were many different types of three-term strings. Rina, at a stage of development equivalent to Seppo's at the time of his second sample, produced two four-term strings from her underlying main verb sentence pattern, and Seppo probably was also capable of this (see 5.1.4). Strings consisting of three major constituents (combinations of subject, verb, object, locative, and adverb) appear to be equivalent in cognitive complexity to those composed of two major constituents, one of which is a modified noun. Utterances of both kinds flourished at the same time in the speech of both children. Similarly, strings with four major constituents seem to be equivalent to those with three, one of which is modified, since the children's earliest four-term constructions include utterances of both types.

The main verb sentences of both children followed a basic subject–verb–object–locative pattern. Rina's pattern also included an indirect object constituent, while Seppo's had an adverb constituent. Rina did not begin to use adverbs for a long time after the sample was collected. Several utterances from Seppo's sample and from the tape taken the week after the sample suggest that Seppo had begun to learn something about the expression of indirect objects:

(*S* takes a finger puppet for
  himself and gives one to *B*)   > *tää..Immi* 'this..Immi'
                                     > *tää..täti*   'this..aunt'
                                       (cf. Rina's 'to-aunt this cracker'
                                       and 'to-aunt (that) cracker')
(*S* trying to get *M* to give him
  another cracker)   > *Immi(kin)..lisää* 'Immi(-also)..
                                                   more'
                               > *lisää Immi..keksi* 'more Immi..
                                                   cracker'
(*S* looking at a picture of a mail-
  man who is a pig carrying mail up
  to a house)   > *possu isi..posti* 'piggie daddy..mail'
                                       (possibly means 'piggie brings
                                       daddy mail')

Both children selected elements from their main verb sentence patterns, most frequently in the order specified, but never produced the maximum strings which can be generated by the grammars: modifier–subject–verb–modifier–object–locative–adverb for Seppo and subject–verb–modifier–object–indirect object–locative for Rina. Constituents did not combine with each other with equal freedom. Certain combinations were more common than others. For example, Seppo rarely combined the object, locative, and adverb constituents. He most often used them individually as complements to verb or subject–verb strings. Similarly, Rina did not combine locatives and indirect objects. She used locatives mainly as complements to subject–verb strings, and paired indirect objects with verbs or direct objects. In the grammars for both children, utterances from the main verb pattern without surface verbs are derived transformationally from underlying strings with verbs, since the syntactic characteristics of subject and object nouns and of prolocatives seem to be closely associated with the selection restrictions of particular 'missing' verbs.

The subjects of main verb sentences differed somewhat in the two samples, but direct objects and locatives were similar. Seppo used simple nouns, modified nouns, and pronouns as subjects, while Rina used only simple nouns. Both children used simple nouns, modified nouns, and pronouns as direct objects. Neither used any personal pronouns. Subject nouns were overwhelmingly (exclusively, in Rina's case) animate, and object nouns were inanimate except with a very few verbs such as 'draws', 'looks-for', 'makes', and 'pushes'.

Demonstrative pronoun–noun and prolocative–noun copular sentences occurred in both samples. Seppo also produced noun–adjective and noun–noun$_{loc.}$ copular sentences, which Rina did not. The nouns in prolocative–noun constructions were modified by genitives and adjectives in both children's samples, but the predicate nominatives in demonstrative pronoun–noun constructions were all simple nouns.

Seppo and Rina had only rudimentary systems of negation and interrogation at this time. Negation involved the placement of a negative marker before one other word, usually a noun or a verb. Rina's negative marker was *ei*, the third person singular form of the negative verb. She also used this appropriately in isolation. Seppo's was *enää*, 'any more', which is not a negative in itself but often accompanies the negative verb in adults' constructions. Both children produced a very few negative constructions which are slightly more complex. Rina's involved the correct use of the copula with the negative verb and a noun, as in *ei oo tyttö*, 'no is girl' ('(it) isn't (a) girl'), while Seppo's involved a more complex verb phrase in two utterances (*ei syödä tämmö*, 'no eat this-kind-of-thing', *enää piirtää tuossa*, 'any more draw there'), and the addition of a sentence-subject in one utterance (*hiiri syö enää*, 'mouse eats any more').

Neither child asked yes–no questions, which require a question inflection and word order changes in Finnish. Both children posed only one type of question at this stage: *missä*, 'where', plus a noun or (Seppo only) a verb. Within a few weeks, the children began to ask simple 'what' questions. Rina used a fixed routine, *mitä tässä*, 'what here?', while Seppo produced several tokens each of *mitä tuolla*, 'what there?', and *mitä tuossa*, 'what there?', and one token of *mitä tuo*, 'what that?' The children's choice of *mitä*, the partitive form of 'what', is curious, since *mikä*, the nominative form, was much more common in the speech of both mothers. The mothers used *mitä* to inquire about the identity of substances or to ask very nonspecific questions about the objects or events in a picture, and *mikä* to ask for the names of particular objects. The children seemed to use *mitä* indiscriminately for both types of questions, evidently not having learned the semantic implications of the nominative and partitive forms.

Although both children produced many utterances designed to influence the actions of others, these were not usually formally marked as imperatives. Neither child used the imperative form of the verb (Rina's *anna*, 'give', was an exception, but it was not always used where required), and neither consistently omitted the subject. Subjectless imperatives did occur, but many nonimperative utterances also lacked subjects. An initial noun such as 'mother' or 'aunt' occurred in some utterances which had imperative intent, but there was rarely a break in intonation to suggest that these should be regarded as vocatives rather than as subjects.

Despite many similarities, the children's approaches to language learning were characterized by distinct styles. Seppo seemed more flexible than Rina in certain respects. His constructions were not so concentrated in a small number of construction patterns as Rina's were. Rina produced a very large number of prolocative–noun, subject–verb, and subject–verb–object strings, and relatively few of other patterns. Seppo's preferred constructions were subject–verb, prolocative–noun, and subject–verb–locative (all with various word orders), but there were substantial numbers of several other patterns as well. Seppo took more advantage of the possibilities for combining different sets of constituents from his underlying main verb pattern than Rina did. His word order was also more flexible than Rina's. He seemed to experiment with various permutations of word order within most of the construction patterns outlined in Table 11. Rina was advanced in other ways, however. She began to use the copula and certain noun inflections long before Seppo did. Judgments about comprehension are difficult to make in the absence of experimental controls, but the characteristics of the children's interactions with their mothers suggest that Rina understood more of what was said to her than Seppo did. For example, she responded appropriately much more often than Seppo to her mother's interrogatives and imperatives. This apparent difference in comprehension may simply have reflected a greater independence on Seppo's part, however. He may have understood as much as Rina, but paid less attention or was less interested in complying.

5.5   Comparison of Seppo and Rina with English-speaking children

The speech of Seppo and Rina in late Stage I is directly comparable to that of the three American children studied by Brown and his associates at the time they were first taped. The MLUs of speech samples from the Finnish and American children are similar:

> Seppo: 1.81
> Rina: 1.83
> Eve: 1.69
> Sarah: 1.74
> Adam: 2.06

The comparison of Seppo's speech at MLU 1.42 (early Stage I) to that of English-speaking children revealed such strong similarities that a single grammar could have been written to account for at least the most basic facts about the children's linguistic knowledge. The same claim can be made for the late Stage I developmental period. Brown (in press) has written a fragmentary transformational generative grammar for Adam, Eve, and Sarah. This grammar, composed only of phrase structure rules, does not perfectly represent each child's ability, but it summarizes some of the basic shared features of the children's speech. Brown's grammar and the phrase structure rules of the grammars written for Seppo and Rina are presented for comparison in Table 12.

The construction patterns generated by the grammars are almost identical. The distinction between copular and main verb sentences is formally represented in each grammar. Copular sentences include noun–locative, noun–adjective, and demonstrative pronoun–noun strings for most of the children. All the children used demonstrative copular sentences like 'this (that)' + N and 'here (there)' + N to signal the 'operation of reference' called 'nomination' by Brown (1970, in press) (see 3.3.2). The underlying subject–verb–object–locative pattern was common to all the children. Brown includes a constituent, N, preceding the direct object NP, which functions as indirect object. This constituent is also present in Rina's grammar, as N after the object NP. Seppo's grammar lacks this, and has a unique constituent, the adverb. All three grammers provide for the modification of direct object nouns. Subject nouns can be modified only in Seppo's grammar. Modifiers are either nouns or adjectives. Noun modifiers usually identify possessors, in

TABLE 12. *Phrase structure rules from the Finnish and American children's grammars, late Stage I*[a]

American children (Adam, Eve, Sarah)	Seppo	Rina
S → Nominal͡ VP	S → (NP ◊ VP)	S_1 → (Dem) (Cop) NP
VP → $\begin{Bmatrix}\text{Predicate} \\ \text{V (N) (NP) (Place)}\end{Bmatrix}$	VP → $\begin{Bmatrix}\text{Predicate} \\ \text{V (NP) (Loc) (Adv)}\end{Bmatrix}$	S_2 → (N) VP
Predicate → $\begin{Bmatrix}\text{Adj} \\ \text{NP} \\ \text{Place}\end{Bmatrix}$	Predicate → $\begin{Bmatrix}\text{Adj} \\ \text{N} \\ \text{Loc}\end{Bmatrix}$	VP → V (NP) (N) (Loc)
Nominal → $\begin{Bmatrix}\text{N} \\ \text{Dem}\end{Bmatrix}$		Dem → $\begin{Bmatrix}\textit{tää}, \text{'this'} \\ \text{Proloc}\end{Bmatrix}$
Place → NP	Loc → $\begin{Bmatrix}\text{N} \\ \text{Proloc}\end{Bmatrix}$	Loc → $\begin{Bmatrix}\text{N} \\ \text{Proloc}\end{Bmatrix}$
NP → (M) N	NP → (M) N	NP → (M) N
M → $\begin{Bmatrix}\text{Adj} \\ \text{N}\end{Bmatrix}$	M → $\begin{Bmatrix}\text{Adj} \\ \text{N}\end{Bmatrix}$	M → $\begin{Bmatrix}\text{Adj} \\ \text{N}\end{Bmatrix}$

[a] Rules for generating 'where' questions and negative constructions are omitted from the Finnish children's grammars, since Brown does not include these in the grammar for the American children.

genitive–noun constructions. The locative constituents of all the children can be realized as simple nouns or (not indicated in Brown's grammar) as prolocative forms like 'here' and 'there'. The locative constituent is rewritten as NP in Brown's grammar, but a modified noun functioned as a locative in only one utterance, produced by Adam. The modification of locative nouns, then, emerged later than the modification of other sentence constituents such as direct object nouns and, in Seppo's case, subject nouns.

The American children, like the Finnish children, produced modified nouns as independent utterances as well as embedded in longer sentences (Brown's grammar does not indicate this aspect of the American children's speech). Brown (in press) notes that his subjects produced genitive–noun strings more frequently than adjective–noun strings both as independent utterances and as sentence constituents. The Finnish children, in contrast, produced about equal numbers of adjective–noun and genitive–noun strings in isolation, but used more adjective–noun strings as sentence constituents.

Most subjects in main verb sentences were animate nouns and most direct objects were inanimate nouns in the speech of all the children.

All of Rina's and Eve's subjects were animate and all but one or two were human. This semantic distinction between nouns functioning as subjects and those functioning as objects was also found in the early Stage I samples from Finnish and American children.

All the children used some pronouns at this time. However, Seppo and Rina, unlike the American children, used no personal pronouns. This may have been an idiosyncrasy of both children, or it may be a general difference between children learning the two languages.

The phrase structure rules of the grammars for Seppo and Rina generate strings which are longer than those either child actually produced. This is also true of the grammar for the American children. The rules of this grammar generate a maximum string of seven constituents (subject–verb–indirect object–modifier–direct object–modifier–locative), but Brown (in press) observes that no construction longer than three constituents, or, in Adam's sample, four, actually occurred. It is interesting that the same 'upper limit' of three terms, with occasional four-term exceptions, characterized the speech of both the American and the Finnish children at similar mean utterance lengths. Brown (in press) points out that the American children's constructions are 'a very liberal sampling of the implied pairs and triplets' in the underlying pattern. The same is true of the Finnish children's constructions. The order of constituents specified by the rules of the grammars is well preserved in this sampling by the Americans, and, with a few exceptions, corresponds to the word order used most frequently by Seppo and Rina. The two sets of children produced almost identical combinations of two and three constituents. Constructions expressing the following grammatical relations occur in all or almost all the samples:

> subject–verb
> verb–object
> subject–object
> verb–locative
> subject–locative
> subject–verb–object
> subject–verb–locative
> verb–object–locative

The children who had indirect object constituents also produced verb–indirect object, direct object–indirect object, and verb–indirect object–direct object strings. Seppo had an adverb constituent, and produced verb–adverb, subject–verb–adverb, verb–object–adverb, and verb–

locative–adverb strings. Both sets of children also produced three-term strings with one elaborated constituent, such as verb–modifier–object and modifier–object–indirect object.

In addition to affirmative, declarative main verb and copular sentences, the Finnish and American children produced rudimentary interrogative and negative constructions. The American children, unlike Seppo and Rina, were able to ask yes–no questions by superimposing a rising intonation on any declarative utterance. They were not yet able to construct formally more correct questions by inserting 'do' or inverting word order. This is parallel to the Finnish children's failure to use the interrogative inflection -*ko/kö* and to make accompanying word order rearrangements. The only questions asked by the Finnish children were composed of 'where' plus a noun or verb. The American children's 'where' questions were similar. Adam's pattern was 'where (N) go?' and Sarah's was 'where N?' Eve, who had the lowest MLU of all the children, asked no 'where' questions at this time. The American children also asked for the names of objects, using fixed routines. Adam's routine was 'who 'at?', Sarah's 'what's that?', and Eve's 'that?' The Finnish children developed 'what there?' and 'what that?' questions a short time after collection of the samples upon which the grammars are based.

Negative constructions were infrequent in the American children's speech (Eve produced none at all). The few examples are similar to the Finnish children's negatives. Most involve a negative word ('no' or 'not') plus a noun or a verb, as in 'no tail?', 'no fall', and 'no put'. Like Seppo and Rina, the Americans produced a very few slightly more complex negatives, such as '(that's not) daddy', '(I not fall)' and 'no pictures innere'. These utterances were so infrequent and diverse that they may have been memorized sentence fragments rather than the result of productive rules for constructing sentences.

In studying the development of syntactic negation in her subjects' speech, Bloom (1970, p. 173) distinguished between three categories of meaning expressed by negative utterances:

1. Nonexistence: the referent was not manifest in the context, where there was an expectation of its existence, and it was correspondingly negated in the linguistic expression...
2. Rejection: the referent actually existed or was imminent within the contextual space of the speech event and was rejected or opposed by the child...

3. Denial: the negative utterance asserted that an actual (or supposed) predication was not the case...

Bloom found that most of her subjects' earliest negative constructions expressed *nonexistence*. Negative constructions which expressed rejection and denial were infrequent at first, and developed in complexity more slowly than those which expressed nonexistence. Rejection preceded denial in this development. The Finnish children's negative constructions are presented in Table 13, with their linguistic and nonlinguistic contexts. Many of these are difficult to interpret. Most of Rina's expressed *denial* rather than nonexistence, as when she disagreed with a name or an interpretation offered by her mother. Several of her negatives which are ambiguous probably also expressed denial. Seppo's negative marker *enää*, 'any more', was used unambiguously only a few times, as in examples (1) and (2) in Table 13. In these utterances, it seemed to express nonrecurrence, an aspect of nonexistence. *Enää* was most often used in a context in which nothing had changed (examples (3), (4), (5), and (6), and Seppo's intention was impossible to determine. Seppo's N+*pois*, 'away', and *pois*+N constructions might also be interpreted as negatives. These utterances occasionally expressed rejection (Seppo didn't want to look at or play with an object any more), or nonexistence (an object had left the field of reference). Most often they occurred when Seppo was looking at a picture of an animal or a vehicle. According to his mother's interpretation, Seppo thought that the referent was about to go away, which could be considered an anticipation of nonexistence, but it is impossible to determine if this was an accurate reading of his intention.

The Finnish and American children all produced utterances with imperative intent, but these were rarely formally distinguished from declaratives. All the children produced some sentences without subjects, but these were not limited to imperatives. In addition, declarative sentences with subjects, like 'mother gives' and 'Rina gets', were often used to influence the behavior of others.

The grammars for Seppo, Rina, and the American children differ in similar ways from those for adult Finnish and English. There are no provisions for inflections, prepositions and postpositions, tense markers, verbal auxiliaries, and other functors (optional markers for the indirect object and the copula in Rina's grammar are the only exceptions). Some of these functors did occur occasionally in the children's samples but most were still too infrequent and unsystematic to

TABLE 13. *Negative constructions in the Finnish
children's speech, late Stage I*

	Rina, MLU 1.83	
(1)	(*M* and *R* looking at a picture of fruit) *Onks siellä omenia ja banaaneja ja kaikkia hedelmia siellä?* 'Are there apples and bananas and all (kinds of) fruits there?' > *ei..täällä*	'not..here' (Denial)
(2)	(*M* and *R* looking at a picture of a horse) *Katoppas, onks täälläkin heppa?* 'look, is here-also (a) horse?' > *ei täällä*	'not here' (Denial)
(3)	(*M* and *R* looking at pictures) *Kuka siinä on?* 'Who there is?' > *ei tässä*	'not here' (Denial)
(4–6)	(*M* and *R* looking at a picture of Donald Duck) *Onks se Aku-Ankka?* 'Is it Donald Duck?' > *ei Aku-Ankka*	'not Donald Duck' (Denial)
	Onhan se Aku-Ankka. 'It is indeed Donald Duck'. > *ei Aku-Ankka o(n)*	'no Donald Duck is' ('it isn't Donald Duck') (Denial)
	Onhan, kulta. '(It) is indeed, dear'. *ei!*	'no!'
	⋮ *Näytä äidille, missä Aku-Ankka?* 'Show mother, where (is) Donald Duck?' > *ei Aku-Ankka!*	'not Donald Duck!' (Denial)
(7)	(*M* and *R* looking at a picture of the Big Bad Wolf) *Iso paha hukka.* 'Big bad wolf'. *iso paha* (B): *iso susi* 'Big wolf'. > *ei susi!*	'big bad' 'not wolf!' (Denial)
(8)	(*M* scolding *R* for misbehavior) *Onko Rina tuhma tyttö?* 'Is Rina (a) bad girl?' *ei oo tyttö*	'no is girl' ('isn't (a) girl') (Denial)
(9)	(*M* and *R* looking at pictures of Pluto in a comic book) *Se on ihan kaikissa kuvissa sama hauva, sen nimi on 'Pluto' hauva.*	

TABLE 13 (*cont.*)

Rina, MLU 1.83 (*cont.*)		
'It is in absolutely all (the) pictures (the) same dog; its name is "Pluto" dog'.		
	tässä hauva	'here dog'
Pluto hauva. 'Pluto dog'.	> *ei Pluto!*	'not Pluto!' (Denial)
(10–11) (*R* trying to get *B* to come sit by her)	*täti tulee istuu Rina viereen*	'aunt comes sit Rina next-to'
Mitä sä sanoit? Täti— Mitä Rina sanoi? Aiti ei käsittänyt. Rina, 'täti'..mitä? 'What did you say? Aunt— What did Rina say? Mother didn't understand. Rina, 'aunt'..what?'		
	> *ei täti*	'not aunt' (Denial?)
Niin, täti.. 'Yes, aunt..'	> *ei täti*	'not aunt' (Denial?)
(12) (*M* trying to get *R* to put her slippers on) *No, ei sitten, Rina saa itse laittaa, hah?* 'Well, no then, Rina gets herself to-put-on, eh?'	> *ei saa!*	'no gets'('doesn't get') (Denial? Rejection?)
Kuka laittaa? 'Who puts-on?'	*äiti laittaa*	'mother puts-on'
(13) (*M* commenting on *R*'s dislike of a food) *Ai, et sä tykännyt siitä.* 'Oh, you didn't like it'.	> *ei tyy*	'no like' (Nonexistence?)
(14) (*M* trying to interest *R* in a book) *Katsos kuin hieno kirja tää on.* 'Look what (a) fine book this is'.	——	'___'
	> *ei (nämä)*	'not (these)' (?)

Seppo, MLU 1.81		
(1) (*M* describing a picture to *S*) *Näin vetää auton pois tuolta hiekasta. Ja sitten auto pääsi pois.. ja mentiin soutelemaan. Kaikki elefantit soutaa. Ja kaikki apinat puussa—* 'Like-this (they) pull (the) car away from there from (the) sand. And then (the) car got out..and		

TABLE 13 (*cont.*)

Seppo, MLU 1.81 (*cont.*)

one-went rowing. All (the)
elephants are rowing. And all
(the) monkeys in (the) trees—'

	> *enää. .vetää*	'any more. .pull'
Ei vedä enää. '(They) don't pull any more'.		(Nonexistence)

(2) (*S* looking at picture of tractor, evidently making up a story about it)
Menikö rikki? 'Did (it) break?'

	setä korjaa	'man fixes'
	setä korjaa	'man fixes'
	> *setä nyt korjaa enää rikki*	'man now fixes any more broken'

(3) (*M* asking about picture which shows Babar and a monkey playing chess)
Mitä tapahtuu siellä? 'What happens there?'

		(Nonexistence)

⋮

	pelaa	'plays'
	fantti pelaa	'elephant plays'

⋮

(several intervening utterances on a different subject matter)

	> *enää pelaa*	'any more plays' (?)

(4) (*M* and *S* looking at a picture of Pinocchio)
Mihin Pinocchio menee, minne—kouluun.
'To-where (does) Pinocchio go, to-where—to-school'.

	> *enää satu*	'any more happen' (?)
Ei satu enää. '(It) doesn't happen any more'.		

(5) (*S* drops the toy dwarf he is playing with)
Päähän pipi tuli, niin, äiti hoitaa.
'To-(the)-head (a) sore came, yes, mother (will) take-care-of'.

	pää. .pipi——	'head. .sore——'
Hoitaaks tätikin peikkoa? '(Does) aunt-also take-care-of dwarf?'	*täti*	'aunt'
Peikkoa hoitaa vähän. Pipi tuli päähän.	*täti——peikko*	'aunt——dwarf'
'Dwarf (she) takes-care-of a-little. Sore came to-(the)-head'.		

TABLE 13 (*cont.*)

Seppo, MLU 1.81 (*cont.*).		
⋮	*putoo sinne*	'falls to-there'
	> *enää pipi*	'any more sore'
		(Nonexistence)

Enää pipi, ei enää pipi. 'any more sore, not any more sore'.

(6) (*S* playing with toy fire engine)

	tuossa palo-auto	'there fire engine'
	⋮	
	> *enää palo*	'any more fire ⟨engine⟩'

(B): *Eikö enää palo?* 'Not any more
(a) fire ⟨engine⟩?'   (?)

	tuossa	'there'
	tuossa palo	'there fire ⟨engine⟩'

(7) (*S* no longer playing with a toy
mouse he had been pretending to
feed earlier; now engaging in
sound play and other monologue
not related to mouse)   > *hiiri syö enää*   'mouse eats any more' (Nonexistence?)

(8) (*S* stopping *B* from drawing on
a page)   > *enää piirtää tuossa*   'any more draw there' (Rejection)

(9) (*M* and *S* talking about a book *S*'s
father brought to *S*)   *isi tätä toi*   'daddy this brought'
Kyllä, isi toi. 'Yes, daddy brought'.
    > *ei..toi*   'no..brought' (Denial?)
Kyllä, toi. 'Yes, brought'.
    enää   'any more'
Ai, ei—ei tuonnut enää. 'Oh, (he)
didn't—didn't bring any more'.

(10) (*S* trying to get a toy mouse to eat
a cardamom seed)   *tämmö syö*   'this-kind-of-thing eats'
Ei, ei. Ei, ei. 'No, no. No, no'.
    > *ei syödä tämmö*   'no eat this-kind-of-thing' ('one doesn't eat this-kind-of-thing'.) (Denial)

be included in the grammars. All the grammars generate strings of finite length. No provisions are needed for recursion through sentence embedding (required in both adult languages to derive relative clauses and sentential predicate complements) or sentence conjoining. There were no relative clauses at all in the children's speech at this time. There were a very few utterances with predicate complements consisting of, or introduced by, catenative verbs, such as Adam's 'I like hit ball', and 'go fall', and Rina's *Rina saa ottaa (lisää) kynä*, 'Rina gets to-take (more) pencil'. Constructions with catenative verbs became productive in the grammars of both the Finnish and the American children by the time their mean utterance lengths were about 2.25. Seppo, for example, at that time began to produce utterances like *tulee hoitaa lintu*, 'comes to-take-care-of bird', and *tämä jaksaa vetää*, 'this is-able to-pull', and the American children used several catenative verbs and modals like 'wanna,' 'hafta', 'gonna', and 'can'.

The late Stage I speech of all the children can be represented by grammars consisting mainly of base component phrase structure rules and lexicon feature rules. The transformational components are of minor importance in that no rules are necessary to derive surface structures which are strikingly different from or more complex than the deep structure strings. The transformational components of the Finnish children's grammars, especially Seppo's, contain more rules for the optional reordering of constituents than would be necessary in grammars written for the American children, however. Since there has been much speculation that rigid word order may be a universal feature of early child language, the significance of this difference will be examined in some detail in the following section.

5.6 Theoretical implications of word order flexibility

One universal of language acquisition which has been proposed is that children use fixed word order in their early constructions. It has often been observed that English-speaking children used fixed order. Brown, Cazden, and Bellugi-Klima, for example, note that Adam, Eve, and Sarah 'scrupulously preserve sentence word order not only with respect to basic relations [such as subject, verb, and object], but also with respect to order of articles, adjectives, auxiliaries, adverbs, and all other words' (1968, p. 42). Braine (1971) reports a child who for a few weeks reversed word order freely with no apparent contrast in meaning (for example, 'rabbit fall down' and 'fall down rabbit'), but most English-speaking children apparently produce few incorrectly ordered constructions.

English, as a relatively uninflected language, relies heavily on word order to convey information about the syntactic function of sentence constituents. It therefore has been unclear whether the use of fixed order by English-speaking children is related to the structure of English or is characteristic of all children, regardless of the flexibility of word order in the language they are exposed to. The discovery that fixed word order was also used by one child who was learning Russian, a language which indicates the syntactic function of sentence constituents with inflections and is flexible with regard to word order (Slobin, 1966a), has lent support to the idea that rigid order is a universal tendency of children regardless of native language. Slobin makes the following assessment of the Russian child's use of fixed word order:

> There must be something in LAD, the built in 'language acquisition device' ...that favors beginning language with ordered sequences of unmarked classes, regardless of the degree of correspondence of such a system with the input language.
>
> It may well be that order is important in the base structure of Russian, thus supporting McNeill's [1966b] proposition that children 'talk base strings directly'. The most economical representation of an inflected language like Russian would order the language in the underlying representation. Inflections could then be added to the characteristic parts of speech and an additional rule or rules would then reorder this string. All of the world's languages make use of order in their grammatical structure, but not all languages have inflectional systems. It would be reasonable, then, for LAD to assume the language to be ordered, to adopt a given order as a first guess, and later learn that it can be changed...this interpretation minimizes the contribution of linguistic input, suggesting that it is more important in providing tests for hypotheses about the organization of language than it is in acting as an observation base for inferences (1966a, pp. 134–5).

Similarly, Fodor (1966b, p. 151) proposes that children acquire cases by assigning positions to words in certain syntactic roles and then adding case markers on the basis of position. Once inflections have been added to mark the syntactic roles of words, transformations could operate to rearrange word order.

McNeill, like Slobin, hypothesizes that children's apparent tendency to use rigid word order results directly from the way in which their innate language acquisition device functions. According to McNeill, one of the contents of LAD is a knowledge of the basic grammatical relations, which are believed by some to be universal (see p. 176). He proposes that the Russian boy's initial use of fixed word order in learning a language which permits relatively flexible ordering reflects the child's innate knowledge of the basic grammatical relations and his active search to express them in his speech:

This phenomenon [the child's fixed order] can be explained if one assumes that Russian children attempt to express abstract structures [basic grammatical relations, in this context] but lack transformational rules of introducing inflections. Indeed, rigid word order is precisely what would be expected on the hypothesis that children include abstract features in their early speech, but must add to this inborn structure the particular transformations employed in their native language (1966a, p. 109).

The data from Seppo's learning of Finnish are a serious challenge to these various proposals. Long before inflections entered his speech, Seppo's word order was very flexible. Not only did different sentences of the same structural description – for example, subject–verb–locative – differ with respect to the order of constituents, but also the order of words in specific sentences was often rearranged within a short period of time while the nonlinguistic context remained the same (see 3.4.2.1 for some examples).

In addition to rearranging orders in spontaneous utterances, Seppo sometimes reversed order in imitating adult utterances. For example:

Mother	*Seppo*
Apina ja elefantti pelaa. 'Monkey and elephant play (a game)'.	*pelaa. .fantti* 'plays. .'phant'
Vetää auto, niin. 'Pulls (the) car, indeed'. ('car' is subject)	*auto vetää* 'car pulls'
Kissan pallo. '(The) cat's ball'.	*pallo kissa* 'ball cat'
Oo, paljon lunta. 'Oh, much snow'.	*oo, lunta paljon* 'oh, snow much'
Tuossa maalaa. 'There (he) paints'.	*maalaa tuossa* 'paints there'
Missä pikku pupu leikkii hiekassa? 'Where (does the) little bunny play sand-in?'	*hie pupu leikkii* 'sand bunny plays'

This behavior is rare among English-speaking children. Brown, Cazden, and Bellugi-Klima note that Adam, Eve, and Sarah 'omit words but seldom confuse order' in imitation tasks (1968, p. 42). Brown and Bellugi observe that

it is conceivable that the child 'intends' the meanings coded by his word orders and that when he preserves the order of an adult sentence, he does so because he wants to say what the order says. It is also possible that he preserves order just because his brain works that way and he has no comprehension of the semantic contrasts involved (1964, p. 137).

Seppo's ability to reorder words in imitation indicates that children who do preserve word order do not do so because their brains automatically work that way. Whether they intend the meanings encoded by the orders they use is still not clear, however.

Seppo appears to have been extremely sensitive to word order as a variable of the input language. He not only learned very early the dominant orders of Finnish, as demonstrated by the relatively great frequency with which he produced these orders in his spontaneous utterances, but also the permissible alternate orders modeled by his mother. The word orders used by Seppo and his mother are compared in Table 14. The table presents the frequencies with which Seppo produced various orders of constituents in his major construction patterns from the time of the first grammar at MLU 1.42 through seven weeks after the time of the second grammar at MLU 1.81, a period of almost six months. Utterances from consecutive tapes have been grouped into six time periods of about one month each. The sample for the first Seppo grammar is from Time 1 and the sample for the second is from Time 4.[1] The first inflections, mainly locative case endings, started to emerge at Time 6. The frequencies with which Seppo's mother produced various orders are taken from the 1000-utterance sample of her speech.[2]

There is a close correspondence between the relative frequencies with which Seppo and his mother produced various word orders. Both produced more subject–verb, noun–noun$_{loc.}$, adjective–noun, subject–verb–object, subject–verb–locative, subject–verb–adverb, and adverb–subject–verb strings than strings with any other orders of these constituents. The mother's most frequent alternate orders, such as subject–locative–verb, locative–subject–verb, and locative–verb–subject, were usually also Seppo's most frequent alternate orders. Orders which were never or very rarely modeled in the mother's speech were also absent or rare in Seppo's speech. Seppo's order preferences differed significantly from his mother's in only a few construction patterns. For example, although the mother produced many more verb–object than

---

[1] All utterance types from the tapes involved are counted, so a few constructions are included in Times 1 and 4 which are not included in the samples upon which the grammars are based.

[2] The frequency counts for the mother's sample include only those utterances which contain the same constituents which appear in equivalent utterances from Seppo, and no additional constituents. The only exception is that although Seppo never used copulas, his mother's utterances with copulas are included so long as the other constituents are limited to those also produced by Seppo. The figures represent utterance tokens rather than types, but in the mother's sample these are only slightly higher than the equivalent figures for utterance types.

TABLE 14. *Frequencies of various word orders in the speech of the Finnish children and their mothers*

Order patterns[a]	Seppo: word orders at six times						Mother
	Time 1 MLU 1.42 Tapes 2–5	Time 2 MLU 1.57 Tapes 6–9	Time 3 MLU 1.48 Tapes 10–13	Time 4 MLU 1.81 Tapes 14–17	Time 5 MLU 2.27 Tapes 18–21	Time 6 MLU 2.36 Tapes 22–24	
subject–verb	32	25	24	74	56	41	47
verb–subject	4	8	15	11	5	8	5
verb–object	3	11	10	6	13	3	16
object–verb	1	1	5	7	5	7	3
noun–noun$_{loc.}$	4	1	2	5	3	10	3
noun$_{loc.}$–noun	2	—	1	—	1	1	1
noun–proloc.	2	10	1	18	4	13	14
proloc.–noun	3	6	10	11	16	17	41
verb–noun$_{loc.}$	—	3	2	1	1	—	3
noun$_{loc.}$–verb	1	—	1	1	2	2	4
verb–proloc.	—	3	1	10	5	6	3
proloc.–verb	—	1	7	6	7	10	8
adjective–noun	2	2	3	12	5	11	37
noun–adjective	—	5	5	5	4	3	8
genitive–noun	3	4	1	9	3	3	8
noun–genitive	1	1	1	1	—	—	—
attrib. noun–noun	1	1	—	4	2	1	7
noun–attrib. noun	2	—	—	—	—	—	—
dem. pron.–noun	1	—	—	1	6	19	31
noun–dem. pron.	—	—	1	—	—	2	2
verb–adverb	—	—	3	4	3	1	6
adverb–verb	—	—	3	6	14	7	13
subj.–verb–obj.	7	3	3	4	6	17	32
subj.–obj.–verb	—	—	—	5	2	—	1
obj.–verb–subj.	—	1	1	—	1	1	1
obj.–subj.–verb	1	—	—	—	—	1	—
verb–subj.–obj.	—	—	—	—	—	1	1
verb–obj.–subj.	—	—	—	—	—	—	—
subj.–verb–loc.	—	3	1	11	8	8	21
subj.–loc.–verb	—	1	—	5	2	11	2
loc.–subj.–verb	—	1	—	1	—	3	5
loc.–verb–subj.	—	—	—	2	2	1	3
verb–loc.–subj.	—	—	—	1	—	—	1
verb–subj.–loc.	—	—	—	1	—	—	1
subj.–verb–adv.	—	—	—	3	7	2	10
adv.–subj.–verb	—	—	—	4	5	8	6
adv.–verb–subj.	—	—	—	—	1	1	4
subj.–adv.–verb	—	—	—	1	—	—	—
verb–adv.–subj.	—	—	—	—	—	—	1
verb–subj.–adv.	—	—	—	—	—	—	—

[a] Constituents functioning as 'subject', 'object', 'indirect object', and, in strings with demonstrative pronouns and prolocatives, 'noun' are both nouns and modified nouns. The 'locative' constituent includes both locative nouns and prolocatives.

TABLE 14 (*cont.*)

| Order patterns | Rina: word orders at three times | | | Mother |
	Time 1 MLU 1.83 Tapes 1–4	Time 2 MLU 1.82 Tapes 5–8	Time 3 MLU 2.39 Tapes 9–12	
subject–verb	21	15	21	14
verb–subject	1	—	3	2
verb–object	5	11	15	14
object–verb	2	3	—	—
noun–noun$_{loc.}$	2	1	2	—
noun$_{loc.}$–noun	—	—	—	—
noun–proloc.	10	6	5	15
proloc.–noun	51	46	47	31
verb–noun$_{loc.}$	—	—	—	—
noun$_{loc.}$–verb	—	—	—	—
verb–proloc.	—	2	3	4
proloc.–verb	—	7	2	2
adjective–noun	3	2	5	3
noun–adjective	1	—	2	—
genitive–noun	4	6	3	1
noun–genitive	—	—	—	—
dem. pron.–noun	5	7	14	55
noun–dem. pron.	1	1	—	4
subj.–verb–obj.	19	8	17	11
subj.–obj.–verb	1	2	—	1
obj.–subj.–verb	1	1	2	—
verb–subj.–obj.	—	1	—	1
verb–obj.–subj.	—	—	1	—
obj.–verb–subj.	—	—	—	—
subj.–verb–loc.	5	1	3	3
subj.–loc.–verb	2	—	—	1
loc.–subj.–verb	1	3	1	2
loc.–verb–subj.	—	2	2	2
verb–subj.–loc.	—	1	—	—
verb–loc.–subj.	—	—	—	—
verb–obj.–indir. obj.	—	—	3	1
verb–indir. obj.–obj.	—	1	2	1
subj.–verb–obj.–indir. obj.	1	—	—	1
subj.–verb–indir. obj.–obj.	—	—	1	1

object–verb strings, Seppo produced a relative large proportion of object–verb strings. In Times 4 and 6, in fact, there are more object–verb than verb–object strings. It is difficult to think of an explanation for this, in view of the close match between mother and child in the relative frequencies of orders for other construction patterns.

Table 14 also presents the frequencies with which Rina and her mother used various word orders. Three time periods are included, the first corresponding to the time of the grammar at MLU 1.83. Rina's mother used somewhat less variable word order than did Seppo's mother, and Rina's word order was correspondingly less flexible than Seppo's. However, Rina, like Seppo, had learned both the dominant orders modeled by her mother and the most frequent alternate orders.

We noted in 4.4.1 that the frequencies with which American children produce various construction patterns closely match the frequencies with which their mothers produce them (Brown, Cazden, Bellugi-Klima, 1968). The correspondence between the relative frequencies with which the Finnish children and their mothers produced various word orders is a similar phenomenon. This makes it difficult to accept Slobin's hypothesis that children's apparent tendency to use fixed word order results from the operation of the innate language acquisition device and 'minimizes the contribution of linguistic input, suggesting that it is more important in providing tests for hypotheses about the organization of language than it is in acting as an observation base for inferences' (1966a, p. 135). It is hard to imagine how the relative frequencies of Seppo's and Rina's various word orders came to correspond so closely to those of their mothers, from a very low MLU in Seppo's case (we do not know about Rina), unless they were relying heavily upon linguistic input as an 'observation base for inference' in at least this matter of word order.

Also not supported by the Finnish data is Fodor's (1966b) suggestion that the acquisition of reordering rules depends upon the prior assignment of inflections on the basis of the position of words in various syntactic roles. Seppo varied word order for several months before he began to add inflections to mark the syntactic functions of words.

Finally, the Finnish data challenge McNeill's argument that 'rigid order is precisely what would be expected on the hypothesis that children include abstract features [basic grammatical relations] in their early speech, but must add to this inborn structure the particular transformations employed in their native language' (1966a, p. 109).

If Seppo was indeed trying to express the basic grammatical relations, he evidently did not feel that order, in the initial absence of inflections, was indispensable to this end.

Although Seppo did not hesitate to reorder strings before inflections emerged in his speech, he displayed clear enough order preferences to demonstrate that he knew the difference between nouns in different syntactic roles and was not simply combining words in random order. Seppo did not seem to be concerned with transmitting as clear a message as possible to the listener, however. In the early tapes, there were few ambiguous utterances. All sentence-subjects were animate or words for cars, and all direct objects were inanimate. The verbs used were such that the listener could easily determine whether a word functioned as subject or object, even when the sentence constituents did not follow the 'normal' subject–verb–object order. For example, *laulaa tipu*, 'sings chick', *ajaa täti*, 'drives aunt', *kirja lukee*, 'book reads', *kivi nostaa*, 'stone lifts', and *bmbm pupu ajaa*, '"car" bunny drives' are all easily interpreted. As Seppo acquired more verbs which can appropriately take inanimate subjects or animate objects, however, animacy ceased to be a reliable clue to syntactic function. He gradually began to produce utterances which were ambiguous when taken out of their nonlinguistic contexts. Examples of such utterances through Time 6 in Table 14 include:

auto vetää	'car pulls'	(subject–verb)
auto vetää	'car pulls'	(object–verb)
vetää auto	'pulls car'	(verb–subject)
vetää bmbm	'pulls "car"'	(verb–object)
tyttö vetää	'girl pulls'	(subject–verb)
kuni⟨ngatar⟩ vetää	'queen pulls'	(object–verb)
vetää lintu	'pulls bird'	(verb–subject)
hiiri vetää lintu	'mouse pulls bird'	(subject–verb–object)
kippi-auto vetää tämä	'dump truck pulls this'	(subject–verb–object)
tämä vetää kippi-auto	'this pulls dump truck'	(object–verb–subject)
tipu syö	'chick eats'	(subject–verb)
syö kissa	'eats cat'	(verb–subject)
syö poika	'eats boy'	(verb–object)
Immi hakee	'Immi looks-for'	(subject–verb)
peikko hakee	'dwarf looks-for'	(object–verb)
äiti korjaa	'mother fixes'	(subject–verb)
tämä korjaa	'this fixes'	(object–verb)
korjaa enkeli	'fixes angel'	(verb–object)
Immi piirtää	'Immi draws'	(subject–verb)
kissa piirtää	'cat draws'	(object–verb)

After reviewing word order in the data from Seppo and Rina, Brown (in press) concludes that 'it would be incorrect to describe the child as *using* order to communicate structural meanings...what we should rather say is that the child has conceptions of the orders used for various structural meanings – including the concept that, for some constructions, order may be rather freely varied. He operates in accordance with his conceptions but he does not try to improve upon them in the interest of communication'.

5.7 Comparison with a Samoan child

Kernan (1969) has presented data from a 26-month-old Samoan girl, Tofi, whose speech is comparable in many respects to that of the Finnish and American children at the stage of development we are considering. Her MLU was 1.60, while Seppo's was 1.81 and Rina's 1.83. As noted in 4.6, Kernan analyzed his subjects' constructions according to the semantic functions of sentence constituents rather than the grammatical relationships they express. The constructions in Tofi's sample have been regrouped in Table 15 according to grammatical relations to allow us to compare her speech directly with that of the Finnish and American children.

Most of Tofi's utterances are variations on a main verb sentence pattern. The only constructions in the sample which can be interpreted as copular sentences are 'Keith there' and two 'where' + N questions. In Seppo's first sample (MLU 1.42), there were also very few utterances which seemed to be modeled on adult copular sentence patterns. Most of these were tokens of N + 'there' and 'there' + N. Other copular sentence patterns, such as noun–adjective and demonstrative pronoun–noun, did not develop until later. Possibly Tofi, like Seppo, initially concentrated on the development of main verb sentences and did not produce many copular sentences until her MLU was closer to 2.00.

Tofi's main verb constructions are very similar to those of the American and Finnish children. The sample includes two- and three-term utterances which express the following relations (in appropriate ordering for Samoan):

subject–verb	subject–verb–locative
verb–object	verb–object–locative
verb–locative	verb–object–indirect object
modifier–noun	verb–modifier–object
subject–verb–object	

TABLE 15. *Constructions in Samoan sample (translated):*
Tofi, MLU 1.60

1. *Verb–Subject*
   brought Usu
   won Usu
   took Siaoloau
   rides girl
   sits baby⎫
   sits baby⎭ (two utterance types)
   walks baby
   sleeps baby
   is-headstrong baby
   goes car
   is-finished thing
   oh, fell thing
   fell thing
   oh, fell girl
   fell candy
   fell car
   baby sleeps

2. *Verb–Object*
   bring other
   get-rid-of thing
   bring baby
   hold hand
   move-away hand
   put-down hand
   give doll
   look-at the hand
   unwrap candy
   hold baby
   hold boy
   hold girl
   bring candy
   cross legs
   do baby
   baby bend
   feet hit

3. *Noun–Genitive*
   baby your
   eyes baby

4. *Noun–Locative*
   Keith there

5. *Verb–Locative*
   set down
   put down
   bring there
   go there
   take elsewhere

6. *Verb–Object–Subject*
   got-rid-of baby you
   wants clothes baby

7. *Verb–Subject–Locative*
   goes Usu there
   oh, fell baby in sea
   oh, fell baby down

8. *Verb–Object–Locative*
   bring baby there⎫ (two utterance
   bring baby there⎭   types)
   bring thing there

9. *Verb–Object–Indirect object*
   bring candy baby

10. *Verb–Object–Modifier*
    give baby toy (baby toy = doll)

11. *Negatives*
    don't be-headstrong

12. *Wh questions*
    where Punefu?
    where baby?

13. *Not classified*
    wants to-eat candy baby
    wants to-sleep baby
    wants to-sleep
    wants to-sleep very-much
    wants to-fall baby
    'sign-of-nominative' baby
    Punefu, baby (vocative)
    Kelina, rabbit (vocative)
    wait, Siaoloau (vocative)
    like-this, baby (vocative)
    cross legs like-this
    lie (down) 'emphasizer'

These are samplings of constituents from the underlying main verb sentence pattern used by most of the Finnish and American children:

subject–verb–modifier–object–indirect object–locative.

The order of constituents in Tofi's pattern, judging from the utterances in the sample, might be:

verb–object–modifier–indirect object–subject–locative.

Tofi did not produce as many different combinations of two and three elements from this pattern as the American and Finnish children did. This difference might be a function of sample size, however, since Tofi's sample was small (625 utterances) compared to those of the American and Finnish children (all 713 utterances). Alternatively, the mean length of utterance in Tofi's sample suggests that she was somewhat less mature linguistically than the other children, so perhaps she had not yet as fully explored the possibilities for combining constituents.

Tofi, like the American and Finnish children, seemed to be able to program a maximum of about three constituents at a time from the main verb sentence pattern. Her three-term constructions, like those of the other children, consist both of three major constituents and of two major constituents with one constituent a modified noun.

Tofi produced a few constructions involving the catenative verb 'want' in conjunction with other verbs. Utterances with catenative verbs were rare in the Finnish and American children's speech at this stage. Only Adam's and Rina's samples contain a few. It is interesting that Tofi's one four-term string: 'wants to-eat candy baby', involves a catenative verb rather than four of the constituents from her six-term main verb pattern. This is parallel to Rina's use of a catenative in her only five-term string, 'Rina gets to-take (more) pencil', rather than five constituents from her six-term pattern. Linguistic development past the point at which three- and four-word constructions can be produced easily may involve both acquiring the ability to program longer simple sentences and learning transformational rules for combining two simple sentences by embedding short constructions into matrix sentences which have catenative verbs.

Tofi's interrogative and negative constructions were similar to those of the American and Finnish children. Her only question form consisted of 'where' plus a noun, and her only negative construction was 'don't be-headstrong'. Kernan notes that 'don't' occurred productively in combination with other words at this time, so it evidently was Tofi's initial negative marker, comparable to Seppo's 'any more', Rina's 'no (not)', and the American children's 'no' and 'not'.

Tofi, like the American and Finnish children, usually omitted functors like tense markers (the verb 'fell' always appeared in the past, and so did not contrast with any other form), prepositions, and articles. Also like them, she seems to have been sensitive to the permissible word orders of her native language. Words in her constructions are ordered as in adult Samoan, with only a few exceptions ('baby sleeps', 'baby bend', and 'feet hit', should be 'sleeps baby', 'bend baby', and 'hit feet', respectively).

5.8   Summary of late Stage I speech

Since Finnish, English, and Samoan are unrelated languages, it is reasonable to hypothesize that features common to the speech of children learning them may characterize the language acquisition process universally. The late Stage I speech of the children investigated here was very similar. The most important aspects of their speech are summarized briefly below:

1. The constructions of almost all the children can be clearly divided into copular and main verb sentences. The copular construction patterns of most of the children include:

> demonstrative–noun ('this (that)' + N, 'here (there)' + N)
> noun–noun$_{loc.}$ ('airplane garage', 'Rina floor')
> noun–adjective ('duck big', 'aunt nice')

Rina was the only child who sometimes included the copula, although the American children occasionally used 'that's' or 'it's', apparently in free variation with 'that' and 'it'.

Main verb constructions consisted of two, three, or, in the case of the two children with the highest MLUs (Adam and Rina), four constituents selected from an underlying pattern which had the following form for most of the children:

> subject–verb–modifier–object–indirect object–locative

(The order of constituents is different for the Samoan child.) Seppo's pattern lacked the indirect object constituent but included an adverb constituent and an optional modifier for the subject. Utterances consisting of three major constituents seemed to be equal in cognitive complexity to those with two major constituents, one of which was a modified noun.

2. Modified nouns occurred both as independent utterances, as in earlier Stage I speech, and as constituents of longer utterances. The constituent

most often modified was the noun in the role of direct object. Some of the children occasionally modified locative nouns, subject nouns, and nouns following demonstrative pronouns or prolocatives. Most modifiers were adjectives or genitive nouns. Attributive noun modifiers also occurred in the speech of some of the children.

3. Nouns functioning as sentence-subjects in main verb sentences tended to be animate, and nouns functioning as direct objects inanimate. There were more exceptions than earlier in Stage I, however.

4. Other construction patterns included rudimentary negatives, usually consisting of a negative word plus a noun or verb, and simple 'where N?' or 'where N go?' questions. The American children also had fixed routines such as 'what's that?' for asking about the identity of objects, and the Finnish children developed such routines shortly after the samples considered in this chapter were collected.

5. Pronouns were rare or absent in the early Stage I speech samples investigated in Chapter 4. In the late Stage I samples, in contrast, all the children used pronouns (the status of pronouns in the Samoan girl's speech is uncertain, since only one token each of 'you' and 'your' occur in the sample). Unlike the American children, the Finnish children used no personal pronouns. All the American and Finnish children used pronouns more often as direct objects than as subjects (there are too few instances of pronouns in the late Stage I Samoan sample to allow this judgment to be made; however, the same pattern is suggested by the distribution of pronouns in the early Stage I Samoan sample – see Table 10).

6. The children's word order usually corresponded to the dominant or only adult order. The Finnish children, who were learning a language which is more flexible with respect to word order than English, Samoan, or Luo, also used acceptable alternate orders with approximately the same rank order frequencies as their mothers did.

7. As in earlier Stage I speech, obligatory functors such as inflections, prepositions and postpositions, articles, conjunctions, tense markers, verbal auxiliaries, and copulas were usually absent, although there were a few exceptions in the speech of all the children.

5.9 Conclusions: do children talk base strings directly?

Observation of children learning English has led to the hypothesis that children's early utterances can be generated almost entirely by the base component of a transformational grammar. The transformational component is thought to be largely absent early in development (McNeill, 1966*b*, p. 51; Brown, Cazden, Bellugi-Klima, 1968, p. 40). McNeill has suggested that 'it is not too unreasonable to think of

children "talking" base strings directly' (1966*b*, p. 51). This characterization has been criticized on the grounds that morphophonemic and
phonological rules do not operate on the abstract symbols present in
base structure but only on the output of the base and transformational
components, that is, upon surface structures. The claim might therefore
be reworded to state that the surface structures of most of children's
utterances can be generated directly by the rules of the base component
and do not require transformational modification. The data from the
Finnish, American, Luo, and Samoan children's early and late Stage I
speech samples support this hypothesis, with a few qualifications.

The base component of a transformational grammar is responsible
for representing several types of knowledge:

1. The hierarchical organization of sentence constituents.
2. The grammatical relationships holding between these constituents.
3. The subcategorization or co-occurrence restrictions.

The basic features of the children's constructions can be accounted
for by rules which provide this information. The children lacked transformations for embedding and conjoining sentences (which allow the
generation of strings of infinite length in adult grammars), for inter-
rogating and negating any affirmative, declarative sentence they were
able to produce, and for assigning most inflections. The reduction
transformation specified in the grammars for Bloom's English-speaking
subjects and the verb deletion transformation of the Finnish children's
grammars may actually be performance rules rather than representations
of underlying competence. If so, they are distinct from the kinds of
rules usually regarded as transformations. However, the children's
grammars do contain certain rules which would be considered transformations in grammars for the adult language: those which reorder
sentence constituents. Reordering may be psychologically the simplest
operation performed by transformations, since it appears very early in
the speech of some children, long before other transformations emerge.
According to McNeill,

If children begin their productive linguistic careers with a competence
limited to the base structures of sentences, it is difficult to see how it can be
explained by any theory of language acquisition that restricts attention to
what a child might obtain from the observable surface characteristics of
parental speech. Such theories would have to predict the opposite course of
development: first, surface structure; then, base structure (1966*b*, p. 52).

In other words, since children's early utterances are base structures, and base structures are abstract and never directly observable in speech, a child cannot acquire language only by observing and making inferences from the speech he is exposed to. McNeill (1970, p. 1088) argues that children's early utterances in fact reflect their innate linguistic knowledge:

A language is thus acquired through discovering the relations that exist between the surface structure of its sentences and the universal aspects of the deep structure, the latter being a manifestation of children's own capacities. The interaction between children's innate capacities and their linguistic experience occurs at this point, in the acquisition of transformations – and it is here that parental speech must make its contribution.

The conclusion that children must have a body of innate linguistic knowledge does not follow from the observation that their utterances look rather like base structure strings of adult grammars. While it is evidently true that most of children's early constructions can be generated without transformations (other than occasional reordering), they are not in themselves base structures, those abstract and unobservable entities to which McNeill refers. The great majority of them are very similar to the simple, active, declarative sentences which abound in parent-to-child speech, such as 'the bunny is hopping', 'this is a book', and 'the ball is on the table'. These parental constructions are not base structures any more than are sentences with more complex transformational histories, such as 'this isn't a book' and 'does the bunny hop?', but they provide models from which children can derive the rules they need to produce utterances like 'bunny hop', 'ball table', and 'this book'. Of course, children do not reproduce all aspects of the surface structures they hear. For example, they selectively omit obligatory functors. The problem posed by this selectivity is not how children can possibly learn something that is abstract and never directly observable without a considerable amount of help from innate knowledge, but rather, why they are attracted to some elements and relationships expressed in the surface structures of the speech they hear and not to others. For example, why should 'bunny hop' be selected rather than 'the hopping' or 'does the', and 'ball table' rather than 'is on the?'. Answering these questions will involve finding out more about the general cognitive capacity of children and the kinds of semantic concepts they are capable of comprehending at different stages of development.

Children produce few constructions which differ dramatically from the surface structure patterns modeled for them in adult speech. Constructions which seem to correspond to abstract base structure representations of sentences in the adult grammar rather than to surface structures have probably been overemphasized in arguments that children cannot acquire language by observing and making inferences directly from the speech they hear. Bellugi (1967) observed that early negation among English-speaking children involves the placement of a negative marker 'no' or 'not' either before or after an affirmative sentence. McNeill (1970, p. 1109) suggests that sentence-external negation could be considered the deep structure representation of negative sentences in all languages, and that children start with the direct expression of this and must learn the transformations which account for the syntax of negation in their local language. However, Bellugi's conclusion that early negative constructions involve the placement of a negative marker external to an otherwise undisturbed affirmative sentence is based on a very few utterances from Brown's subject Adam, such as 'no the sun shining' and 'no I see the truck'. Most of Adam's negative constructions and all of Eve's and Sarah's consisted of a negative placed either before or after a simple noun, verb, or verb phrase, rather than external to a well-developed affirmative declarative sentence with a subject. Bloom (1970) studied negation in her children's linguistic development and found that inclusion of a negative marker initially entailed omission of the sentence-subject; later, when subjects were included, negative words were placed after the subjects and before the verbs. The acquisition of syntactic-negation by the Finnish children followed the same general history. Thus, there is very little evidence that children's early negative constructions correspond to the adult grammar's base structure representation of the negative marker external to the entire sentence. Once sentences become long enough that there are constituents with respect to which the negative *can* be internal, it is usually found after the subject and before the verb, corresponding to its ultimate position in surface structure in adult English and Finnish.

Contrary to McNeill's hypothesis, when there is a great discrepancy between deep structure and surface structure children's utterances usually follow the surface structure pattern modeled most frequently in adult speech. For example, although in a transformational grammar the surface structure noun phrases 'John's book' and 'the big ball' would be derived transformationally from underlying strings of the form 'John has a book' and 'the ball is big', children produce utterances of the former type long before those of the latter. In another example, when Brown's subject Adam began to produce separable verbs with direct objects, he ordered the constituents verb–noun–particle rather than verb–particle–noun, although the latter order is what is found in base structure according to Chomsky (Brown, in press).

To summarize, the fact that most of children's utterances can be generated by the base structure rules of a transformational grammar without the intervention of transformational rules does not constitute evidence that children have innate linguistic knowledge corresponding to the abstract and unobservable base structure representations of sentences. It appears instead that almost all the the rules needed for generating children's constructions could be derived directly from the surface strings modeled by parents. Whenever a large discrepancy exists between the underlying and surface structure representations of utterances, children usually follow the model provided by the surface structure.

In the last two chapters, we have found that the theory of transformational generative grammar in many respects provides a useful approach to child language. Unlike the pivot grammar, which takes into account only the superficial form and arrangement of words, it enables us to formalize some of the significant syntactic and semantic characteristics of children's utterances and to make fruitful comparisons among children learning different languages. However, the use of transformational generative grammars to represent children's competence involves postulating certain kinds of linguistic knowledge for which there is little evidence in child speech. This and other possible drawbacks to the transformational approach are considered in the following chapter.

6 Problems with the transformational grammar approach

Grammar writing involves giving rigorous and concise formal representation to the kinds of facts about linguistic structure which speakers of a language must in some sense know in order to understand and produce novel sentences. Characteristics of a speaker's competence cannot be examined directly but must be inferred from the way they are expressed in linguistic behavior. When a grammar is written, rules are formulated in a certain way because they seem able to account for observed linguistic behavior more accurately and comprehensively than rules of another type. The selection of a particular theoretical framework for grammar writing, then, entails at least partial commitment to certain assumptions or inferences about the characteristics of the speaker's knowledge. Representing competence with a transformational grammar of the sort described by Chomsky involves the postulation of a base component which gives formal representation, by means of the subconfigurations of the constituents of phrase-markers, to certain grammatical relations like 'subject of', 'predicate of', and 'direct object of' (see 4.1 for definitions of these relations). Are we justified in crediting children with an understanding of these relations and of the constituent structure which they entail?

According to transformational generative theory, the grammatical relations which hold between constituents in deep structure are found in all the world's languages. Katz and Postal make the proposal that in general theory there be a universal characterization of these 'basic grammatical relations' (1964, p. 159). Similarly, Chomsky writes that 'these definitions must be thought of as belonging to general linguistic theory; in other words, they form part of the general procedure for assigning a full structural description to a sentence given a grammar' (1965, pp. 71–2).

McNeill proposes that universals of language structure result from the characteristics of children's capacity for acquiring language, and that evidence of them will therefore be found in children's earliest utterances. He notes that this hypothesis 'requires that the basic grammatical relations will be honoured in the very early speech collected from children' (1966*a*, p. 102). McNeill presents some evidence for the view that children's 'language acquisition device' contains innate knowledge of the basic grammatical relations. After studying 400 utterances collected from Brown's subject Adam, he concludes that every sentence the child produced was a combination of word classes compatible with one or another of the basic grammatical relations (he includes the concept 'modifier of a noun phrase' among these). For example, the sample contained utterances like 'Adam run' and 'change Adam diaper', which express such notions as subject–predicate and verb–modifier–object, but it did not include constructions like 'come eat pablum', which does not express a basic grammatical relation but must be derived transformationally from simpler sentences (McNeill, 1966*a*, p. 103). Brown (in press) has reviewed McNeill's interpretation of the data and concludes that although there are certain flaws in the analysis, most of the early sentences did manifest one or more grammatical relations. He adds that they could also be interpreted as expressing one or more semantic relations.

If children's early competence indeed includes an understanding of the basic grammatical relations, representing their utterances with phrase-markers which by their configurations implicitly indicate these relations is desirable. However, it is not clear whether children's utterances conform to certain patterns because they express the basic grammatical relations or whether the apparent presence of the relations can be interpreted more accurately in some other way.

An important first step in determining whether children have a knowledge of the basic grammatical relations early in their development is to examine the characteristics of their utterances closely, without preconceptions. In particular we need to guard against assuming that children's utterances have a certain structural organization simply because an adequate description of the adult language must specify such a form for equivalent adult utterances. We may find that those structural phenomena of adult speech which motivate the postulation of various syntactic concepts are absent in child speech.

In a transformational grammar, the most fundamental division in the deep structure representation of sentences is between constituents with the grammatical functions 'subject of' and 'predicate of'. Let us consider first whether there is justification for analyzing the constituent structure of children's utterances in this way, and second, whether there is any evidence that children understand the grammatical relation 'subject of'.

6.1   Constituent structure

Transformational grammar provides an account of constituent structure in which strings like 'the man drives a car' and 'Mommy goes to the store' are hierarchically organized along the traditional lines. The initial noun or noun phrase makes up one constituent, while the verb plus an optional direct object and/or other optional elements such as a locative phrase constitute another. This hierarchical organization of sentence elements is indicated by a phrase-marker such as this:

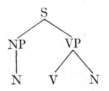

In this NVN string, the initial noun functions syntactically as subject of the sentence (defined as the noun phrase immediately dominated by S), while the verb and the final noun together compose the verb phrase, which functions as predicate of the sentence (defined as the verb phrase immediately dominated by S). The V and N of the verb phrase are immediate constituents, with the N functioning as direct object of the verb. According to McNeill (1971), this hierarchical organization of sentence constituents results automatically from the child's application to sentences of his innate knowledge of the basic grammatical relations.

What is the justification for this analysis of the constituent structure of children's early three-term constructions? Chomsky notes that there are various ways to justify assigning constituent structure. One must show, for example, that the postulated intermediate phrases 'must receive a semantic interpretation', or 'are required for some grammatical rule', or 'define a phonetic contour', or that 'there are perceptual grounds for the analysis' (1965, p. 197, fn. 7).

The few attempts to use strictly linguistic criteria to determine the constituent structure of children's early utterances have had inconclusive results. For example, Brown (unpublished materials) asked whether

Adam, Eve, and Sarah regularly used VP as an answer to 'what are you doing?' or 'what is it doing?' questions, as adult speakers do. He found that the children often did not respond to these questions at all and almost never answered them appropriately. The same is true of Kendall and of my two Finnish subjects. Brown also tried to determine whether in Adam's speech the privileges of occurrence of V + N were the same as those of V alone, which might have suggested that V + N should be considered as a single constituent. He found that the privileges of occurrence were the same, since both V and V + N could occur after initial nouns or pronouns. This finding does not constitute sound evidence for a VP constituent, however, since N + V, or the subject plus the verb, also had the same privileges of occurrence as V alone: both could precede nouns or prolocatives. On the basis of this test, then, either V + N *or* N + V could be considered a constituent substitutable for V alone. This was true not only in Adam's speech but also in that of Kendall, Seppo and Rina.

Other linguistic grounds which might be used to justify postulating a VP constituent in children's early utterances are also lacking. For example, children do not initially use phrases like 'do (so)' which make reference to a preceding VP. In samples of speech from the earliest stages of word combining, one does not find sentences like 'Daddy like cake. Mommy does too', or 'Johnny went home (and) so did Jimmy'.

In sum, no one has yet to my knowledge succeeded in demonstrating on purely linguistic grounds that the verb 'belongs with' the direct object or the locative in child speech rather than, for example, with the subject – in other words, that verb plus direct object or locative is a constituent in a way in which subject plus verb is not. Arguments for a verb phrase constituent in children's utterances have been based on another sort of evidence – weaker linguistically but of just as great interest for us – evidence which bears on the question of whether the verb plus the direct object or the locative element has a psychological unity for the child which the subject plus the verb lacks.

One such argument draws on the observation that verb–object strings are more common in early speech than subject–verb strings. This was true of Brown's subjects Adam, Eve and Sarah at MLUs of about 1.75 and of Bloom's three subjects at MLUs of below 1.50. McNeill notes that the predominance of predicates without subjects over predicates with subjects in Adam's speech 'would result if the sentences with subjects were all recent acquisitions and the sentences without subjects had existed in Adam's repertoire for some time' (1970, p. 1090). On the basis of this and other arguments, McNeill hypothesizes that the early speech of children consists largely of predicates in isolation, to which subjects later begin to be added. He also suggests that subject noun phrases may initially be practiced in isolation, with the child only later realizing that subjects and predicates can be brought together into one sentence (1966*b*, pp. 44–5). He writes that the difficulty in hypothesizing about the origin of subject noun phrases or predicate verb phrases in children's speech 'lies in describing a reasonable mechanism by which children might arrive at hierarchical structures. Imitation is obviously inappropriate because it cannot account for the emergence of a constituent with psychological unity...' (1966*b*, p. 45). McNeill appeals to the child's innate knowledge of basic grammatical relations to account for this apparent 'psychological unity'.

The argument presented above that children's verb–object constructions are predicates with psychological unity depends upon the observation that verb–object strings are more common in early speech than subject–verb strings. According to this line of reasoning, if some children from an early stage of development produced more subject–verb strings than verb–object strings, we might argue that for them, subject–verb had a psychological unity which verb–object lacked. Similarly, if even full subject–verb–object strings were more frequent than verb–object strings, perhaps subject–verb should be considered an initial unit to which 'object' is added only later, just as McNeill suggests that verb–object is a unit to which 'subject' is added later. These were, in fact, the characteristics of the speech of two Finnish children and of at least one American child, Kendall. All of these children produced far more subject–verb than verb–object strings, and they produced either about equal numbers of verb–object and subject–

TABLE 16. *Frequency of Production as a Clue to Constituent Structure*[a]

	Kendall (English) MLU 1.10	Kendall (English) MLU 1.48	Seppo (Finnish) MLU 1.42	Seppo (Finnish) MLU 1.81	Rina (Finnish) MLU 1.83
subject–verb	19	31	25	64	21
verb–object	5	10	3	9	4
subject–verb–object	—	7	7	8	19

[a] Figures refer to utterance types.

verb–object strings or more of the latter. Table 16 presents the relevant figures for samples of their speech.

If we follow to its logical end the argument that constituent structure is revealed in the relative frequency with which these various strings are produced, we should have to conclude that for these children the hierarchical organization of sentence elements was not

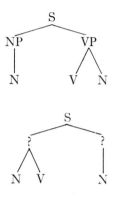

but rather,

Such an organization would be a false step towards the adult understanding of constituent structure which we assume they will ultimately attain.

Another sort of argument that predicates have psychological unity is presented by Braine (1971). Like McNeill, Braine has suggested that the first English sentences consist of a predicate with an optional subject, and that 'most of the large, apparently heterogeneous collection of one-word utterances consisting of an English adjective, adverb, verb, or noun come out as sentences consisting of a predicate phrase occurring alone'. He finds evidence for this in children's 'replacement sequences', a term he uses to describe sequences of utterances in which a short utterance is followed or preceded by a longer string which incorporates it and suggests what grammatical relations were intended by it. Braine found that these sequences tend to consist of an utterance without a subject followed by the same utterance with a subject. For example:

> chair..pussycat chair
> want that..Andrew want that
> off..radio off
> fall..stick fall
> go nursery..Lucy go nursery
> build house..Cathy build house (Braine, 1971).

Replacement sequences also occurred, although relatively infrequently, in the speech of the Finnish children and of Kendall. Some of these did involve producing a predicate and then adding a subject. But many involved instead the operation of producing a subject first and then adding the predicate, or, even more interestingly, of producing the subject and the verb and then adding a direct object or a locative. The following are some examples:

Seppo: *Humma. Humma. Humma aa-aa.*
          'Horsie. Horsie. Horsie "sleeps"'.
          Tipu. Tipu laulaa.
          'Chick. Chick sings'.
          Aiti. Aiti avaa.
          'Mother. Mother opens'.
          Isi pestään. Isi pest—
          Isi. .Isi joo pestään juna.
          'Daddy wash. Daddy wash—Daddy. .
          Daddy already wash train'.
          Tää kuuluu. Tää kuuluu tuohon.
          'This belongs. This belongs to-there'.
          Immi piirtää. Immi piirtää tuohon.
          'Immi draws. Immi draws to-there'.
          Setä kappe (= kapteeni). Tulee. Hoitaa.
          Setä kappe tulee. Hoitaa. Lintuu.
          Setä kappe hoitaa lintuu.
          'Man captain. Comes. (To)-take-care-of.
          Man captain comes. (To)-take-care-of. Bird.
          Man captain takes-care-of bird'.

Rina: *Aiti, isi. Aiti, isi tulee.*
          'Mother, daddy. Mother, daddy comes'.

Kendall: 'Lissa. 'Lissa. 'Lissa write.
          Kendall. Kendall gone.
          Kristin. Kristin sit chair.
          Kendall innere. Kendall innere bed.
          Kendall pick up. (O + V) Daddy pick up. (S + V)
          Kendall. (O) Mommy pick up Kendall. (S + V + O)

To summarize, arguments about constituent structure which are based upon the relative frequency of production of different types of strings or upon the characteristics of replacement sequences are not conclusive. Using these criteria on data from certain children leads to an analysis of constituent structure which specifies subject plus verb as one constituent and direct object or locative as another. It appears that frequency of production and the characteristics of replacement sequences may not be reliable clues to hierarchical organization. In short, we still do not know whether children produce their early subject–verb–object and subject–verb–locative constructions with the particular understanding of constituent structure which has been ascribed to them, or even with any concept of hierarchical organization at all. Thus, the constituent VP, dominating N + V, is gratuitous in the phrase structure rules of the transformational grammars written to represent the linguistic competence of the two Finnish children, and would also be so in a grammar for Kendall. There is in fact less reason to postulate the existence of such a constituent for the children than of one dominating N + V. In this respect, then, the analysis of the children's knowledge provided by a transformational grammar is difficult to justify.

6.2 The grammatical relation 'subject of'

The children whose speech we have been considering all produced utterances with constituents which would be identified as 'subjects' in adult speech. However, there may be other ways to interpret these constituents as well. What evidence is there that the concept of 'subject' is part of children's early competence?

In transformational theory, the deep structure subject of a sentence is defined as the noun phrase immediately dominated by S. We have just seen that the analysis of constituent structure upon which this definition depends may not be applicable to children's utterances. If this is the case, then justification for crediting children with the concept 'subject of' must come from elsewhere.

Fillmore (1968) has shown clearly that syntactic functions like subject and direct object are not consistently associated with particular semantic roles. A verb may take several noun arguments, each performing a different semantic function in the sentence such as 'agent', 'object acted upon', 'location', 'instrument', and so on. It is not the case that sentence–subjects, for example, always play a particular semantic role such as 'agent'. Consider the subjects in the following English sentences:

(1) *John* broke the stick.
(2) *The stick* broke.
(3) *The key* opened the door.
(4) *John* sees Mary.
(5) *Chicago* is windy.

In (1), 'John' initiates the action of breaking and so has an agentive relationship to the verb. In (2), 'the stick' does not initiate the action but rather is the object acted upon. In (3), 'the key' is the instrument used (presumably by someone) to effect the action. In (4), 'John' does not initiate 'seeing' Mary; rather, he is passively affected by a stimulus coming from her. In (5), 'Chicago' names a location where there is much wind. Like subjects, direct objects do not have a constant semantic function. The subject and direct object for any particular verb, however, identify noun phrases in particular semantic roles. For example, the subjects of 'drive', 'eat', 'hit', and 'jump' identify the agent. The subjects of 'see', 'hear', 'want', and 'receive', in contrast, identify a 'person affected' by a state or stimulus. The subjects of verbs like 'fall' and 'revolve' identify neither an agent nor a person affected, and are rather difficult to characterize semantically.

Why do we need the concept 'deep structure subject' for an adequate analysis of adult speech? Why, for example, do we not simply identify each noun phrase in a sentence by reference to its semantic function? This is a difficult question. In my understanding, the answer might go something like this: In linguistic theory, the relationships which hold between underlying meanings and actual sentences are indicated by transformations. The operations involved in transformations cannot be specified simply by reference to the semantic functions of words in sentences. For example, a rule for deriving passive sentences which specified that the word functioning as agent of the verb should become the object of the preposition 'by' would be inadequate. Passives can also be created out of sentences in which there is no agent, like 'your mother wants you' or 'John sees Mary'. The constituent which becomes the object of 'by' in passive sentences can only be defined in an abstract way, as a noun phrase with a certain syntactic function which we call 'subject'. The semantic function of this noun phrase is different for different subclasses of verbs.

Put differently, the need for the concept 'deep structure subject' arises because there are transformations – including the one which derives passive sentences – which for the purposes of a particular operation treat a certain noun argument for each verb in the same way across a number of different verbs, even though these noun arguments do not necessarily have identical semantic functions in their respective sentences. Such transformations can cause a deep structure subject to yield its characteristic location in a phrase-marker (as the noun phrase immediately dominated by S) to another deep structure constituent. This constituent then becomes the surface structure subject in the phrase-marker which is derived from the operation of the transformation. For example, in the passive sentence 'Mary is seen by John', the deep structure direct object 'Mary' appears as surface structure subject, while the deep structure subject 'John' appears in final position as the object of the preposition 'by'.

Fillmore (1968, p. 58) notes that some languages have been described as not having passives, and others as able to express transitive sentences only passively. He argues that since these languages offer no choice of surface structure subject, the concept of subject is not applicable to them. To pursue this argument further, if a particular language lacked syntactic operations which treated a particular noun argument for each verb in the same way across a number of different verbs, and which could cause deep and surface structure subjects to differ, why would there be any need for the syntactic abstraction of 'deep structure subject'?

The language of children appears initially to lack such operations. As we noted earlier (5.9), children's early utterances can be generated almost entirely by the base component of a transformational grammar, with the occasional aid of simple reordering operations and perhaps a verb deletion transformation. Virtually all constructions follow the simple active declarative pattern, although certain elements obligatory in adult speech are absent. Thus, no transformations need to be specified which require reference to a sentence constituent with the abstract syntactic function which characterizes subjects in adult speech. Deep structure and surface structure subjects are therefore always identical.

On what grounds can the abstraction of 'subject' be made in the case of a language which lacks transformations requiring it? In simple active declarative sentences of adult English and Finnish, the particular noun argument of a verb which functions as deep and surface structure subject governs person and number concord in the verb, is in the nominative case (pronouns only in English; nouns and pronouns both in Finnish), and has a characteristic position. In early child speech, subjects cannot be identified on the basis of either verbal concord or case. In the Finnish children's early speech, for example, almost all nouns were nominative, not just those which would be subjects in equivalent adult utterances. Verbal agreement was automatic, since all verbs were in the third person singular form, no personal pronouns were used, and nouns were never marked for plural. On grounds of case and verbal agreement, then, *any* noun in one of Seppo's or Rina's utterances could be considered a subject. Similar arguments apply to English-speaking children. When the Finnish children began to use case-marked pronouns, they did not consistently distinguish them with regard to syntactic function, since sometimes they used nominative pronouns as direct objects.

This leaves only position as a basis for the abstraction of 'subject'. The particular noun argument of the verb which functions as deep and surface structure subject in simple active declarative sentences typically occurs in preverbal position in both English and Finnish (other orders are possible as well in Finnish). This ordering is generally observed in children's early constructions. Thus, in studies of child speech, the noun which occurs in preverbal position is identified as the subject – provided that it would be considered the subject in an adult utterance too. But when the child produces constructions like 'ball hit' and 'apple eat' we simply conclude that he has reversed the normal verb–object order. We do not consider the possibility that he might have mistakenly identified the wrong noun argument of a particular verb as subject, perhaps by analogy with sentences like 'the toy broke', 'the door opened', or 'the page ripped'. All of these sentences involve verbs which share a special property: if they occur in sentences in which no agent is expressed, the noun referring to the object acted upon or otherwise affected by the action specified by the verb can occur as deep structure subject. If an agent is expressed, however, this noun must give up the function of subject to the agent and become a deep structure direct object. The verbs 'hit', 'eat', and many others do not have this flexibility. It is conceivable that a child might at first not recognize this distinction between verb classes, and so would assume that all 'objects acted upon' can be subjects in agent-less sentences. For such a child, 'ball' in 'ball hit' and 'toy' in 'toy broke' would perform the same syntactic function, and it would be incorrect to interpret the former as a misordered direct object and the latter as a subject. However, this is what we ordinarily do. In summary, then, we do not even make consistent use of position to help us identify subjects in children's utterances, even though it is the only cue we have available. Instead, we simply rely on our knowledge of what the subject would be in equivalent adult utterances.

Occupation of identical position is in any event not a sufficient reason to assume identical syntactic function. For example, in the sentences 'John eats cake' and 'John goes home', the nouns 'cake' and 'home' occur in the same position but they do not perform the same syntactic function. Similarly, then, why should the first words in typical child utterances such as 'John eat cake' and 'John want cake' be considered to perform the same syntactic function when their semantic functions are different?

To summarize, the structural phenomena which require the concept of subject in adult speech are evidently missing in early child speech. To credit children with an understanding of the concept is an act of faith based only on our knowledge of the adult language. On the other hand, however, there is no proof that children do *not* have the concept. It is possible, for example, that children use this knowledge in their comprehension of adult sentences before their own productions begin to reflect it, although this has not been demonstrated.

6.3 A semantic interpretation of the structural meanings of children's early utterances

If children do not make use of the concept of subject in constructing their early sentences, how should we interpret the apparent subjects in their speech? An alternative hypothesis about the form of children's early knowledge of language structure has been proposed by Schlesinger (1971). Schlesinger suggests that the components of the structural relationships expressed by children's utterances are semantic concepts like 'agent', 'action', 'object', and 'location' rather than syntactic notions like 'subject' and 'predicate'. He notes that these concepts do not reflect specifically linguistic knowledge, but, rather, are determined by the more general innate cognitive capacity of the children.

Superficially, the characteristics of children's utterances are compatible with either a semantic or a syntactic description. How to decide which provides the closer approximation to the form of children's linguistic knowledge? There is no easy answer to this question. Several possible ways in which the problem can be approached are outlined below.

6.3.1 The semantic functions of subjects in children's utterances.
As noted in 6.2, the deep structure subjects of English sentences can

perform a number of different semantic roles. The same is true of subjects in Finnish sentences. It is reasonable to hypothesize that if children form their earliest utterances in accordance with a knowledge of the grammatical relation 'subject of', those sentence constituents which look like subjects in their utterances should perform the same range of semantic functions as do subjects in adult speech. Is this in fact the case, or are the semantic functions of children's subjects limited?

In Seppo's early Stage I sample (MLU 1.42), all sentences with main verbs (that is, sentences in which the predicate was composed of V (N) rather than Loc), had *agents* in the role of subject. This semantic phenomenon accounts for the fact that Seppo's subjects were almost always animate, the only exceptions being words for cars which performed actions like 'go' and '(go) fast'. Animate beings and vehicles were seen as capable of initiating the actions described by verbs. Every one of Seppo's verbs (discounting *uffuf*, "dirty, naughty", which does not have verb status in adult Finnish), was of the subclass for which the grammatical function 'subject' is identified with the semantic role of agent. This choice of verbs was not imposed upon Seppo by the structure of Finnish, since utterances like 'mother sees', 'the cat wants (or: gets) milk', and 'the boat sinks', in which the subject is a being or an object affected, are also acceptable simple sentences. For Seppo at MLU 1.42, then, the grammatical function of subject apparently was identical with the semantic function of 'agent' in sentences with main verbs. Of course, it is possible that in a larger sample there would have been some occurrences of verbs with nonagentive subjects.

By late Stage I, in contrast, Seppo had acquired several verbs which take nonagentive subjects, and combined them with subjects in utterances like 'tower falls-over', 'mouse is-afraid', 'cat falls', and 'spool goes there'. Rina at a similar stage of development (MLU 1.83) used mainly verbs which take agentive subjects, but also had a few other verbs like 'live', 'fall', and 'get' (in the sense of 'receive'), and used these productively with subjects. For the Finnish children, then, the grammatical function of subject appears to have been strongly associated with the semantic function of *agent*; only towards late Stage I did verbs which take nouns in other semantic roles as subjects begin to emerge.

Subjects in the early Stage I samples of the English, Samoan, and Luo children considered in chapter 4 were also overwhelmingly agents, although there were more exceptions than in Seppo's sample. Moreover, the association found in the Finnish data between higher MLU values and increased diversity of the semantic functions of subjects is also apparent in the English and Samoan data.

The first sample collected from the American child Kendall (MLU 1.10) included no nonagentive subjects with main verbs with the possible exception of 'Kendall' in 'Kendall hurt', which could have meant either 'Kendall hurts' or 'something is hurting Kendall'. In the later sample from Kendall (MLU 1.48), only 'break', 'fall', and 'see' occurred with nonagentive subjects, in one utterance token each. Judgments about the semantic functions of subjects are difficult to make for Bloom's English-speaking children, since Bloom does not list all the utterances in their samples and one cannot tell from the listing of verbs in the children's lexicons whether a particular verb ever occurred in construction with a subject. Gia at MLU 1.12 used only verbs which take agentive subjects. At MLU 1.34, she used 'see', 'stuck', and 'got' as well, but we are not told whether any but the last appeared in construction with subjects. Kathryn at MLU 1.32 used a few verbs which do not take agentive subjects: 'see', 'want', 'stuck', 'hurt', 'fit', and 'have'. Eric at MLU 1.19 used 'want' and 'see', although without subjects, while at MLU 1.42 he used 'fit', 'need', 'want', and possibly 'see' with nonagentive subjects. Non-agentive subjects were fairly frequent in the late Stage I samples (MLUs around 1.75) from Adam, Eve, and Sarah, in utterances like 'Adam sees that', and 'I like jelly'.

The early Stage I Samoan sample from Sipili (MLU 1.52) contains only three subjects with main verbs, but these are all agents. The late Stage I Samoan sample from Tofi (MLU 1.60), however, contains several nonagentive subjects, with the verbs 'want', 'fell', and 'is-finished'. The Luo sample, representing a stage of development perhaps slightly more advanced than that of the other samples classified as early Stage I, includes several nonagentive subjects with verbs such as '(be) sick', 'know', 'see', and 'want'.

To summarize these observations, sentence-subjects apparently tend initially to be restricted largely to the semantic function of 'agent', with a handful of exceptions for some children. As the child matures linguistically, the semantic functions of his subjects become increasingly diverse. This developmental trend provides some support for a semantic interpretation of children's early utterances. It suggests that children initially are not searching for the means provided by their language for expressing the relations between grammatical concepts like subject and predicate, as in McNeill's view, but rather for the way to express the relations between a limited number of semantic concepts. The linguistic knowledge which underlies the earliest two- and three-word constructions may thus be no more complex than simple rules to order words which are understood as performing semantic functions like 'agent', 'action', and 'object acted upon'. Children may find certain semantic concepts easier to understand or more attractive than others for nonlinguistic, cognitive reasons. For example, they may be able to grasp the concept of 'agent' before the concept of 'person affected' by a state or stimulus becomes available to them. The selection of verbs to be learned at an early stage of development and the kinds of grammatical subjects which appear with them may be largely determined by these considerations of what the child can understand or is interested in expressing.

Of course, the semantic categories mentioned here are not necessarily the particular ones children use. They are abstractions, although not at such a high level as syntactic concepts like 'subject', and perhaps children do not even make these abstractions. They could conceivably make an individual rule for each verb specifying that 'the one who drinks', 'the one who drives', 'the one who sings', etc., appears before the verb, whereas 'that which is drunk' and 'that which is driven' appears after the verb. They might also make the abstraction at some intermediate level between the initiators of individual verbs and the concept of agent, and formulate rules which apply to classes of verbs which are semantically similar in some respect.

6.3.2 Other clues to the structural meanings of children's utterances. What other kinds of evidence might we look for to help us decide whether children's early knowledge of language structure is primarily semantic or syntactic? Of particular interest would be information about the levels of abstraction at which children make generalizations to form novel constructions. Finding systematic evidence of this sort will probably require experimental study. However, non-systematic evidence which suggests one interpretation or the other for individual children may be obtainable from samples of spontaneous speech. For example, if a child initially began to observe inflections or verbal concord only for agentive subjects, this would suggest that 'agent' rather than 'subject' was a functional concept for him. One bit of evidence of this sort comes from the Russian child Zhenya (Gvozdev, 1961, p. 173). Initially, Zhenya did not formally mark direct objects, but rather used the nominative form of the noun for all syntactic functions. When he began to acquire the accusative case, he used it only to mark those direct objects which designated the objects of action; particularly those occurring with verbs referring to the transfer or relocation of objects, such as 'give', 'carry', 'put', and 'throw'. At this time Zhenya rarely marked the direct objects of verbs like 'read', 'draw', and 'make', in which the relations between action and object are more complex. This pattern of marking indicates that at first Zhenya did not regard all direct objects as functionally equivalent, but only that subset of them which referred to objects acted upon in certain rather direct ways.[1]

Another kind of information about children's functional concepts and categories might come from a study of whether there are certain patterns in what children 'select' to acquire from the linguistic structures to which they are exposed. For example, we might find that initially some children simply do not learn verbs which take nonagentive subjects even when these are modeled in parental speech with greater frequency than the verbs which they do learn. This would suggest that for them, 'agent' rather than 'subject' is a functional concept.

To examine this possibility for Seppo, the frequency with which Seppo's mother produced verbs of various types was analyzed. The most striking finding was that she modeled verbs which take agents as subjects over $4\frac{1}{2}$ times as frequently as all verbs which take other semantic concepts as subjects combined (imperative sentences were excluded from this count, since the verbs of these automatically take (deleted) agents as subjects; if imperatives are included, the figure goes up to $5\frac{1}{2}$). In nonimperative sentences in the mother's sample, there were 259 occurrences of verbs which take agents as subjects, 38 of those which take 'objects or persons involved' (Fillmore's Objective case; see p. 198), and 18 of those which take 'persons affected' (Fillmore's Dative case). Of the latter two types of verbs, the mother modeled only *putoo*, 'falls', much more frequently than she modeled many of the verbs Seppo used at MLU 1.42. *Näkee*, 'sees', *saa*, 'gets, receives', *osaa*, 'knows how to', *hukkuu*, 'is lost', *paistaa*, 'shines', *kaatuu*, 'falls down', *pysyy*, 'stays', and *palaa*, 'burns' (intransitive) were modeled

---

[1] I am grateful to Dan I. Slobin for drawing my attention to this example.

two to four times each, which was as often as many of the verbs which Seppo did use were modeled.

There is thus a very small amount of evidence that Seppo overlooked verbs which take nonagentive subjects in favor of no more frequently modeled ones which take agentive ones. Our main conclusion, however, must simply be that Seppo's early restriction of sentence-subjects to agents is not too surprising, considering how much more often verbs which require such subjects were modeled. As is always the case when children's frequency profiles are similar to those of their parents, possible explanatory variables are confounded. It is impossible to determine whether Seppo initially lacked the concept of nonagentive subject for cognitive reasons which were independent of the speech he heard, and chose his verbs accordingly, or whether the characteristics of his mother's speech simply called his attention to the concept of agent and did not push him strongly towards the early acquisition of verbs which take other semantic concepts in the role of subject.

6.4   Accounting for the acquisition of syntactic concepts

When the structural relations expressed in children's early constructions are given a semantic interpretation, the problem arises of how Chomsky's level of syntactic deep structure is acquired, if, in fact, it is acquired at all. Several investigators have argued that learning theories cannot account for the acquisition of information represented only in deep structure, since this is abstract and never directly exhibited in the speech to which the child is exposed (e.g. Bever, Fodor, Weksel, 1965; McNeill, 1971). In particular, McNeill has argued that because the basic grammatical relations 'can be consistently defined only in the deep structure of sentences, they are beyond the reach of any linguistic experiences a child may have' (1971, p. 23).

Some researchers who advocate a semantic interpretation of children's early utterances, such as Schlesinger (1971) and Kernan (1970), resolve the problem of how children can learn something which is never directly represented in speech by arguing that they do not have to – that an abstract syntactic level of deep structure does not exist. Acquiring a language simply involves learning how to translate semantic intentions directly into surface structures.

Doing away entirely with syntactic deep structures need not be the inevitable outcome of a theory of language acquisition which holds that knowledge of grammatical relations is not innate. It seems plausible that certain abstract representations of linguistic structure are included in a speaker's knowledge of his language, even though these may not correspond exactly to those outlined by Chomsky. It is possible that achieving an understanding of the abstract syntactic relationships which hold between parts of sentences is an important part of the language acquisition process.

The argument that the basic grammatical relations are unlearnable simply because they are definable only in the abstract underlying representation of sentences is not very convincing. If we accept this, we must agree that *all* aspects of deep structure are unlearnable for the same reason. But many aspects of deep structure as specified in transformational generative theory are language-specific, such as the underlying order of constituents. If the deep structure representation of sentences is to be considered part of adult competence, we can only assume that these language-specific aspects of deep structure are learnable. To argue otherwise would be to support the untenable position that children are born with a bias toward acquiring the particular language they in fact learn. And if children command some process of learning powerful enough to make these abstractions purely on the basis of linguistic experience, why should the same process not also be able to deal with abstract concepts which are believed by some to be universal, such as the basic grammatical relations?

There is, however, some evidence that the basic grammatical relations themselves are not universal. As noted earlier, Fillmore (1968) observed that certain languages do not offer a choice of subjects and therefore appear to lack the process of subjectivalization. If, in fact, the subject–predicate division is language-specific, we must rule out the possibility that it constitutes part of children's innate knowledge.

It is possible that children can acquire an understanding of the basic grammatical relations through an increasing comprehension of the way various semantic relationships are formally dealt with in their language. The concept of 'subject', for example, might develop in the following way: the child initially formulates rules specifying that words designating initiators of actions precede words designating actions (or, alternatively, that the name of the one who initiates a particular action precedes the name of the action). As the child acquires verbs which take nonagentive noun arguments as subjects, he learns additional rules for the placement with respect to the verb of words performing such semantic functions as 'person affected' and 'instrument'. The concept of 'subject' emerges when the child eventually realizes that nouns in various semantic roles are treated identically across different subclasses of verbs not only with respect to position but also with respect to transformational possibilities, and thus have an equivalence of function at a higher level of abstraction than the particular semantic functions they perform.

The foregoing discussion of the possibility that children do not have knowledge of the basic grammatical relations from the beginning of word combination, but rather acquire it gradually through linguistic experience, must end inconclusively. As some of the arguments extended above indicate, we still do not know whether children have an early knowledge of grammatical concepts like 'subject' and of the constituent structure upon which they depend. The evidence which has been adduced that they have such concepts is weak and does not withstand careful scrutiny. On the other hand, there is as yet no proof, but only some suggestive material, that they lack these concepts. One conclusion that can be drawn from the discussion is clear, however: using the transformational framework for writing grammars for children forces us to postulate deep structure constituents and grammatical relations which have not been justified and which thus may not correspond to the characteristics of children's linguistic knowledge. We do not need such powerful and abstract grammatical concepts as 'subject' and 'predicate' to represent the facts of children's speech early in development, and to write grammars which give them formal representation is to rely too heavily upon concepts needed for an adequate explanation of adult speech without recognition that the phenomena which necessitate them may be absent from child speech.

6.5 Should semantic relationships be represented in a grammar?

Implicit in some of the preceding arguments is an additional way in which transformational grammar, as it is conceived by Chomsky and his followers, perhaps provides an inadequate representation of children's knowledge of sentence construction. Certain semantic concepts which may play an important role in children's early syntactic development are not formally recognized within this framework. In the syntactic component of a transformational grammar, different semantic concepts are not distinguished unless they have an effect on syntax. For example, sentence-subjects are not subclassified on the basis of their semantic relationships to the verb because these relationships have not appeared to affect rules for constructing sentences. A semantic feature like animacy of the subject, in contrast, is formally recognized because it limits the choice of verb. Fillmore (1968) has argued that certain semantic concepts which have not been formally recognized because they seem to have no grammatical consequences do in fact subtly influence such aspects of syntax as selection constraints and transformational possibilities. In both of the following sentences, 'table' receives the same syntactic interpretation in transformational grammar, as the direct object of the verb:

(1) John ruined the table.
(2) John built the table.

However, the first sentence but not the second can be queried appropriately by asking 'what did John do to the table?' and, while the first can be paraphrased as 'what John did to the table was ruin it', the second cannot be paraphrased as 'what John did to the table was build it' (Fillmore, 1968, p. 4). In a transformational grammar, these sentences could be distinguished by reference to the particular verbs involved, which, for example, might be marked differently with respect to transformational possibilities. Fillmore, however, would give more explicit formal recognition in the syntactic component of a grammar to certain semantic distinctions which have subtle but systematic grammatical consequences, such as the difference in the semantic functions of the direct objects in (1) and (2).

In children's utterances, the expression of different semantic concepts often does not result in discoverable differences in syntax. In Seppo's speech at MLU 1.81, sentence-subjects had such relationships to the verb as agentive, ('elephant climbs'), person affected ('mouse is-afraid'), and object or person involved ('tower falls-down'). However, no aspect of the grammar seemed to be affected by the distinction between these relationships. For example, it was not the case that subject–verb strings could be reversed to verb–subject when the subject had a 'person-affected' relationship to the verb but not when it had an agentive relationship. It could be argued, therefore, that a grammar written for Seppo at this stage should not take into account such interesting but grammatically irrelevant semantic details.

However, the goal of writing grammars for children, as it has been defined in this study, is not only to provide an accurate account of the details of children's utterances, but to do so with formulations which approximate as closely as possible the functional concepts, categories, and rules for word combination of children's linguistic competence. The data from the children whose speech is analyzed in this study suggest that children may construct their early sentences out of semantic rather than syntactic building blocks, and that these building blocks and the ways they combine at different stages of development are similar across languages. An approach to grammar writing which does not distinguish among different semantic concepts might cause us to overlook important similarities in the way different children acquire language. Therefore, a psychologically revealing account both of the competence of individual children and of cross-linguistic similarities in language acquisition may require that we analyze child speech within a theoretical framework which permits the semantic functions of sentence constituents to be explicitly identified.

This possibility is pursued in more depth in the following chapter, in which the potential fruitfulness of using a semantically based approach to writing grammars for children is investigated.

7 The case grammar approach

A semantic approach to grammar writing is offered by Fillmore (1968). His suggestions for a theory of case grammar were motivated purely by linguistic considerations and were not influenced by the characteristics of child speech. Nevertheless, case grammar seems well suited in several respects to represent children's linguistic knowledge. It gives formal recognition to semantic relationships which appear to be important in the early speech of children, and, unlike transformational grammar, does not postulate the presence in deep structure of the constituent structure, or subconfiguration of sentence elements, which defines the basic grammatical relations.

While Fillmore's linguistic theory is similar to Chomsky's (1965) in certain respects, such as in the insistence on the centrality of syntax and on the need to give sentences underlying as well as superficial representations which are linked by transformations, their ideas of what is appropriate to deep structure differ. Fillmore considers Chomsky's deep structure 'an artificial intermediate level between the empirically discoverable "semantic deep structure" and the observationally accessible surface structure, a level the properties of which have more to do with the methodological commitments of grammarians than with the nature of human languages' (1968, p. 88). He regards grammatical relations like 'subject of' and 'predicate of', which are basic to deep structure in transformational generative theory, as surface structure phenomena which occur in some but probably not all languages and which should be accounted for transformationally where needed. In Fillmore's theory, syntactically significant semantic concepts called *case relations* are the basic elements of deep structure. The case relations 'comprise a set of universal, presumably innate, concepts which identify certain types of judgments human beings are capable of making about the events that are going on around them, judgments about such matters as who did it, who it happened to, and what got changed' (1968, p. 24). Case relations can be marked in surface structure by a variety of devices including both overt morphological elements like inflections of the nominal system, prepositions, or postpositions, and 'configurational' markers, which are dependent on word order or the like. Languages differ in the particular devices they employ to mark given case relations. Fillmore hypothesizes that observations made about case relations and the structures containing them 'will turn out to have considerable cross-linguistic validity' (1968, p. 5).

Some of the cases which appear to be most necessary are described as follows (1968, pp. 24–5):

Agentive (A), the case of the typically animate perceived instigator of the action identified by the verb.

Instrumental (I), the case of the inanimate force or object causally involved in the action or state identified by the verb.

Dative (D), the case of the animate being affected by the state or action identified by the verb.

Factitive (F), the case of the object or being resulting from the action or state identified by the verb, or understood as part of the meaning of the verb.

Locative (L), the case which identifies the location or spatial orientation of the state or action identified by the verb.

Objective (O), the semantically most neutral case, the case of anything representable by a noun whose role in the action or state identified by the verb is identified by the semantic interpretation of the verb itself; conceivably the concept should be limited to things which are affected by the action or state identified by the verb. The term is not to be confused with the notion of direct object, nor with the name of the surface case synonymous with accusative.

Other cases suggested more tentatively are the *Essive*, to characterize predicate nominatives, as in 'that is *a book*', the *Benefactive*, as in 'he is too tall *for you*', and the *Comitative*, as in 'he is coming *with his wife*'.

In the deep structure of a case grammar, a sentence is analyzed at the most basic level into a 'proposition' and a 'modality'. The proposition consists of a verb and one or more nouns each associated with the verb in a particular case relationship. The concept of 'verb phrase' is eliminated; all the nouns have equal status with respect to the verb. Each case relation can occur only once, although two or more nouns can be conjoined to represent that relation. Case relations and the verb they are associated with are considered unordered. The modality constituent contains markers for modalities on the sentence as a whole, such as negation, tense, mood, aspect, interrogation, and certain adverbs.

Surface structures are derived from underlying structures by transformations which involve operations like selection of the overt morphological markers (if any) for cases, subjectivalization and objectivalization, sequential ordering, nominalization, and registration of elements in the verb. Recursion is accomplished by the embedding of one simple sentence into another through one of the cases. In some languages subjectivalization transformations might create surface structure subjects out of deep structure agents, datives, instrumentals, or locatives. In other languages no case would appear in a syntactic role which could be identified as 'subject'.

In the next sections, we shall evaluate the applicability of case grammar to child language. A case grammar for the first Seppo sample at MLU 1.42 is presented to provide some concrete issues to consider. Although some modifications have been made where this seemed desirable for greater clarity or accuracy, the grammar stays relatively close to Fillmore's proposals. The advantages of case grammar as a method of representing children's early linguistic competence is then discussed, and a partial set of deep structure rules for a 'universal case grammar' for early Stage I child speech proposed. Finally, the drawbacks of the case grammar approach are considered.

7.1 Case grammar for Seppo at MLU 1.42

The deep structure rules, lexicon feature rules, and transformational rules of a case grammar for Seppo based on the speech sample with an MLU of 1.42 are presented below. The lexicon for nouns is identical to that presented in Appendix D for the transformational generative grammar. Verbs, classified according to 'frame features' which indicate the set of case frames into which they may be inserted, are given in Appendix P. Constructions generated by the grammar are presented in Appendix Q, classified according to their deep structure case relations. Constructions not generated by the grammar are identical to those not generated by the transformational grammar, listed in Appendix G, with the addition of *rake⟨ntaa⟩..tuf tuf*, 'builds.."train"'. According to Fillmore, constructions with verbs like 'make' or 'build' involve direct objects in the Factitive case. The occurrence of the Factitive case in one utterance was considered insufficient evidence for postulating a Factitive case in Seppo's grammar at this stage.

Deep Structure Rules

$$1.\ S \to \left\{ \begin{array}{l} V\ (A)\ (O) \\ \left\{ \begin{array}{l} D \\ L \end{array} \right\}\ O \end{array} \right\} \qquad\qquad 2.\ \left\{ \begin{array}{l} A \\ O \\ D \\ L \end{array} \right\} \to N$$

Lexicon Feature Rules

1. $N \to [+N, \pm\text{animate}, \pm\text{proloc}]$
2. $[-\text{animate}] \to [\pm\text{vehicle}]$
3. $[+N] \to \left\{\begin{matrix}[+\text{animate}]\\[+\text{vehicle}]\end{matrix}\right\} / ^A[X\text{——}Y]^1$
4. $[+N] \to [+\text{animate}]/^D[X\text{——}Y]$
5. $[+N] \to \left\{\begin{matrix}[-\text{animate}]\\[+\text{proloc}]\end{matrix}\right\} / ^L[X\text{——}Y]$
6. $[+N] \to [\pm\text{animate}]/^O[X\text{——}Y]$
7. $V \to [+V]$
8. $[+V] \to +[\text{——}(A)]/\text{——}(A)^2$
9. $[+V] \to +[\text{——}(A)\ (O)]/\text{——}(A)\ (O, [-\text{animate}])$
10. $[+V] \to +[\text{——}(O)]/\text{——}(O)$
11. $[+\text{proloc}] \to$ *tuossa*, 'there'

Transformational Rules

1. T ordering: obligatory
   (a) $\{V\ (A)\ (O)\}^3 \Rightarrow (A)\ V\ (O)$
   (b) $\{D, O\} \Rightarrow D+O$
   (c) $\{L, O\} \Rightarrow O+L$

2. T reordering: optional
   (a) Placement of *pois*, 'away', and *kiinni*, 'closed'
   $$\text{S.D.}: \left\{\begin{matrix}pois\\kiinni\end{matrix}\right\} N$$
   $$\text{S.C.}: x_1 - x_2 \Rightarrow x_2 - x_1$$
   (b) Placement of *tuossa*
   $$\text{S.D.}: N + tuossa,\ N + tuossa$$
   $$\text{S.C.}: x_1 - x_2 \Rightarrow x_2 - x_1$$

3. T verb deletion: optional
   $$\text{S.D.}: N + V + N$$
   $$\text{S.C.}: x_1 - x_2 - x_3 \Rightarrow x_1 - x_3$$

7.1.1 Absence of the modality constituent. According to Fillmore's formulations, the deep structure of a sentence contains a modality constituent and a proposition. This can be represented as $S \to M + P$.

---

[1] The form of rules 3–6 is that suggested by Fillmore (1968, p. 26) to provide for insertion of noun lexical items into deep structures. Rule 3 is to be read 'any N in an A phrase must contain the feature [+animate] or [+vehicle]'.

[2] See 7.1.4 for an explanation of the verb insertion rules.

[3] Braces are used here to indicate that the elements enclosed are to be considered unordered.

Neither the symbol M nor the symbol P appears in Seppo's grammar. M is absent because there is nothing to include in a modality constituent. Seppo's grammar at MLU 1.42 lacked operations which apply to sentences as a whole, such as negation, interrogation, or tense marking. The imperative, also an operation on the sentence as a whole, was not formally distinguished from the declarative. An alternative representation of these facts would be to introduce the symbol M and simply rewrite it in all contexts as zero.

All of Seppo's utterances, as generated by the grammar, consist of a proposition. The symbol P does not appear because the rule S → P is unnecessary, given the absence of M. The elements to the right of the arrow in the rule

$$ S \rightarrow \left\{ \begin{matrix} V\ (A)\ (O) \\ \left\{ \begin{matrix} D \\ L \end{matrix} \right\}\ O \end{matrix} \right\} $$

represent possible rewritings of P, however, and would be generated in this way if S were rewritten initially as M + P.

7.1.2 Absence of the verb in some deep structures. According to Fillmore, the proposition of every deep structure contains one or more nouns in case relations to a verb. Sometimes the V constituent is lexically empty. In this case, a form of 'be' or 'have' is inserted into the empty verb slot to absorb the tense and other modalities specified by the modality constituent. For example, when the deep structure V + O + L is realized as 'the book is on the table' ('the book' is in the Objective case and 'the table' is in the Locative case), the V constituent is lexically empty and so is represented by an appropriate form of 'be'. In English, according to Fillmore, a form of 'have' is inserted into a lexically empty verb slot whenever the subject of the sentence is not in the Objective case. For example, in the sentence 'John has a book', the sentence-subject 'John' is in the Dative case, so the V constituent is rewritten as 'has'.

The grammar written for Seppo generates certain deep structures which do not contain a V constituent at all. S may be rewritten simply as D + O or L + O. D + O is the deep structure proposition of utterances like 'father clock' ('father's clock'), and L + O is the proposition of utterances like 'chick shoe' ('chick is on the shoe'). Fillmore's formal requirement that all deep structures contain a verb could have been satisfied by including a verb in the deep structures of such utterances and then specifying that V is rewritten as zero in the contexts ——D + O and ——L + O. This formulation was not adopted because there is no way to justify postulating a V constituent in the deep structures of such utterances. Seppo, unlike adult Finns, did not fill lexically empty verb slots with a form of 'be', and did not have any modalities which needed expression through such a marker.

The word 'case' must be redefined slightly when not all deep structures contain a verb. Fillmore defines cases in terms of the relationships nouns may have to the actions or states identified by the verbs with which they are associated. For example, the Locative is 'the case which identifies the location or spatial orientation of the state or action identified by the verb' (1968, p. 25). The definition of 'case' is extended in Seppo's grammar to include the relationships nouns may have to other nouns as well as to verbs. Justification for this redefinition is that even when all deep structures are said to contain verbs, as Fillmore specifies, the nouns in sentences with lexically empty verb slots really seem to have relationships to each other rather than to the form of 'be' or 'have' which is inserted. For example, in 'the book is on the table', the object referred to by 'table' is in a locative relationship to the object referred to by 'book', not to the copula 'is'. In 'John has a book', the person referred to by 'John' is in a dative relationship to the object referred to by 'book' rather than to the verb 'has'.

7.1.3 Rewriting case symbols. Fillmore suggests that case symbols such as A, O, D, and L be rewritten as K + NP. The K (for *Kasus*) is then rewritten as the morphological marker of the case. Depending on the language and the case, K might be a preposition, postposition, case affix, or zero. In English, for example, the case marker for A is 'by'. For I it is 'by' if there is no agent, otherwise it is 'with'. For O and F it is zero. In Finnish, K could be a case ending such as -*lla* for I, a case ending plus a postposition, or zero, depending on the case and the context.

In the grammar for Seppo, cases are rewritten simply as N. The symbol K is not included because it is always zero. Seppo at this time omitted virtually all case endings and postpositions, so nouns in his constructions were not marked to indicate the case relations they had to verbs or to other nouns.

According to Fillmore, NP (in the case symbol → K + NP) is to be rewritten as N(S). When S, the embedded sentence, contains a lexical item identical to N, the result is an NP consisting of a noun modified by a relative clause. Genitive constructions like 'John's books' are derived 'from relative clauses built on sentences which, by themselves, would have assumed the form X *has* Y [the deep structure of which is $V + D + O$]. The N in the modified NP is the same as the N contained in the D of the adjunct sentence, and the V is empty' (Fillmore, 1968, p. 49). 'John's books' is derived from a deep structure like 'books (books to John)' by 'deleting the repeated noun...and the "empty" verb and reattaching the D to the dominating NP'. The case marker of the D is then changed to '-s' (Fillmore, 1968, pp. 49–50).

Seppo's genitive constructions are not derived in this way for three reasons:

1. Genitive constructions like 'father clock' occurred only as independent utterances, never as constituents of longer utterances. It is therefore usually impossible to tell what case, if any, they represent. If they are generated as Fillmore proposes, however, they must originate as noun phrases in given case relations.

2. It is impossible to justify deriving Seppo's genitive constructions as NPs since there is no evidence that they had psychological unity for Seppo and could be replaced by simple nouns. They did not share privileges of occurrence with nouns.

3. There was no contrast in Seppo's speech between utterances like 'John has books' (in Finnish, literally, 'John-at is books') and those like 'John's books'. Fillmore would derive the former from the simple proposition $V + D + O$ and the latter from a sentence with the same proposition embedded in a noun phrase. Seppo simply produced noun–noun constructions in which the person referred to by the first noun had possessive rights over the object referred to by the second noun. Since there is no need to distinguish between two types of construction which both contain the proposition $V + D + O$, all genitive constructions are generated simply as $D + O$, with the verb lacking for reasons explained in 7.1.2.

Fillmore does not indicate how prolocatives like 'here' and 'there' are to be introduced into a case grammar. Since all cases are to be rewritten as nouns, however, prolocatives might be considered as special nouns which can be substituted for 'true' nouns naming locations just as pronouns can be substituted for nouns in other case relations such as Agentive or Objective. This interpretation is supported by the fact that in Finnish, prolocatives consist of pronouns which are inflected with the same locative case endings used with nouns. In the grammar for Seppo, nouns in the Locative case are rewritten either as inanimate nouns or as prolocatives, as indicated by the rule

$$[+N] \rightarrow \left\{ \begin{matrix} [-\text{animate}] \\ [+\text{proloc}] \end{matrix} \right\} /^{L} [X\text{——}Y].$$

7.1.4   Verb insertion. According to Fillmore, entries for verbs in the lexicon contain 'frame features' which 'indicate the set of case frames into which the given verbs may be inserted. These frame features have the effect of imposing a classification of the verbs in the language' (1968, p. 27). Some verbs can appear in several case frames. In English, for example, 'open' can occur in the context [——O] (as in 'the door opened'), [——O + A] ('John opened the door'), [——O + I] ('a key opened the door'), and [——O + I + A] ('John opened the door with a key'). These facts can be summarized by giving 'open' the frame feature + [——O (I) (A)]. This indicates that 'open' must occur with a noun in the Objective case and can optionally also occur with nouns in either the Instrumental or Agentive cases, or both.

In Seppo's grammar, the lexical entries for verbs contain one of three frame features:

$$+ [\text{——}(A)]$$
$$+ [\text{——}(A)\,(O)]$$
$$+ [\text{——}(O)]$$

Fillmore does not indicate how rules for inserting verbs into deep structures should be formulated. The method adopted in the grammar specifies what contexts verbs with each of these frame features can occur in:

1. The rule [+ V] → + [——(A)]/ ——(A) indicates that a verb with the feature + [——(A)] can be inserted into a context which contains either only a noun in the Agentive case or no other element at all. Verbs with this feature correspond to the intransitive verbs of the transformational generative grammar.

2. The rule [+ V] → + [——(A) (O)]/ ——(A) (O, [–animate]) indicates that a verb with the feature + [——(A) (O)] can occur in isolation, with a noun in the Agentive case or the Objective case, or with nouns in both the Agentive and the Objective cases. It can occur with a noun in the Objective case only if that noun has the feature [–animate]. These verbs correspond to the transitive verbs of the transformational grammar.

3. Following Fillmore, adjectives have been considered a form of verb with the frame feature + [——(O)]. The rule [+ V] → + [——(O)]/ ——(O) indicates that these can occur in isolation or with nouns in the Objective case, both animate and inanimate.

According to Fillmore, adjective–noun constructions like 'little fish' are derived from noun phrases with embedded sentences. The embedded sentences in noun phrases of this type have the deep structure proposition V + O, which, by itself, would assume the form X *is* Y, as in 'fish is little'. After the repeated noun and the lexically empty verb are deleted and the the remaining constituents reordered, 'fish (fish is little)' becomes 'little fish'. Adjective–noun constructions are not derived in this way in Seppo's grammar for the same reasons that genitive–noun constructions are not derived from underlying noun phrases of the form 'X (X *has* Y)' (see 7.1.3). Instead, adjective–noun strings are generated as simple sentences with the deep structure proposition V + O.

In the case grammar for Seppo, the deep structure proposition V + O underlies utterances which, in the transformational grammar (chapter 4), have two distinct deep structures with different syntactic interpretations. The syntactic relation expressed by 'drives car', for example, is directive objective, while that expressed by 'little fish' is modificational. Utterances of the two types can be distinguished in the case grammar by reference to the frame feature of the verb they contain. If the verb has the feature + [——(A) (O)], the relationship is directive objective, while if it has the feature + [——(O)], it is modificational. Moreover, if the noun in the Objective case is animate, the relationship must be modificational, since transitive verbs can take only inanimate direct objects.

7.1.5 Verb deletion. In the transformational grammar for Seppo, subject–object strings are derived by deletion of an underlying verb. Agentive–Objective strings are derived in this way in the case grammar for a similar reason. In the transformational grammar, insuring that all subject nouns are either animate or words for vehicles and all direct object nouns are inanimate depends on the specification of an underlying verb. In the case grammar, the syntactic features of agents (subjects in the transformational grammar) can be specified without reference to an underlying verb by the rule

$$[+N] \rightarrow \left\{ \begin{matrix} [+\text{animate}] \\ [+\text{vehicle}] \end{matrix} \right\} /^{A} [X\text{——}Y].$$

The Objective case, however, unlike the Agentive case, is not always associated with nouns with certain syntactic features. Nouns in the Objective case can be either animate or inanimate depending on the contexts in which they occur. When they occur with verbs which have the frame feature + [——(O)] (adjectives), they can be either animate or inanimate. However, when they occur either with agents alone or with verbs which have the frame feature $+[\underline{\quad\quad}(A)(O)]$ (transitive verbs), they must be inanimate. The inanimacy of Objective nouns in these latter two contexts can be accounted for most economically by reference to an underlying verb. Absence of the verb in some surface structures is accounted for by the verb deletion transformation.

7.2   Advantages of the case grammar approach

The case relationships which are important in deep structure for Seppo in early Stage I are *Agentive, Objective, Locative,* and *Dative.* The vast majority of his constructions consist of no more than two cases or one case plus a verb. The only three-term constructions (aside from structurally unique utterances which are not accounted for by the grammar) are composed of the cases A and O plus a verb.

The case grammar and the transformational grammar based on Seppo's early Stage I speech sample account for essentially the same set of utterances. There is almost a one-to-one correspondence between deep structures analyzed in terms of case relations and those analyzed in terms of grammatical relations. Only the V + O constructions of the case grammar have two distinct syntactic interpretations in the transformational grammar.

Case grammar deep structure	*Syntactic interpretation in the transformational grammar*
V + A	subject–verb
V + O	verb–object
	modifier (adjectival)–noun
A + O	subject–object
D + O	modifier (genitive)–noun
L + O	noun–locative
V + A + O	subject–verb–object

Although the two grammars account for the same utterances and seem virtually intertranslatable, the case grammar account of Seppo's linguistic competence has certain advantages over the transformational grammar account. First, it allows us to dispense with the deep structure division between subject and predicate, a division which I have suggested credits the child with a more abstract linguistic knowledge than his behavior gives evidence for. The case grammar allows us to introduce the concept of subject with a subjectivalization transformation only when it seems justified, rather than forcing us to assign the grammatical function of subject to certain sentence constituents from the very beginning of word combination. Children acquiring languages which lack the syntactic relationship 'subject of' naturally would never acquire such a transformation, while children acquiring languages like Finnish and English may well go through a period of learning before mastering the concept. There is no justification for according the special grammatical status of 'subject' to nouns with the semantic function of agent in Seppo's early utterances. The most desirable grammar for him is one which allows nouns which function as agents to be generated and ordered with respect to other sentence constituents by rules which are conceptually equivalent to those which generate and order other elements like locatives and possessives.

A second advantage of the case grammar is that it offers a concise and non-language-specific account of many of the elements 'missing' from early child speech. The Finnish, American, Luo, and Samoan children we have investigated in Chapters 4 and 5 omitted almost all functors, such as prepositions, postpositions, and case endings. Their speech consisted mainly of nouns and verbs in various implicit semantic relationships, but with the exact nature of these relationships not marked as in adult speech. In case grammar terms, Fillmore's symbol K, which represents the morphological marker of the case in the rule Case Symbol $\rightarrow$ K + NP, is generally zero. Case grammar thus allows us to give the same formal account of, for example, both the Finnish child's initial failure to inflect nouns with locative case endings, in utterances like Seppo's 'chick shoe', and the American child's omission of prepositions, in utterances like Kendall's 'Kendall water'. In case grammars for the children investigated, as illustrated in the grammar for Seppo, case symbols would be rewritten as simple nouns in the early period of word-combining. By the time mean length of utterance approaches 2 morphemes (late Stage I), case symbols would be rewritten as nouns optionally modified by adjectives and genitives, with case markers still largely absent.

Like case markers, many modalities, such as tense, aspect, negation, and interrogation, were either rudimentary or entirely absent in the Stage I speech of the Finnish, American, Samoan, and Luo children. The account of the deep structure of sentences proposed by Fillmore allows these absences to be represented in the same way across languages: M is rewritten in most cases simply as zero. The modality constituents of those children whose languages can mark questions by intonation alone would also include interrogation. Early constructions seem to consist primarily of the elements of deep structure propositions: nouns in various case relationships to each other and to verbs. Judging from the children investigated, a mean utterance length of under about 1.30 to 1.50 morphemes is associated with a sentence length limitation of two terms, with most constructions consisting of no more than a verb plus one noun or of two nouns in given case relationships. In the late Stage I speech samples of most of the children (MLUs of about 1.60 to 2.00), the maximum constructions contained three terms, either a verb and two cases or three cases without a verb.

A third advantage of the case grammar approach is that it provides for the generation of deep structure elements in unordered sets. Our comparison of Finnish, American, Samoan, and Luo children suggests that children's early utterances in all languages may share certain semantic and syntactic characteristics. We might best formalize our knowledge of these universal aspects of language acquisition in a sort of 'universal grammar' for early child speech. The purpose of such a grammar would be to represent the shared foundation of linguistic knowledge, perhaps partially innate and partially learned, from which children work towards the grammars of their particular languages. It should therefore omit features of children's utterances which clearly result from exposure to specific languages. Since children are not predisposed to learn one language rather than another, they probably come to the language acquisition task without preconceptions about the particular word orders they will be required to learn. The data from the Finnish children suggest that children rely heavily on their observations of acceptable order patterns in their native language in formulating their own order rules (see 5.6). Since the order rules acquired depend on the language being learned, the order of elements in the deep structure of a 'universal child grammar' must be left unspecified. Case grammar, unlike transformational generative grammar, provides this representation. Order is not specified in deep structure, but is introduced by various transformational rules. Case grammar therefore appears better able than transformational grammar to give a revealing account of the process of language acquisition in this respect.

7.2.1 A universal case grammar for child language.

What deep structures would be generated by a universal case grammar for children? Table 17 presents the combinations of verbs and case relations found

TABLE 17. *Case grammar classification of utterances in English, Finnish, Luo and Samoan samples, early Stage I[a]*

Case grammar deep structure	Syntactic interpretation according to trans-formational grammar	English (Kendall) MLU 1.48	Finnish (Seppo) MLU 1.42	Luo MLU unknown	Samoan (Sipili) MLU 1.52
Two-term utterances		*Frequencies in utterance types*			
V+A	subject–verb	28	34	4	3
V+O	verb–object	14	9	13	6
	adjective–noun	7	4	2	1
	subject–verb	2	—	1	—
V+L	verb–locative	3	1	—	1
V+D	subject–verb	1	—	3	—
V+F	verb–object	1	1	—	—
A+O	subject–object	5	3	—	—
L+O	subject–locative	13	12	3	1
D+O	genitive–noun or noun–(*has*)–noun	14	4	5	23
	noun–indirect object	—	—	—	1
O+E	dem. pronoun–noun	6	1	7	—
	noun–noun	5	—	—	—
Three-term utterances					
V+A+O	subject–verb–object	7	7	4	—
V+D+O	subject–verb–object	—	—	4	—
V+A+L	subject–verb–locative	4	—	2	—
V+D+L	subject–verb–locative	—	—	1	—
V+O+L	subject–verb–locative	—	—	1	—
	verb–object–locative	2	—	—	—
O+E, E = D+O	dem. pronoun–genitive–noun	1	—	1	—
O+L, O = D+O	genitive–subject–locative	—	—	—	2

[a] Headings such as V+A and D+O indicate the deep structure combination of cases with each other or with verbs. The symbols are to be considered unordered; therefore they do not necessarily correspond to the order of elements in the children's utterances.

in the speech of the Finnish, American, Samoan, and Luo children considered in Chapter 4, at a stage of development marked by MLUs of approximately 1.30 to 1.50. (Kendall is the only English-speaking child represented, since full listings of utterances from Bloom's subjects were not available. Their utterances were very similar to Kendall's, however, except that they produced fewer three-term strings.) Kendall's constructions and those of the Luo and Samoan children are reclassified in case grammar terms in Appendix R. This procedure may have resulted in occasional errors of classification for the latter two sets of utterances, since some translations may have suggested a case which is not really accurate. For example, if the Luo equivalent, in case terms, of 'John sees' were translated into English as 'John looks-at', the Agentive rather than the correct Dative case for 'John' would be

BES

suggested. Despite some possible errors in frequencies, however, we can still get a general idea of which cases are important.

The *Agentive*, *Objective*, *Locative*, and *Dative* cases appear in all the samples. The *Essive*, used for predicate nominatives in utterances like 'that doggie', occurs in at least one utterance in all the samples except the Samoan, in which the constructions 'the' + N and 'sign of the nominative' + N seem to substitute for it in function. The *Instrumental*, *Benefactive*, and *Comitative* cases were absent in the samples (but see the footnote in Appendix R for the Samoan sample), and may therefore represent more difficult semantic concepts. Most constructions consisted of no more than two cases or one case plus a verb.

Case grammar deep structure rules which summarize the characteristics of the children's two-term constructions and some of their three-term constructions are given below:

1. $S \rightarrow M + P$

2. $M \rightarrow \begin{cases} \emptyset \\ Q \text{ (rising intonation for interrogation, for children} \\ \quad \text{ whose languages offer this possibility)} \\ \text{Neg (only for some children, and limited to very} \\ \quad \text{ simple utterances)} \end{cases}$

3. $P \rightarrow \begin{cases} V \text{ (A) (O) (L)}^1 \\ \begin{Bmatrix} L \\ D \\ E \end{Bmatrix} O \end{cases}$

The syntactic relationships expressed by utterances with these deep structures are similar for all the children. For example, V + A always corresponds to subject–verb. Datives are mainly genitive noun modifiers, occasionally subjects, and almost never indirect objects. The deep structure V + O underlies utterances expressing either the verb–direct object or modifier–noun relationship. Only in the Luo and English samples does it ever express the subject–verb relationship but in only one and two utterances respectively. Direct object nouns are almost always in the Objective case. Seppo had one utterance with a Factitive direct object, 'builds "train"'. Bloom's subject Kathryn used the verb 'make' with Factitive objects, so perhaps the Factitive is more common at this stage than the samples investigated suggest.

In the late Stage I speech samples from the Finnish, American, and Samoan children, A, O, L, D, and E remain the most important cases.

---

[1] Choice should be limited to no more than three elements, a verb and one or two of the three cases. For some children, L would not yet appear with verbs.

They combine more freely with each other in longer strings than in the early Stage I samples. Factitive direct objects become more common as verbs like 'draw' and 'make' enter the vocabulary. The Dative case is still found primarily in genitive–noun constructions, but it also appears more frequently than before as indirect object, although not yet as direct object. Almost all sentence-subjects are in the Agentive case in the earlier samples, but by late Stage I they are sometimes in the Dative case (with verbs like 'want', 'get', and 'see') or the Objective case (with verbs like 'fall', 'come', and 'go'). The Instrumental, Benefactive, and Comitative cases are still absent, with only a few exceptions (Adam, for example, produced the V + I combination 'sweep broom', which probably meant something like 'sweep with a broom').

Modalities in late Stage I speech include rising intonation to mark yes–no questions in the grammars of those children whose languages offer this means of interrogation, and negation for very simple sentences, most of which lack subjects. Imperative intent is still not formally marked by the consistent omission of subjects, or, in the Finnish samples, by use of an imperative verb form. Seppo, unlike the other children, had an adverb modality in late Stage I.

7.3 Disadvantages of the case grammar approach

Although the case grammar approach to writing grammars for children has certain advantages over the transformational generative approach, it also has drawbacks of its own. Some of the semantic categories postulated by Fillmore seem either too abstract to apply to child language or too empty semantically to be useful. Fillmore's Dative case is defined as the 'case of the animate being affected by the state or action identified by the verb'. In adult Finnish and English, nouns in the Dative case can function as subjects ('*John* sees George', '*John* has a book'), as indirect objects ('John gave a book to *George*'), as direct objects ('John murdered *George*'), and, following transformational operations, as possessive noun modifiers ('*John's* book'). In early child speech, however, almost all Dative nouns name possessors. There are no Dative direct objects in the children's early Stage I samples and very few indirect objects or Dative subjects. Therefore, the Dative case, defined as 'the animate being affected by the state or action identified by the verb' is a more abstract concept than is needed to represent the characteristics of children's utterances. Its inclusion

14-2

in a child grammar is therefore difficult to justify. This argument is analogous to the one made earlier (6.3.1) against postulating the deep structure syntactic function 'subject' in children's grammars: if all or almost all subjects are *agents* of the action identified by the verb, it is plausible that children are operating with the semantic notion 'agent' rather than the more abstract syntactic concept 'subject'. If children start out with a concept such as 'possessor' (or, alternatively, with a group of even less abstract concepts corresponding to the particular possessive relationships involved in different situations), they would not discover the abstract concept 'Dative' until they produced utterances with indirect objects, Dative subjects, and Dative direct objects, and eventually 'realized' in some sense that these are all manifestations of the same underlying semantic concept.

The Objective case also causes problems in writing grammars for children. Fillmore defines it as the 'semantically most neutral case, the case of anything representable by a noun whose role in the action or state identified by the verb is identified by the semantic interpretation of the verb itself' (1968, p. 25). Unlike the other cases, the Objective case does not name a particular semantic relation, but rather is used for nouns in roles which are not clearly assignable to other cases. O appears in several different deep structures in child speech, at least one of which has more than one syntactic interpretation:

1. O identifies the object possessed in the deep structure D+O (as formulated in Seppo's grammar). For example, 'father *clock*'.
2. O identifies the object located in the deep structure O+L: '*chick shoe*'.
3. O identifies the non-Essive noun or pronoun in the deep structure O+E underlying predicate nominatives: '*this clock*'.
4. O identifies the direct object of the verb in the deep structures V+O and V+A+O: 'drives *car*', 'bunny drives *car*'.
5. O identifies the noun modified by an adjective in some V+O deep structures (as formulated in Seppo's grammar): 'little *fish*'.
6. O identifies the sentence-subject in some V+O deep structures: '*tower* falls-down'.

When a case performs a relatively clear-cut semantic function such as agentive or locative, the syntactic features of nouns in that case can usually be specified directly by reference to the case symbol. In Seppo's grammar, for example, all Agentive nouns are rewritten as nouns with the syntactic feature [+animate] or [+vehicle]. All Locatives have the feature [−animate] or [+proloc]. However, the syntactic features of nouns in the Objective case vary according to the semantic or syntactic functions performed by the nouns, and so cannot be specified in one context-free rule simply by reference to O. In Seppo's grammar, for example, O is inanimate when it is the direct object of a verb, but it is either animate or inanimate when it is the object located by a noun in the Locative case. The fact that certain verbs occur only with inanimate Objective nouns in the deep structures V + O and V + A + O is accounted for in the grammar by the rule $[+ V] \rightarrow + [\text{\textemdash}(A)(O)]/$ \text{\textemdash}(A)(O, $[-\text{animate}]$). The presence of this rule in the grammar (other rules could be designed to indicate the same restriction) is necessitated by the use of the semantically neutral case O, and does not result from a hypothesis about the form of linguistic knowledge which accounts for the particular syntactic features of Objective nouns in various contexts in Seppo's speech. In the transformational grammars written for Seppo, the animacy of subjects and the inanimacy of direct objects is insured by rules specifying the permissible arrangements of animate and inanimate nouns in relation to verbs. When Seppo's speech is analyzed according to case grammar categories, the reason that all subjects are animate (or vehicles) becomes clear: they all function semantically as *agents*, and must therefore be seen as capable of initiating an action. The case grammar allows us to specifically label these sentence constituents as agents and to specify that all nouns functioning as agents must have certain syntactic features. The case grammar thus provides a meaningful explanation for the animacy of nouns functioning as subject, and therefore presumably comes closer in this respect to representing Seppo's linguistic knowledge than the transformational grammars written for him do. The syntactic features of nouns in the Objective case are also closely associated with the semantic functions they perform in Seppo's utterances. For example, nouns referring to objects receiving the force of an action are inanimate, while nouns referring to objects located and nouns modified by adjectives are either animate or inanimate. When these nouns are all said to be in the same case, the opportunity to specify their syntactic features by reference to their semantic function is lost, and *ad hoc* rules must be devised to distinguish between the different sorts of Objective nouns in order to give their features.

Another drawback of the case grammar is that its account of modified nouns is difficult to apply to child speech. As noted in 7.1.3, Fillmore suggests that all case symbols should be rewritten as K + NP, and NP as N(S). Noun modifiers are derived from S, the sentence embedded in NP. The NP as a whole constitutes the realization of a particular case symbol. In the speech of the children investigated in Chapters 4 and 5, nouns in some case relations were never modified. Typically, O and E were sometimes modified, as in Seppo's 'here little tractor' (L + O), Kendall's 'that Kimmy ball' (O + E), and Seppo's 'lifts big stone' (V + O), while A, D, and L were rarely or never modified. Even if each case symbol were rewritten individually by rules such as

$$\begin{Bmatrix} O \\ E \end{Bmatrix} \rightarrow NP$$

$$NP \rightarrow N(S)$$

$$\begin{Bmatrix} A \\ D \\ L \end{Bmatrix} \rightarrow N$$

so that the NPs for O and E contained an optional embedded sentence and the NPs for A, D, and L did not, certain problems would remain. In Rina's speech, for example, O was sometimes modified when it functioned syntactically as direct object but not when it functioned as subject. A general rule such as O → N(S) would therefore be unsatisfactory for her grammar. How to represent the information that nouns in certain cases can be modified only in certain contexts is unclear.

Deriving modified nouns from N(S) is also unsatisfactory because the children's nouns were not modifiable by any embedded sentence, as in adult speech, but only by adjectives, names for possessors, and sometimes attributive nouns. Relative clauses, which are more complex expansions of the embedded S in N(S), did not occur in the Stage I speech samples investigated.

Finally, as mentioned in 7.1.3, and 7.1.4, it is not clear that children's genitive and adjectival modifiers should be derived from sentences embedded in noun phrases at all. Genitive–noun and adjective–noun strings are primitive utterance types which occur earlier than the Noun (*is*) Adjective and Noun *has* Noun strings from which both Fillmore and Chomsky would derive them. Moreover, there is no evidence that they are organized as NPs and share privileges of occurrence with nouns.

Formulating the modality constituent of case grammars for children is also difficult. Modalities are supposed to be operations upon the sentence as a whole. In adult Finnish and English, modalities such as negation, interrogation, tense, and certain adverbs do apply to entire sentences. This is not true in child speech, however. By late Stage I, almost all the children investigated produced negative constructions, but their negative markers were usually conjoined only with simple nouns or verbs. Many affirmative sentences had subjects and were three or occasionally even four morphemes long, but sentences of this complexity were never negated. Case grammar rules such as

$$S \rightarrow M + P$$
$$M \rightarrow Neg$$

would be an inaccurate representation of children's competence, since children are capable of constructing many propositions (P) which they cannot yet negate. In writing grammars for children, it would be necessary to specify that the modality *Neg* could apply only to certain one- or two-term propositions, the nouns of which are often in unknown case relations. (What, for example, is the case of 'fire engine' in Seppo's 'any more fire engine', or of 'tail' in Sarah's 'no tail?'?) How this limitation can be specified is unclear.

In a case grammar for Seppo in late Stage I, adverbs should probably be represented as modalities. They did not operate on any sentence, however, but only on noncopular sentences. Like the negative marker, they seemed to be involved in the constraint on sentence length, just as elements internal to the proposition (A, O, V, etc.) were. Sentences were composed of no more than three constituents, whether from the proposition or the modality. These facts do not fit the case grammar's representation of the modality as external to the proposition but operating upon it as a whole.

Fillmore regards interrogation as a modality. The children whose languages offer special intonations for yes–no questions were able to question sentences of any length or composition, so this kind of interrogation can easily be represented as an operation of the modality constituent upon the sentence. Fillmore does not indicate how Wh questions should be dealt with, however. Wh questions do not apply to whole sentences but only to certain constituents within them, such as the agent ('*Who* said that?'), the locative ('*Where* are you going?'), or the object ('*What* did you hit?'). It is unclear how Wh interrogation can be made to operate only upon one constituent of the sentence rather than upon the entire sentence.

There is an additional difficulty with the representation of Wh questions. When Wh question words like 'where' and 'what' entered the children's speech, they were at first used only with single words, usually nouns or pronouns. The presence of a Wh question modality, then, constrained the length of the proposition to two constituents, the case which was questioned, such as the Locative or the Objective, and a verb or one other case. This constraining influence, like that of the negative marker, cannot be represented when S is expanded simply as $M + P$ regardless of how M is rewritten.

These problems suggest that the case grammar's basic division between modality and proposition is not quite right for child speech. The process by which children gain control of the operations of the modality constituent, as it is formulated for the adult grammar, seems to involve an interaction between the elements of the modality and those of the proposition. This interaction cannot be accounted for when the modality is introduced into deep structure independent of the proposition and is defined as a set of operations on the sentence as a whole. Rules can perhaps be formulated to make generation of the desired kinds of utterances technically possible, but this is difficult and would probably result in a misrepresentation of children's linguistic knowledge in the interests of maintaining a representational schema better suited to adult grammar.

To summarize, the formulations of case grammar do not provide a fully adequate account of the competence underlying children's speech production. The chief value of case grammar for a theory of language acquisition may lie in its insistence on the grammatical significance of semantic concepts and in its rejection of certain fundamental assumptions of transformational generative grammar which seem to be inappropriate for child speech, such as the basic division between subject and predicate.

8 *Summary and conclusions*

In the preceding chapters, the early steps children take in acquiring the syntax of their native language have been analyzed in an effort to discover whether some characteristics of the language acquisition process are language-independent. A comparison of the speech of two Finnish children with that of American, Samoan, and Luo children has suggested some possible universals of language acquisition.

The method of analysis chosen was the writing of grammars for the Finnish children at two stages of development. The comparison of their speech with that of children learning other languages was carried out in connection with discussions of the features of the grammars. According to Chomsky, 'a fully adequate grammar must assign to each of an infinite range of sentences a structural description indicating how this sentence is understood by the ideal speaker-hearer' (1965, pp. 4–5). Different kinds of grammars make different assumptions about the nature of the knowledge which underlies linguistic performance. In this study, the ultimate goal of grammar writing has been to come to some conclusions about what features a grammar must have to give an accurate account of the details of children's utterances with rules which capture the cognitively functional concepts and categories of children's linguistic competence. The accuracy and revealingness of three kinds of grammars – the pivot grammar, transformational generative grammar, and case grammar – were evaluated.

The pivot grammar appears to be inadequate in two ways as a representation of children's linguistic knowledge. Most critically, it does not account for the observable characteristics of children's utterances. Even the individual American children upon whose speech the pivot grammar was based were found not to have had pivot grammars at all, as the concept is usually understood. It is not surprising, therefore, that the speech of other American children and of Finnish and Samoan children failed to conform to the rules of the pivot grammar as well. It proves to be impossible to make a division of the words in any one child's vocabulary such that one class contains only words which have the characteristics attributed to 'pivots' (occur with high frequency relative to other words, have fixed position, combine with any word not of this class, and, according to McNeill (1966*b*), do not occur in isolation or in combination with each other), and the other class contains only words which have the characteristics attributed to 'open class' words (can occur in either initial or final position, occur in isolation or in combination with any pivot or with each other, and cannot be further subdivided on distributional grounds). The characteristics of children's early two-word utterances were found to be much more complex than the two-class pivot–open model suggests. Many of the words used in constructions by the children studied had combinations of the characteristics of both the pivot and open classes. For example, some high frequency words did not have fixed position, some had fixed position but combined only with nouns and not with all the clearly non-pivot words of the child's vocabulary, and so on. Most words which occurred in many different constructions, with or without fixed position, were also among the most frequent of single-word utterances, contrary to McNeill's (1966*b*) assertion.

In addition to representing the privileges of occurrence of words in children's early constructions inaccurately, the pivot grammar is inadequate in another respect. It is fundamentally incapable of expressing as much information about sentence structure as children appear to possess, even very early in their syntactic development. The pivot–open model of child speech arose from the attempt to discover children's syntactic classes by distributional analysis. Such an analysis takes into account only the form and arrangement of words in utterances and ignores their meanings. Many of the regularities in children's first constructions appear to be related to children's apparent intentions, however. For example, the Finnish and American children demonstrated, by their relatively consistent placement of words in initial or final position according to their syntactic or semantic functions, that they had learned the dominant word orders used in their respective languages to express relations of subject–verb–object (or, alternatively, agent–action–object acted upon), possessor–object possessed, and object located–location. A grammar which aims to represent children's linguistic competence must take this knowledge into account. The pivot grammar, which disregards meaning and represents most noun–noun, noun–verb, and verb–noun strings as $O + O$, an unordered combination of two words from the same class, cannot do so.

The investigation of the pivot grammar's adequacy revealed many specific similarities in the speech of the children studied, even though the grammar itself cannot account for them. Each child for whom relatively complete data are available had a few words which appeared in a large proportion of constructions. These high-frequency words can be divided into two groups. Some, called 'syntactic operators' by Bloom (1970), 'operated' semantically and syntactically in a fairly constant fashion on the words with which they were combined. Deixis, or 'nomination' as Brown (1970, in press) has termed it, was the most common semantic function of syntactic operators in several different languages: the child names and often points to an object or event in the immediate context and couples the name with a word such as 'this', 'that', 'it', 'see', 'here', or 'there'. The particular nominative words adopted by the American children were most often 'this' and 'that', while the Finnish children used the translation equivalents of 'here' and 'there'. This difference seems to be related to the way parents typically pose questions about the identity of objects in the two languages. Other operators used by both Finnish and American children, such as 'no', 'away', 'any more', and 'no more', signaled 'nonexistence' or 'disappearance'. The position of syntactic operators in children's utterances generally seems to be a function of their position in adult utterances, although there are exceptions. 'This' and 'that', for example, generally precede the name of the object pointed out in the speech of both Finnish and American children, while 'here' and 'there' occur both before and after the name; this corresponds to adult privileges of occurrence in both languages.

Other high frequency words did not operate in a constant way upon the words with which they combined, but entered into constructions which seemed to express a variety of semantic or syntactic relationships. These words were most often animate nouns, including names for the self, the mother, other important family members, playmates, and animals. Animate nouns, whether frequent or infrequent, tended to occur in initial position in two-word utterances, and inanimate nouns in final position. This regularity of positioning evidently resulted not from the child's belief that the individual words themselves 'belonged' in certain positions, as the rules of the pivot grammar indicate, but from the convergence of other factors. As noted, the children followed the dominant word orders of their languages in expressing subject–verb–object, possessor–object possessed, and object located–location relationships. Constructions involving these relationships constituted a large proportion of two-word utterances. In the children's speech, subjects, possessors, and – to a lesser extent – objects located tended to be animate nouns, while direct objects, objects possessed, and location names tended to be inanimate nouns. Animate nouns therefore most often occurred in sentence-initial position, and inanimate nouns in sentence-final position.

The flaws of the pivot grammar indicate that in order to do justice to children's competence, we must represent their linguistic knowledge with grammars which are able to take semantic and/or syntactic meanings into account. Departing from observable linguistic data to make inferences about children's probable intentions is risky, since it involves the danger of overinterpreting, thereby crediting the child with more knowledge than he actually possesses. However, such inferences appear to be necessary if we are to gain insight into the process by which children generate their utterances. At each point, care must be taken to avoid postulating a more complex or abstract kind of knowledge than is really necessary to account for the characteristics of the data.

Transformational generative linguistic theory provides a grammatical framework which enables us to represent information about certain kinds of meanings. The analysis within this framework of the speech of two Finnish children and the comparison of their speech with that of American, Samoan, and Luo children (Chapters 4 and 5) revealed that the children's utterances were semantically and syntactically very similar at two stages of development with respect to the kinds of constructions produced, the length and internal complexity of utterances, the omission of obligatory elements, and the absence of certain construction patterns and operations.

In the samples from early Stage I (mean length of utterance about 1.30 to 1.50 morphemes), most constructions were only two morphemes long. The construction patterns which appear to have been productive for most or all of the children are subject–verb, verb–object, and modifier–noun (modifiers include both adjectives and genitive nouns, and, for some children, attributive nouns). Noun–locative, demonstrative pronoun–noun, and subject–object strings were also productive in somewhat fewer samples. Productive three-term construction patterns began to emerge during early Stage I, but were still infrequent. Of these, subject–verb–object strings appeared in the most different samples. However, other strings with three major constituents, such as subject–verb–locative or verb–object–locative, seem to have emerged at about the same time for many children, along with still other three-term strings such as verb–modifier–object and demonstrative pronoun–modifier–noun, which consist of two major constituents, one of which is a modified noun.

In late Stage I (mean length of utterance about 1.60 to 2.00 morphemes), there were many productive three-term construction patterns. The distinction between copular and noncopular sentence patterns had become clearer. Noncopular sentences seem to have been constructed by a selection of two or three constituents from a main verb sentence paradigm which had the following form for most of the children (with language-appropriate word order):

subject–verb–modifier–object–indirect object–locative

(One Finnish child lacked the indirect object constituent and included an adverb constituent and an optional modifier for subjects.) Copular sentence patterns included noun–locative, noun–adjective, and demonstrative pronoun–(modifier)–noun strings.

Wh questions and negative constructions were rudimentary or absent in the early Stage I samples. By late Stage I, most of the children combined negative words and Wh question words with one or two other words. Yes–no questions were present in the speech of children learning languages which provide a special questioning intonation which can be superimposed on declarative sentences, but absent in the speech of the Finnish children, whose language does not offer this device.

In both early and late Stage I speech, transformational operations for embedding and conjoining sentences were lacking. Obligatory functors such as inflections, conjunctions, prepositions and postpositions, articles, and copulas were also largely absent. A few functors did appear to be productive in the Luo sample and in one of the Samoan samples. However, all but one of these performed semantic or syntactic functions which were important in the other samples as well, but which could be expressed without functors in the other languages.

Virtually all the children had learned the dominant or only word orders used by adult speakers of their language. Inappropriately ordered strings were exceptional. The Finnish children had also learned something about the permissible alternate orders of their language: the relative frequencies with which the children and their mothers produced various word orders of given construction patterns, such as subject–verb–object, were very similar.

The theory of transformational grammar was found to provide a representation of the linguistic knowledge underlying sentence production at an early stage of development which is satisfactory in certain respects. It is possible to use the formulations of this theory to write a grammar which can both generate the set of utterances in a speech sample which are judged to have resulted from productive rules for sentence construction and give these structural interpretations which presumably have some correspondence to the child's intentions. However, the use of transformational generative grammars for child language involves making some assumptions which are difficult to justify. In transformational grammar, as it has been formulated by Chomsky (1965) and applied to child language by Bloom (1970), a basic division is made in deep structure between subject (the noun phrase immediately dominated by S) and predicate (the verb phrase immediately dominated by S, consisting of a verb plus an optional direct object and other optional elements). This analysis of constituent structure is implicit in the subconfiguration of symbols in phrase-markers. Arguments that predicates have psychological unity for children have been based upon the relative frequencies with which children produce verb–object, subject–verb–object, and subject–verb strings, and upon the characteristics of their 'replacement sequences'. These arguments can be turned around to justify the unity of subject–verb as a constituent for some children, however. It was concluded that the relative frequencies of various constructions and the characteristics of replacement sequences provide little insight into the constituent structure of children's utterances. Thus, the constituent structure assigned to children's utterances by a transformational generative grammar is largely gratuitous. It seems plausible that at an early stage of grammatical development, children are able to produce combinations of words without having the same implicit understanding of their constituent structure as an adult speaker has. An understanding of the hierarchical organization of sentence constituents is probably not a necessary prerequisite at all for producing simple two- and three-term constructions. It is possible that children learn about constituent structure as their grammars gradually develop rather than controlling this information from the very beginning of word combination.

In addition to imposing a certain constituent structure analysis upon utterances, transformational grammar postulates that a particular deep structure constituent functions as sentence-subject. We found that 'subject' is a more abstract and powerful grammatical concept than is needed to represent the characteristics of children's early utterances adequately. First, the transformational characteristics of adult speech which necessitate this concept are absent in children's speech. Second, the apparent sentence-subjects of children's earliest constructions almost always identify *agents*, or the initiators of the actions described by the verbs. As children mature, the semantic functions of their subjects gradually become more diverse, and therefore more like those of subjects in adult speech.

These observations indicate that the transformational grammar account of 'chick' and 'bunny' as subjects in utterances like Seppo's 'chick sings' and 'bunny drives car' may be an inaccurate representation of the knowledge which enables children to produce such utterances. Instead, they may construct sentences from elements which, as they understand them, perform semantic functions like 'agent', 'action', 'object acted upon', and 'location'. Certain semantic notions may be more easily grasped than others for nonlinguistic, cognitive reasons. 'Agent', for example, appears to be understood earlier than, or at least is more attractive than, the concept of 'person affected' by a state or action. According to this view, the early linguistic knowledge of Finnish and American children would include the information that the name for the initiator of an action precedes the name for the action, and that the name for an object receiving the force of an action follows the name for the action. As the child's grammar develops, he may gradually notice that various semantic notions are dealt with syntactically in similar ways, and only eventually come to the syntactic abstraction of 'subject'.

We do not yet know for certain whether children's early constructions are generated primarily with knowledge which makes use of semantic rather than syntactic categories, and whether children's utterances lack the constituent structure which would be assigned to them by a grammar for an adult speaker of the language. However, it makes sense to analyze child speech within a grammatical framework which permits us to entertain such possibilities rather than adopting a grammar which forces us to postulate that certain concepts are functional in the child's competence from the beginning. Thus, we should be able to conceptually distinguish syntactic concepts like 'subject' from less abstract notions like 'agent', and to introduce them only when the data justify it. Similarly, we should be able to generate the earliest constructions without a particular constituent structure, if no justification for a breakdown one way or another can be found, and to gradually introduce such structure, rule by rule if necessary, as justification becomes more apparent.

In Chapter 7 we considered the possibility that the rules of a case grammar approximate the form of children's linguistic knowledge better than those of a transformational grammar. Case grammar gives formal representation to semantic concepts which seem to be important in the early speech of children, and, unlike transformational grammar as formulated by Chomsky, it introduces elements into deep structure without imposing upon them a constituent structure which specifies that the verb and the direct object are more closely related than the subject and the verb. Moreover, it avoids altogether the assumption that one constituent in deep structure must function as 'subject'. In addition to these advantages, case grammar appears to give a concise and non-language-specific account of many of the elements which are missing in children's utterances in several languages. According to Fillmore, noun inflections, prepositions, and postpositions are all morphological markers of the case relations nouns have to verbs. A noun in a particular case is generated as $K + NP$; the K (for *Kasus*) symbolizes the case marker, which takes different forms in different languages. In Stage I speech, K generally seems to be zero. A large proportion of utterances consists of nouns and verbs in various implicit semantic relationships, but the exact nature of these relationships is not marked.

The speech of the Finnish, American, Samoan, and Luo children for whom data are available suggests that the Agentive, Objective, Locative, and Dative cases may all occur in children's early Stage I utterances regardless of language. The Essive case, used in predicate nominative constructions, occurred in the American and Luo samples, but not in the Finnish and Samoan samples. Most productive construction patterns contained either nouns in two of these case relationships or one noun and a verb: $V + A$, $V + O$, $A + O$, $L + O$, $D + O$, $E + O$. By late Stage I, many three-term construction patterns were productive. These consisted of three nouns in various case relations or of a verb and two nouns. Nouns in the Factive case began to occur more often than before, as direct objects of verbs like 'draw' and 'make', but other cases proposed by Fillmore, such as the Instrumental, Comitative, and Benefactive, were still absent in constructions.

Although a case grammar approach to child speech permits us to generate children's utterances with categories and rules of concatenation which perhaps approximate the functional categories and rules of children's linguistic competence better than the formulations of transformational generative grammar do, it is not entirely satisfactory. At least two of the semantic categories it employs probably do not correspond to the functional categories of children's linguistic competence. In adult speech, the Dative, which Fillmore defines as 'the case of the animate being affected by the state or action identified by the verb', can be the case of subjects, direct objects, and indirect objects. In children's earliest constructions, however, it functions virtually exclusively as the name for a possessor in genitive noun–noun constructions. The Dative case is therefore undoubtedly a more abstract category than children actually work with. If, as in a case grammar, we are going to label nouns according to their semantic functions, it would probably be better simply to label children's genitive nouns as 'possessives'. Even this might be a more abstract category than is appropriate, since perhaps children conceive of nouns which function in different sorts of 'possessive' relationships as fundamentally distinct – consider, for example, the difference between 'Rina nose' and 'Rina pencil'.

The Objective case, like the Dative case, probably does not correspond to any functional category in children's grammars. It seems to be a semantically neutral case which is applied to all nouns not clearly belonging to some other case. Do children really see any similarity between nouns which function as objects located ('*chick* shoe'), objects possessed ('father *clock*'), objects acted upon ('bunny drives *car*'), initial nouns or pronouns in predicate nominative constructions ('*this* fish'), and nouns in predicate adjective constructions ('*fish* is little')? Probably not. Why should words in such utterances not be distinguished according to the semantic functions they perform, just as words which function agentively or locatively are distinguished? This would enable us to specify the syntactic features of these nouns, such as animacy or lack of it, by reference to their semantic function, which may well be analogous to what children do, rather than by the kind of *ad hoc* rules needed in the case grammar for Seppo.

Another drawback to case grammar is that its account of noun modification is probably not right for children. In case grammar, modifiers (both genitive and adjectival) are derived from S, the sentence embedded in NP. In early Stage I speech, however, there is no evidence

15

that genitive–noun and adjective–noun combinations are organized as noun phrases, since they appear initially as independent utterances, just as agent–action and agent–object strings do, and they do not share distributional privileges of occurrence with single nouns. As with respect to other aspects of constituent structure, a grammar for children should allow us to represent modifiers and nouns as immediate constituents of noun phrases only when there is evidence for this organization. In late Stage I speech, evidence for a noun phrase constituent does begin to emerge, but the case grammar derivation of the modifier from an embedded sentence is still inappropriate. Nouns at this time are not modified by any type of sentence the child is able to produce, but only by adjectives and by other nouns. Limiting the expansion of the embedded sentence to these is difficult. It is likely in any event that children do not understand genitive–noun and adjective–noun combinations like 'father clock' and 'little fish' as transformationally modified versions of strings like 'father (father has clock)' or 'fish (fish is little)': the simple genitive–noun and adjective–noun strings are primitives of the children's grammars, emerging long before strings like 'father has a clock' and 'fish is little'.

We found that evidence for making the case grammar's deep structure division between a modality and a proposition is lacking in Stage I speech. According to Fillmore, modalities like negation, interrogation, and certain adverbs are operations upon a sentence as a whole. But in the speech of the children studied, negative words and Wh question words were usually conjoined only with simple nouns or verbs rather than with propositions as long and complex as the children were able to produce in affirmative declarative sentences. This suggests that in the process of language acquisition, those elements which case grammar assigns to the modality and those it assigns to the proposition interact in a way which cannot be accounted for when the modality and the proposition are introduced into deep structure independently.

In summary, the representations of children's early linguistic competence which are provided by the formulations of the pivot grammar, transformational generative grammar, and case grammar are all unsatisfactory, each in different respects. The pivot grammar was found to be the most inadequate, since it does not even provide an accurate account of the superficial characteristics of children's utterances. Transformational grammar and case grammar both incorporate certain features which appear to be essential to a grammar which can generate, in a cognitively revealing fashion, the kinds of utterances children produce. For example, both are capable of taking the apparent meanings of utterances into account in giving them structural interpretations. Both make a distinction between deep and surface structure, which is necessary if we are to distinguish between combinations of word classes which are superficially identical but which apparently express different structural meanings. Providing adequate structural interpretations for some utterances seems to involve postulating deep structures which are more complex than the surface structures associated with them. For example, the characteristics of noun–noun strings judged to express a subject–object (or agent–object) relationship are best accounted for in the grammars for Seppo and Rina by specifying an underlying verb which is transformationally deleted.

The points at which the formulations and basic assumptions of both transformational generative grammar and case grammar apparently fail to provide an appropriate model of children's developing linguistic competence suggest other features which an optimal grammar for child language should incorporate. It should be completely flexible in assigning constituent structure. Hierarchical relationships should be postulated only when there is evidence in the data that children understand the elements of their utterances to be hierarchically organized, rather than because a certain hierarchy of sentence constituents must be specified in an adequate adult grammar for the language. The optimal grammar should also be flexible with regard to the kinds of concepts and categories it postulates as functional in the child's competence. We have suggested that the kinds of concepts children use in generating their earliest two- and three-word constructions may be primarily semantic. As the child matures linguistically, according to this view, he begins to recognize regularities in the way different semantic concepts are dealt with and to gradually reorganize his knowledge into syntactic concepts, which are more abstract. At any point in time, some of the concepts which are functional in the child's competence may be primarily semantic and others primarily syntactic. If this is true, the optimal grammar for child language must be capable of operating with both semantic and syntactic concepts. It must also be flexible enough to represent shifts over time to new levels of abstraction, so that, for example, a sentence constituent which at one time might be represented as an 'agent' would at a later time be represented as 'sentence-subject'.

In this study, we have come to some tentative conclusions about universal aspects of early syntactic development and about the form a grammar must take to represent the linguistic competence underlying children's initial sentence production in a maximally revealing way. The data collected from the Finnish children have widened the available data base, and so have been fundamental to these formulations. We still have far too little comparative material, however. The hypotheses advanced in this investigation must be tested against material from children learning still other languages before firm conclusions about universals of early syntactic development can be reached.

Appendix A

Outline of Finnish grammar

The following discussion of the structure of Finnish is very incomplete. It deals mainly with aspects of the language which are relevant to the present study.

Phonology

Vowel harmony is one of the most outstanding features of Finnish phonology. The back vowels (a, o, u, aa, oo, uu) and the front vowels (ä, ö, y, ää, öö, yy) cannot occur together in the same word (unless it is compound), although the front vowels /e/ and /i/ occur in words with vowels of either group. The children did not observe vowel harmony consistently. They tended to pronounce the front vowels /y/ and /ä/ as [u] and [a] respectively, especially in final syllables. Thus, Rina's *kynä*, 'pen', was usually rendered as [kuna], and Seppo's *missä*, 'where', as [mis:a].

Vowel and consonant length are both phonemic. There are few consonant clusters, and these are restricted to medial environments. Unallowed clusters which would result from inflection are reduced. Primary stress is always on the first syllable of a word.

Morphophonemics

1. The requirements of *vowel harmony* dictate that every inflection which contains a vowel (unless the vowel is /i/ or /e/) have two forms, one for use with back vowel words and one for use with front vowel words. The alternation between two allomorphs occurs in inflections for all parts of speech.

2. *Consonant gradation*: The consonants k, t, p, kk, tt, pp, and clusters in which they occur are subject to reduction to what is known as their 'weak grade' when the immediately following syllable is short (i.e. contains a single vowel), and is changed from open to closed (i.e. when inflection causes the syllable to terminate in a consonant). Some examples:

Strong grade	Weak grade	Nominative	Genitive	Gloss
kk	k	takki	takin	'coat'
tt	t	hattu	hatun	'hat'
pp	p	kauppa	kaupan	'store'
k	ø	sika	sian	'pig'
t	d	katu	kadun	'street'

Strong grade	Weak grade	Nominative	Genitive	Gloss
p	v	tapa	tavan	'custom'
lk	l	jalka	jalan	'foot'
rk	r/rj	märkä	märän	'wet'
		kurki	kurjin	'crane'
nk	ng ([ŋ:])	kenkä	kengän	'shoe'
uku	uvu	puku	puvun	'dress'
yky	yvy	kyky	kyvyn	'ability'
lp	lv	halpa	halvan	'cheap'
rp	rv	turpa	turvan	'muzzle'
mp	mm	kumpu	kummun	'hill'
lt	ll	silta	sillan	'bridge'
rt	rr	parta	parran	'beard'
nt	nn	ranta	rannan	'shore'
ht	hd	kehto	kehdon	'cradle'

(These examples are limited to nouns and adjectives, but the same gradation occurs in every part of speech.)

Seppo's and Rina's words were generally invariant, most often based on the nominative singular form of nouns and the third person singular form of verbs. In the absence of inflection, the children did not yet need to observe consonant gradation. However, they occasionally produced words in a grade appropriate for inflection but omitted the inflection. For example, Seppo produced *kengä*, the uninflected weak grade of *kenkä*, 'shoe'. This was probably modeled on the nominative plural form *kengät*, 'shoes'. Similarly, Rina produced *hampa*, the strong grade of *hammas*, 'tooth'. This was probably modeled on the nominative plural, *hampaat*, 'teeth'.

3. *Vowel and consonant stems*: All inflectable words have a vowel stem to which inflections are added. For nouns, this is often identical to the nominative singular form of the word; for example, *kello-*, 'clock'. Words which undergo consonant gradation have two vowel stems, one in strong grade and one in weak grade. For example, *kukka-*, *kuka-*, 'flower'. Some inflections are added to the strong grade stem and others to the weak grade stem; this is phonologically conditioned. Some words also have a consonant stem, which is used with certain inflections. For example:

Nom. sing. or 3rd pers. sing. form	Vowel stem	Consonant stem
pieni 'small'	piene-	pien-
	pienessä 'in (the) small'	pientä 'small' (partitive)
	pienen 'of (the) small'	

Nom. sing. or 3rd pers. sing. form	*Vowel stem*	*Consonant stem*
käsi 'hand'	käte-	kät-
	käde-	kättä 'hand' (partitive)
	käteen 'to (the) hand'	
	kädet 'hands'	
pesee 'washes'	pese-	pes-
	pesen 'I wash'	pestään 'one-washes'
		pes + nyt → pessyt 'washed'

The child learning Finnish must discover whether or not a given word has both a vowel and a consonant stem, and which inflections are used with which stems. In addition, he must observe the rules of consonant gradation and apply inflections only to stems in the appropriate grade. Data from four Finnish children I have studied in all, including Seppo and Rina, suggest that when Finnish children begin to inflect words, they make errors from failure to use the appropriate stem (the vowel stem was occasionally used where the consonant stem was required), from failure to observe consonant gradation, and from using the nominative singular form of nouns ending in a vowel as the vowel stem for all nouns, although this is inappropriate for some nouns.

Morphology

Suffixation is the chief morphological device of Finnish.

1. Nouns

There is no article and no gender in Finnish. Number (singular and plural) is marked. There are fourteen cases, many of which denote relationships expressed by prepositions in English. A sample noun is declined below. Case endings are italicized. The *i* (or *j*) in the plural forms is the plural marker.

	talo 'house'		
	Singular	*Plural*	
Nominative	talo	talo*t*	
Genitive	talo*n*	talo*jen*	'of the...'
Essive	talo*na*	talo*ina*	(expresses the state of a person or thing)
Partitive	talo*a*	taloj*a*	'some...' 'some of...', 'any...'
Translative	talo*ksi*	taloi*ksi*	(denotes the state a person or thing passes into. Follows verbs of change and becoming)

talo 'house' (*cont.*)

	Singular	Plural	
Inessive	talo*ssa*	taloi*ssa*	'in(side) the...'
Elative	talo*sta*	taloi*sta*	'out of the...'
Illative	talo*on*	taloi*hin*	'into the...'
Adessive	talo*lla*	taloi*lla*	'on the...', 'by means of the...'
Ablative	talo*lta*	taloi*lta*	'from the...'
Allative	talo*lle*	taloi*lle*	'to the...'
Abessive	talo*tta*	taloi*tta*	'without the...'
Comitative	—	taloi*ne*(nsa)	'with the...'
Instructive	(talo*n*)	taloi*n*	(expresses instrument with which or manner in which an action is performed)

(Many of the case endings have additional or derived meanings as well. See pp. 142–3 for a partial explanation of the meanings of the Adessive and Allative, and pp. 125–7 for a discussion of the use of the Genitive (also called the Genitive/Accusative) and Partitive to mark direct objects.)

Nouns may also carry a possessive suffix, which follows the case ending:

talossa*ni*	'in my house'
talo*si*	'your house'
talosta*mme*	'out of our house'

Pronouns are declined, on the whole, like nouns.

2. Adjectives

Adjectives precede the nouns they modify, and agree with them in case and number:

suuri talo	'big house'
suuren talon	'of the big house'
suuressa talossa	'in the big house'
suuret talot	'big houses'

The comparative and superlative nominative singular forms of adjectives are formed by adding *-mpi* and *-in* respectively to the vowel stem. These forms must also be declined. A few adjectives, such as *pikku*, 'little, wee', are not inflectable.

3. Verbs

Three persons are marked in singular and plural. In standard Finnish, the verb agrees with the subject in number and person (with one exception, irrelevant to the present discussion). In the colloquial speech of the children and their parents, however, third person singular verbs were often used with third person plural subjects.

The voices are active and passive. The passive is always impersonal, and lacks a subject. In English translation, the subject would often be 'it', 'one' or 'you'. An agent cannot be expressed when the passive is used. Colloquially, the passive form of the verb is routinely used in place of the first person plural form in active sentences, usually with *me*, 'we'.

The moods are indicative, potential (rare in spoken Finnish), conditional, and imperative. The indicative is conjugated in the present, imperfect, perfect, and pluperfect. The other moods have present and past tense only. The present tense indicates future time as well as present, according to context. The imperfect (translated, for example, both as 'I said' and 'I was saying') is marked by an *i* inserted after the verb stem and before the personal endings. This may result in morphophonemic changes. Two sample verbs are conjugated in the present and imperfect indicative below:

Present

	sano-, 'say'		mene-, 'go'	
	sing.	pl.	sing.	pl.
1st	sanon	sanomme	menen	menemme
2nd	sanot	sanotte	menet	menette
3rd	sanoo	sanovat	menee	menevät

Imperfect

	sing.	pl.	sing.	pl.
1st	sanoin	sanoimme	menin	menimme
2nd	sanoit	sanoitte	menit	menitte
3rd	sanoi	sanoivat	meni	menivät

The perfect and pluperfect are formed with the present and imperfect tenses of the verb 'to be', conjugated for person and number, plus the past participle of the main verb. This is analogous to the use of 'have' as an auxiliary in English, and identical to the use of 'be' for certain verbs in French, Italian, and German: *je suis allé*, 'I have gone'.

4. *Adverbs*

Adverbs are usually formed by adding *-sti* to the vowel stem of adjectives:

Adjective		*Vowel stem*	*Adverb*	
kaunis	'beautiful'	kaunii-	kauniisti	'beautifully'
kauhea	'awful'	kauhe-	kauhesti	'awfully'

5. *Prepositions and postpositions*

Finnish has both prepositions and postpositions; the later predominate. The noun which a postposition follows is usually in the genitive case. Many postpositions must be inflected with locative case endings, and appear in one of three forms: one for use in sentences with a copula or stationary verb, one for use with verbs of motion away from, and one for use with verbs of motion to. For example:

päällä	'on top of'	vieressä	'next-to'
päälle	'to the top of'	viereen	'to next-to'
päältä	'from the top of'	vierestä	'from next-to'

Postpositions also mark the relationships 'under', 'across', 'because of', 'through', 'near', and others.

Sentence types of special interest

1. Negatives

Negative constructions are formed with a special negative verb which has two series of personal forms, one for the imperative and another for the other moods.

	Imperative	*Other moods*
1st sing.	—	en
2nd sing.	älä	et
3rd sing.	älköön	ei
1st pl.	älkäämme	emme
2nd pl.	älkää	ette
3rd pl.	älkööt	eivät

In a nonimperative negative construction, the appropriate form of the negative verb precedes the verb to be negated, which is placed in a 'neutral' form for present tense and in its past participle form for imperfect tense. The neutral form is the weak grade vowel stem plus an 'aspiration' which manifests itself as a glottal stop between vowels or as a doubling of an initial consonant in the following word. For perfect and past perfect, the past participle is preceded by the verb 'be' in its stem and past participle forms respectively. To illustrate, we shall imagine that there is a verb 'to not' in English. Parallel constructions would then take these forms (words in corresponding sentence positions are translation equivalents, except that the Finnish forms of 'be' are translated as 'have', since these verbs function similarly in their respective verbal systems):

Present:	hän ei mene	'he nots go'	('he doesn't go')
Imperfect:	hän ei mennyt	'he nots gone'	('he didn't go')
Perfect:	hän ei ole mennyt	'he nots has gone'	('he hasn't gone')
Past Perf.:	hän ei ollut mennyt	'he nots had gone'	('he hadn't gone')

A present tense conjugation for all persons is as follows:

1st sing.	minä en mene	'I don't go'
2nd sing.	sinä et mene	'you don't go'
3rd sing.	hän (se) ei mene	'he/she (it) doesn't go'

1st pl.	me emme mene	'we don't go'
2nd pl.	te ette mene	'you don't go'
3rd pl.	he (ne) eivät mene	'they-animate (they-inanimate) don't go'

In the colloquial speech the children were exposed to, the negative verb is often placed before the subject in sentence-initial position:

en minä sano	'I don't say'
et sinä mene	'you don't go'
ei hevonen syö	'(the) horse doesn't eat'

In negative imperative constructions, the imperative negative verb form is placed before the consonant stem of the verb to be negated (if it has one; otherwise, the vowel stem), to which *-ko/kö* is added. In the 2nd person singular, the vowel stem is used without *-ko/kö*. The negative imperatives to which the children were exposed were almost exclusively in the 2nd person singular:

| älä sano! | 'don't say!' |
| älä mene! | 'don't go!' |

Direct objects in negative constructions are in the partitive case.

2. *Imperatives*

There is a present tense imperative form for all persons except the 1st singular. The children most often heard the 2nd person singular form (this is the only form that occurs in the mothers' speech on the tapes). The 2nd person singular verb form is identical to the 'neutral' form used in negative utterances. An understood 2nd person singular pronoun is omitted, as in English. See pp. 126–7 for a discussion of the case of the direct object. Some examples:

syö!	'eat!'
katso puuta!	'look-at (the) tree!'
nosta se ylös!	'pick it up!'
tule tänne!	'come here!'

3. *Yes–No questions*

In stylistically neutral questions, an interrogative particle *-ko/kö* is added to the verb, which is placed in sentence-initial position:

kissa menee pois	'(the) cat goes away'
meneekö kissa pois?	'does (the) cat go away?'
kissa on mennyt pois	'(the) cat has gone away'
onko kissa mennyt pois?	'has (the) cat gone away?'
tämä on kala	'this is (a) fish'
onko tämä kala?	'is this (a) fish?'

The interrogative particle may be added to words other than the verb if special emphasis is required. This word is then placed in sentence-initial position:

kissako menee pois?	'is it the cat that's going away?'
metsäänkö kissa menee?	'is it into the woods that the cat is going?'
kissako?	'cat?'
tämäkö?	'this one?'

4. *Wh questions*

Many Wh question words are derived from *mi-*, the stem for 'what', which is inflected to produce related forms:

mikä	'what' (nominative)
minkä	'of what' (genitive)
mitä	'what' (partitive)
missä	'in what, where' (inessive)
mihin	'to what, whither' (illative)
millä	'by what, how' (instrumental)
	etc.

Kuka, the equivalent form for 'who', is also inflected to produce 'whose', 'to whom', etc. Other Wh word equivalents are *kumpi*, 'which (of two)', *koska* and *milloin*, 'when', and *kuinka*, 'how'.

These interrogative words come first in the sentence, but, in contrast to English, they do not disturb the order of the remaining sentence constituents:

mikä tämä on?	'what this is?'
mitä sinä sanoit?	'what you said?'
missä minä olen?	'where I am?'
koska he lähtevät?	'when they leave?'
mistä sinä otit tuon?	'from where you took that?'

Word order

The normal, unmarked order is subject–verb–direct object–indirect object. Adverbs of time and place are usually sentence-initial or sentence-final (other orders are possible), but adverbs of manner often occur next to the verb. Orders other than the dominant are used for special emphases. No confusion results, since the grammatical function of sentence constituents is marked by inflection. See Table 14 for the frequencies with which Seppo's and Rina's mothers used various word orders.

Appendix B

Kendall, Mean Length of Utterance 1.10
All Nonimitated Constructions

Utterance	Gloss or nonlinguistic context
Kendall sit	K describing ongoing activity
Kendall read	K describing ongoing activity
Kendall walk	K describing ongoing activity
Kendall bounce	K describing ongoing activity
Daddy sit	K describing ongoing activity
Daddy hide	K describing ongoing activity
Daddy write (2)[a]	K describing ongoing activity
Daddy walk	K describing ongoing activity
Mommy read	K describing ongoing activity
Mommy tie-it[b]	K wants M to tie her shoe
Kimmy read	K recalling that Kimmy, a friend, also reads
read, Kimmy read	K recalling that Kimmy, a friend, also reads
Kimmy bite	K demonstrating how Kimmy bites with her teeth
horse walk	K looking at a horse walking
horse run	K looking at a horse running
Kendall Mommy walk	K and M are walking along, side by side
spider move (6)	K describing ongoing activity
Melissa walk	K describing ongoing activity
Bill talk	K describing ongoing activity
doggie bye	K remembering that a dog had run by earlier. K and M use phrase 'go bye bye' meaning 'to leave', 'go away'
Daddy teeth	K touching sink, just after M has said to Melissa '. . .while Shawn (= Daddy) is brushing his teeth'
Dad sock	D has left room to find sock. Could mean 'Dad's sock' or something like 'Dad find sock'
Mommy spider	K trying to get M to come watch a spider with her. No vocative intonation
Mommy 'oops'	M has just said 'oops'
Melissa eye	Melissa drawing eye in a face for K
Kimmy B.M.	K having her diapers changed; evidently remembering that Kimmy has B.M.s too
Kendall B.M.	Same context as above

[a] Numbers in parentheses refer to the number of times a construction appears in the sample, if more than once.

[b] V-it combinations apparently were produced as single units. They did not contrast with V alone (with one exception) or with V plus another direct object.

Utterance	Gloss or nonlinguistic context
Kendall leave	D has just said to K 'Can you grab some leaves'?
Mommy curly	Not a direct imitation, but shortly before, Melissa had said, 'Mommy has curly hair'
find Mommy (3)	K exiting to look for M
taste cereal (2)	K eating cereal; M has recently said 'taste it'
close..door	K pulling door shut
close..bathroom	K pulling bathroom door shut
tie-it (2)[b]	K wants M to tie her shoe
carry-it[b]	K wants M to carry her
carry-it, Mommy	Same context as above
horse..see-it[b]	K looking at horse. Possibly imperative
Daddy here	'Daddy is here'
Bill here	'Bill is here'
Mommy bathroom (2)	M is in the bathroom
pig water	K looking at a pig standing in water
pig house (2)	Pig has gone into own house. Could be 'pig's house' or 'pig goes into house'
Melissa car	Melissa is about to get into the car of K's family
penny innere	K looking into pair of overalls where she has put penny
slipper doggie (2)	M has recently been talking about putting the slipper on the doggie
doggie slipper	Same context as above
purse 'way	K putting purse aside
Melissa 'way	Melissa has just left room
ant 'way (2)	Ant has gone into crack in sidewalk
go house	K being carried towards a house; M and D have already gone inside
sit lap	K wants to sit on M's lap
Kendall chair (2)	'Kendall's chair'
Kendall house	'Kendall's house' (a routine)
Kendall foot	K wants to take her shoe off
lady car	K looking at picture of lady standing beside a car
Daddy book (5)	'Daddy's book'
Melissa house (2)	'Melissa's house' (in response to 'whose house is this?')
Bill house	'Bill's house' (in response to 'whose house is this?')
Kimmy house (2)	'Kimmy's house'
doggie..house	'Doggie's house'
Bill book	'Bill's book'
no, Mommy..hand	K doesn't want to hold Melissa's hand, wants M's hand
animal house (2)	K walking by a barn at a farm
my penny	K playing with her own penny
our car (4)	In response to 'whose car is this?' (A routine)
doggie..sleepy	K lying down, pretending to be a dog
(rocks..broken) (2)	K has been told not to touch pieces of a broken sculpture
hand clean (3)	K holding out hands, wants M to wash them
more walk	Everyone continuing to walk along

Utterance	Gloss or nonlinguistic context
more lights	*K* looking at lots of lights
more lights, Mommy	Same context as above
that..book	In response to 'what's that?'
walk self	*K* walking by herself
tie-it self	*K* tying her shoe by herself
Mommy, down	*K* wants to be lifted down
Mommy, telephone	*K* pointing out telephone to *M*
no, self (2)	*K* rejecting help; wants to do something herself
no, sit	In response to 'do you want to go to sleep now?' *K* wants to continue sitting on couch
no, carry	*M* has suggested that *K* walk up a ramp, but *K* wants to be carried
no, 'way	*K* rejecting food *M* offers
no, cereal	In response to 'are you all done?' *K* continuing to eat cereal
no, Mommy	In response to 'can you tie it yourself?' *K* wants *M* to tie shoe for her
Kimmy Pam	Kimmy is *K*'s friend, Pam is Kimmy's mother. Neither are present
open, close	*K* has been opening and closing a door
lady man	*K* watching a lady and a man walk by together
Daddy pat	*K* patting *M*'s arm; *D* is sitting nearby on floor. Could be that *K* wants to pat Daddy too, but she doesn't persist, or she is remembering that Daddy sometimes pats Mommy
lady hat	In response to 'what did the lady have?'
lady car	'lady's car' or 'lady (near) car'. *K* watching a lady standing near a car
Bill car	'Bill's car' or 'Bill in car'
Melissa car	'Melissa's car' or 'Melissa in car'
door..find	*K* exiting to find Daddy who she thinks is hiding. Perhaps she thinks he is hiding behind a door
animal dog	'a dog is an animal' (?)
no more	In response to 'do you want more of anything?'
Kendall hurt	'Something is hurting Kendall', or 'Kendall hurts'
Kimmy girl	'Kimmy is a girl'. *M* has just said 'Kendall is a girl'
back doggie (2)	*K* putting toy dog behind her on sofa
inna Mommy	*K* wants to come in past screen door; *K* is outside and *M* is sitting just inside
'frigerator on	*K* has heard the refrigerator start to make a noise
slipper on	*K* putting her slipper on
tummy off	*K* wants shirt off of her tummy
Mommy in	*K* shutting bathroom door on *M* so *M* is inside bathroom, *K* outside
in Daddy	*K* getting ready to shut door on Daddy, who is inside a room

Appendix C

Kendall, Mean Length of Utterance 1.48
Constructions in the Sample Classified According
to Grammatical Relations

1. *Subject–verb*
    (a) N + V
        Kendall bark
        Kendall swim
        Kendall bite
        Kendall break
        Kendall turn
        Kendall fix-it^a (2)^b
        Kimmy spit
        Kimmy come
        Kimmy swim
        Kimmy blow (2)
        Kimmy bite
        Kimmy running
        Kimmy eat (2)
        Mommy bounce
        Mommy sleep
        Mommy read
        Mommy break-it^a
        Daddy pick-up
        Daddy break-it^a
        Melissa bounce
        Melissa read
        Phil running (2)
        Pam running
        Scott scream
        cow moo (4)
        doggie bark
        pillow fell
        thread break
        Kendall Kristin sit ('Kendall and Kristin sit')
    (b) V + N
        hug Mommy ('Mommy hugs')
        see Kendall ('Kendall sees')

^a V-it combinations apparently were produced as single units. They did not contrast with V alone or with V plus other direct objects.
^b Numbers in parentheses refer to the number of times a construction appears in the sample, if more than once.

2. *Verb–Object*
    (a) V + N
        look Kendall ('Look at Kendall')
        read..book
        writing book
        leave-it heel
        break Fur-Book (name of a book)
        bite..finger
        open..lotion
    (b) N + V
        doggie sew (5) ('sew doggie')
        Kimmy kick ('kick Kimmy')
        Kendall pick-up ('pick up Kendall')
        doggie lookit ('look at doggie')
        shoe off ('take shoe off')
        hat on ('put hat on')
        lotion away ('take lotion away')

3. *Subject–Object*
        Kendall bath (6) ('Kendall takes a bath')
        Kendall shower ('Kendall takes a shower')
        Kendall book ('Kendall reads (looks at) a book')
        Kendall spider ('Kendall looked at a spider')
        doggie woof (3) ('doggie says woof') (alternatively, could be subject–verb)

4. *Subject–Verb–Object*
        Mommy..sew doggie
        Kimmy ride bike
        Kendall turn page
        Kimmy eat hand
        Mommy pick-up..Kendall
        Mommy fix-it..ear
        Mommy hit Kendall (reversal of subject and object: means 'Kendall
            hit Mommy')

5. *Modifier–Head*
    (a) Adj + N
        poor doggie (2)
        red Kendall (refers to a picture of *K* with a reddish cast)
        blue Mommy (refers to a picture of *M* with a bluish cast)
        big bed
        dear..horsie
        more lotion
    (b) N (genitive) + N
        Kendall rocking-chair (could also be interpreted as N + Adj + N)
        Kimmy bike
        papa door (2)
        Kendall turn
        Kimmy pail (3)
        Kendall pail

6. *Noun–Locative*
    (a) N + Loc
        Kendall bed ('Kendall is in bed')
        Kendall water

Kendall pool
lotion tummy
ear outside
towel bed (2)
Kendall innere
Kendall innere bed
Kendall down
mess here
pillow here
(*b*) Loc+N
there cow
here mess
7. *Verb–Locative*
play bed (2)
sit pool
sit here (2)
fell off
8. *Subject–Verb–Locative*
Ben swim pool
Kristin sit chair
Kendall play bed (2)
Kendall crying there
9. *Object–Verb–Locative*
Kimmy change here (2) ('change Kimmy here')
Kimmy kick there ('kick Kimmy there')
10. *Predicate Nominative*
that Kimmy (2)
that Scott
that lady
that hole
that. . candy
that Daddy's
that Kimmy ball
Mommy lady (response to 'what's Mommy?')
Daddy Shawn (response to 'what's Daddy?' *D*'s name is Shawn)
Kendall monkey (*M* has just said 'you're a monkey')
Kimmy monkey
boy, Kurt boy
11. *Predicate Adjective*
hair wet
12. *Conjunction*
Kimmy Phil (*K* looking at a picture of Kimmy and Phil)
13. *Wh question*
where doggie go? (3)
where pillow go?
14. *Negatives*
no page (*K* doesn't want *M* to turn page. Could be anaphoric, as in 'no, this page', or with an implied verb, as in 'no turn page')
no rabbit (*M* has just sat on toy rabbit. Could be anaphoric, as in 'no, (there's the) rabbit', or with an implied verb, as in 'no sit rabbit')
no Kimmy, no (reference unclear; Kimmy is not present)
no Kimmy (same context as above)

Daddy tail. .nope (*K* has been listing things which do have tails. Daddy
    does not)
Melissa carry room no bed (*K* upset when Melissa put tape recorder on
    her bed. Melissa has just said she would take it away)

15. *Miscellaneous and uninterpretable constructions*
    upside-down
    too red (imitation of *M*'s 'that's red too')
    Scott monkey too ('Scott is a monkey too')
    picture Kendall ('picture of Kendall')
    Kendall picture (same context as above)
    picture water ('picture of water')
    bless you, papa (routine from a book; *K* added the vocative)
    thank you much (3) (a routine)
    Kendall box (2) (*K* looking at picture of herself sitting on floor
        surrounded by Christmas boxes)
    birthday Kimmy (*K* remembering that Kimmy had a birthday party
        a month earlier)
    pail Kimmy (*K* looking at picture of *K*'s own pail; Kimmy not present)
    moon book (*K* looking at a book with a picture of the moon on one page)
    here moon book (same context as above)
    sita rabbit (*K* playing with toy rabbit. Meaning unclear)
    night night crib (reference unclear; no crib is present, and it is daytime)
    Melissa hand (*K* demonstrating how Melissa is holding her hands)
    see running (*K* looking at a picture of a man running)
    these pictures go (follows *M*'s 'where are these pictures?'
        Addition of 'go' probably influenced by *M*'s 'where', since *K* has
        Wh question routine 'Where N go?')
    Kendall out bed crib (reference unclear. *K* looking at picture of a bed)
    picture Mommy see Kendall (follows *M*'s 'did Daddy show you these
        pictures already?')

16. *Syntactic interpretation uncertain*
    Kendall birthday ('Kendall had a birthday' or 'Kendall's birthday')
    pig tail ('pig's tail' or 'pig has a tail')
    cow tail ('cow's tail' or 'cow has a tail')
    doggie hole (4) ('doggie's hole' or 'doggie has a hole')
    Kendall presents ('Kendall's presents' or 'Kendall got presents')
    Kendall dinner ('Kendall's dinner' or 'Kendall has dinner')
    Kendall book (2) ('Kendall looks at a book' or 'Kendall's book')
    Kendall doggie ('Kendall has a doggie' or 'Kendall's doggie')
    Kimmy doggie ('Kimmy has a doggie' or 'Kimmy's doggie')
    doggie pillow ('doggie's pillow' or 'doggie is on the pillow')
    Mommy kiss ('Mommy kisses' or 'kisses Mommy')
    that blow ('blow that' or 'that's (a picture of) blowing' – *K* looking
        at picture of Kimmy blowing out candles)
    Kimmy look-at Kimmy (2) (probably verb–object: 'look at Kimmy')
    Daddy read Kendall ('Daddy reads to Kendall' or 'Daddy reads with
        Kendall' – *K* looking at a picture of *D* and *K* looking at a book together)
    Kendall read Daddy (same context as above)
    water Ben ('Ben is in the water' or 'in the water with Ben')
    Kendall see Kendall (*K* looking at picture of herself. Could be
        subject–verb–subject, subject–verb–object, or object–verb–object)
    read Kendall ('Kendall reads' or 'read to Kendall')

Appendix D

Seppo, Mean Length of Utterance 1.42
Lexicon for the Transformational Generative Grammar

[+N]		[±animate][a] [±vehicle][a] f: type/token[b]		
isä	'father'	+	.	2/7
setä	'man, uncle'	+	.	4/4
tyttö	'girl'	.	.	1/1
täti	'lady, aunt'	+	.	6/7
vauva	'baby'	+	.	2/2
äiti	'mother'	+	.	7/9
ammu	'moo-cow'	.	.	1/1
ankka	'duck'	.	.	2/2
api⟨na⟩	'monkey'	+	.	2/3
fantti	'elephant'	+	.	2/3
hauva	'doggie'	+	.	4/5
humma	'horsie'	+	.	2/2
kala	'fish'	.	.	1/1
kissa	'cat'	+	.	2/2
nalle	'teddy bear'	+	.	3/3
nöf	"piggie"	+	.	2/2
pupu	'bunny'	+	.	10/14
tipu	'chick'	+	.	10/16
auto	'car'	.	+	5/5
bmbm	"car"	.	+	14/18
kan	"tractor"	.	.	2/2
kuorma⟨-auto⟩	'truck'	.	.	2/2
tuf tuf	"train"	.	.	6/6
kahvi	'coffee'	.	.	2/2
mamma	"food"	.	.	4/7
omena	'apple'	.	.	1/1

[a] Lexical items which are not marked positively for a syntactic feature should in general be considered negatively marked. Items are not marked positively for a feature unless in the sample on which the grammar is based they appear in contexts in which negatively marked items do not appear. However, a larger sample would probably reveal that additional words should be marked positively for certain features. For example, Seppo's *kala*, 'fish', could probably potentially appear in the contexts in which 'duck' or 'chick' appear, and so was also probably [+animate].

[b] Frequency figures indicate the number of constructions a word appears in. When a word is given two lexical entries, some occurrences of the word cannot be clearly assigned to either entry and so are not included in the count.

[244]

[+N] *(cont.)*		[±animate] [±vehicle]	f: type/token
piirakka	'pie'	. .	1/1
pulla	'coffee cake'	. .	1/1
ruoka	'food'	. .	1/1
vettä	'water'	. .	1/1
kenkä	'shoe'	. .	4/5
takki	'coat'	. .	3/3
kello	'clock'	. .	3/7
kirja	'book'	. .	1/1
kukka	'flower'	. .	1/1
lauta⟨nen⟩	'plate'	. .	1/1
pipi	'sore'	. .	1/1
puu	'tree'	. .	1/1
talli	'garage'	. .	4/4
talo	'house'	. .	1/1

[+V]		[±——(N)]	f: type/token
aa-aa	"sleeps"	.	6/6
ajaa	'drives'	+	11/14
avaa	'opens'	.	1/1
hakkaa	'pounds'	.	1/1
heittää	'throws'	.	1/3
itkee	'cries'	.	1/2
juo	'drinks'	+	1/1
katsoo	'watches, looks (at)'	.	1/2
kiinni	'(put) closed, fasten'	+	1/1
korjaa	'fixes, repairs'	.	1/1
kuorii	'peels'	.	1/1
kovaa	'(goes) fast'	.	4/5
kuti⟨ttaa⟩	'tickles'	.	3/3
käy	'goes'	.	2/3
laittaa	'prepares, fixes, sets up'	+	2/2
iaulaa	'sings'	.	3/4
leikkii	'plays'	.	1/1
lentää	'flies'	.	1/1
lukee	'reads'	.	2/4
pippaa	'injures'	.	1/1
pois	'(take) off, away'	+	3/4
pois	'(goes) away'	.	5/8
polttaa	'burns'	.	1/1
rake⟨ntaa⟩	'builds'	+	1/1
tanssii	'dances'	.	2/2
tuu	"blows horn"	.	1/1
uffuf	"dirty, naughty"	.	2/3
ui	'swims'	.	1/1
vetää	'pulls'	+	3/3

[+Adj]			f: type/token
pikku	'little'		1/1
rikki	'broken'		7/7

Not classified		f: type/token
hinaa	'tows'	1/1
hyppää	'jumps'	1/1
istuu	'sits'	1/1
kaikki	'all'	1/1
kukkuu	'yoo hoo'	1/2
meni	'went'	1/1
nami	'goody'	1/1
on	'is'	1/1
pamma	"closed"	10/10
taas	'again'	5/5
ulo⟨s⟩	'outside' (directional)	1/1

Appendix E

Seppo, Mean Length of Utterance 1.42
Constructions Generated by the Transformational
Generative Grammar[a]

1. *Subject–Verb*

äiti..avaa	'mother..opens'
äiti lukee (3)[b]	'mother reads'
isä itkee (2)	'father cries'
setä tuu	'man "blows horn"'
setä polttaa	'man burns'
setä tanssii	'man dances'
vauva aa-aa	'baby "sleeps"'
tipu laulaa (2)	'chick sings'
tipu katsoo (2)	'chick watches'
tipu..lentää	'chick..flies'
tipu..ui	'chick..swims'
tipu kuti⟨ttaa⟩	'chick tickles'
tipu pois (3)	'chick (goes) away'
pupu ajaa (2)	'bunny drives'
pupu heittää (3)	'bunny throws'
pupu leikkii	'bunny plays'
pupu..korjaa	'bunny..fixes'
hauva..pippaa	'doggie..injures'
hauva pois (2)	'doggie (goes) away'
kissa pois	'cat (goes) away'
ammu pois	'moo-cow (goes) away'
nöf pois	'"piggie" (goes) away'
nöf..hakkaa	'"piggie"..pounds'
fantti..lukee	'elephant..reads'
fantti uffuf (2)	'elephant naughty'
nalle aa-aa	'teddy bear "sleeps"'
humma aa-aa	'horsie "sleeps"'
bmbm..käy (2)	'"car"..goes'
bmbm kovaa (2)	'"car" (goes) fast'
auto auto auto..käy	'car car car..goes'

[a] A few constructions are included which contain a repeated word. Such repetitions are probably due to performance factors and are therefore not provided for by the grammar.

[b] Numbers in parentheses indicate the number of times the construction occurs in the sample. Numbers in parentheses preceded by 'T' indicate the transformation which must be applied to derive a construction pattern or a particular construction.

2. *Verb–Object*
   (a) V + N
     ajaa bmbm (2)   'drives "car"'
     rake⟨ntaa⟩..tuf tuf   'builds.."train"'
     laittaa..bmbm   'sets-up.."car"'
   (b) N + V (T 1 a)
     takki pois   'coat (take) off'
     kirja..pois   'book..(take) away'
     mamma pois (2)   '"food" (take) away'
     takki kiinni   'coat (put) closed, fasten'

3. *Subject–Object* (T 2)
     tipu mamma (2)   'chick "food"' (see p. 90)
     täti mamma (2)   'lady "food"' (see p. 90)
     humma kukka   'horsie flower' (see p. 90)

4. *Subject–Verb–Object*
     nalle ajaa..kan   'teddy bear drives.."tractor"'
     pupu ajaa bmbm (2)   'bunny drives "car"'
     kissa ajaa bmbm   'cat drives "car"'
     pupu ajaa tuf tuf   'bunny drives "train"'
     pupu laittaa bmbm   'bunny sets-up "car"'
     äiti juo kahvi   'mother drinks coffee'

5. *Modifier–Head*
   (a) Adj + N
     rikki..bmbm   'broken.."car"'
     pikku kala   'little fish'
   (b) N (genitive) + N
     täti auto   'aunt car'
     isä kello (5)   'father clock'
     setä kello   'man clock'

6. *Noun–Locative*
   (a) N + N
     auto talli   'car garage' (see p. 89)
     ankka vettä   'duck water' (see p. 89)
     ankka puu   'duck tree' (see p. 89)
     tipu kenkä (2)   'chick shoe' (see p. 89)
   (b) N + Proloc
     pipi tuossa   'sore there'
     tipu..tuossa   'chick..there'
   (c) Proloc + N (T 1 b)
     tuossa kenkä   'there shoe'
     tuossa ammu   'there moo-cow'
     tuossa..tuf tuf   'there.."train"'

7. *Syntactic interpretation uncertain*
     tyttö hauva   'girl dog' (genitive–noun or conjunction)
     täti..täti kahvi   'aunt..aunt coffee' (genitive–noun or subject–object)
     täti..vauva   'lady..baby' (genitive–noun or subject–object)

Appendix F

Seppo, Mean Length of Utterance 1.42
Single-word Utterances and their Frequencies of Occurrence

isä (3)	'father'	*kasvo⟨t⟩ (2)	'face' (lit. 'features')
*kam	"cowboy"		
setä (4)	'man, uncle'	*hattu (4)	'hat'
täti	'lady, aunt'	kenkä	'shoe'
tyttö (2)	'girl'	*käsi⟨neet⟩ (4)	'mittens'
vauva	'baby'	*paita	'shirt'
äiti (8)	'mother'	*saappa⟨at⟩ (3)	'boots'
		takki (14)	'coat'
ammu (8)	'moo-cow'		
ankka	'duck'	*pallo (2)	'ball'
api⟨na⟩ (12)	'monkey'	*paperi (2)	'paper'
fantti (8)	'elephant'	pipi (6)	'sore'
hauva (8)	'doggie'	*pyörä	'wheel, bicycle'
humma (15)	'horsie'	talli (7)	'garage'
kissa (6)	'cat'	talo (2)	'house'
*lintu	'bird'	*tutu	"horn"
nalle	'teddy bear'		
nöf	"piggie"	ajaa (5)	'drives'
pupu (8)	'bunny'	aa-aa (12)	"sleeps"
tipu (20)	'chick'	*hakee	'fetches, looks-for'
		heittää	'throws'
auto (6)	'car'	hyppää (8)	'jumps'
bmbm (2)	"car"	katsoo (2)	'watches, looks (at)'
kan (2)	"tractor"	kuti⟨ttaa⟩ (11)	'tickles'
kuorma⟨-auto⟩	'truck'	käy (4)	'goes'
*lentokone (8)	'airplane'	laittaa (2)	'makes, prepares, sets up'
tuf tuf (20)	"train"		
		laulaa	'sings'
kahvi	'coffee'	leikkii	'plays'
mamma (7)	"food"	lentää (2)	'flies'
omena	'apple'	lukee	'reads'
pulla (5)	'coffee cake'	pippaa (2)	'injures'
ruoka (2)	'food'	pois (20)	'away, off'
*sokeri	'sugar'	polttaa	'burns'
vettä	'water'	rake⟨ntaa⟩	'builds'
		tanssii (3)	'dances'
*hampa⟨at⟩ (2)	'teeth'	uffuf	"dirty, naughty"
*käsi	'hand'	ui (5)	'swims'
*tukka	'hair'		

* Starred words occur only in single-word utterances.

*korkea	'high'
rikki (4)	'broken'
*tuolla	'(over) there'
tuossa (10)	'(right) there'
*ei (3)	'no'
*hau hau	'bow wow'
*kiitos	'thank you'
*kipi kapi (2)	(sound effect to indicate walking)
*mnaa (2)	(idiosyncratic signal to request a drink)
*no (7)	'no' (English)
pamma (15)	"closed"
taas	'again'
*tip tip tip	(sound used to call chickens)
*ui ui (4)	'oh, oh'

Appendix G

Seppo, Mean Length of Utterance 1.42

Constructions not Generated by the Transformational

Generative Grammar

Forty-eight construction types (51 tokens) in the sample are not accounted for by the grammar. These include:

Nine constructions which express grammatical relations in a different order from that provided for by the grammar. Most of these could have been generated by extending the scope of the reordering transformations. See 4.3.4 for a discussion of the reason this was not done.

1. *pois api⟨na⟩*	'away monkey'	(verb–subject)
2. *laulaa tipu*	'sings chick'	(verb–subject)
3. *kuorii äiti*	'peels mother'	(verb-subject)
4. *kovaa kovaa*	'(goes) fast fast	
kovaa kovaa..bmbm	fast fast.."car"'	(verb–subject)
5. *auto vetää*	'car pulls'	(object–verb)
6. *bmbm pupu ajaa*	'"car" bunny drives'	(object–subject–verb)
7. *hauva..tädi(n)*	'doggie..lady('s)'	(noun–genitive)
8. *talli..bmbm*	'garage.."car"'	(locative–noun)
9. *ulo⟨s⟩ takki*	'to-outside coat'	(locative–noun)

Three constructions in which one word occurs both before and after another word:

10. *rikki..auto..rikki*	'broken..car..broken'	(modifier–head–modifier)
11. *rikki bmbm rikki*	'broken "car" broken'	(modifier–head–modifier)
12. *kuorma..talli..kuorma*	'truck..garage..truck'	(noun–locative–noun)

One construction with an inanimate noun functioning as sentence-subject with a word classified as a verb in Seppo's lexicon. The grammar allows only animate nouns to appear in such contexts.

13. *mamma uffuf..uffuf*	'"food" "dirty".."dirty"'

Four constructions with vocatives (involving clear vocative intonation):

14. *äiti, pulla*	'mother, coffee cake'
15. *äiti, tuf tuf*	'mother, "train"'
16. *api⟨na⟩, kukkuu* (2)	'monkey, yoo hoo'
17. *äiti, taas taas*	'mother, again again'

[251]

Two instances of possible locative phrases:

18. *pois talli*	'away garage'	(*S* has been talking about a broken car. *M* interprets this as *pois talliin*, 'away garage-into', meaning that the car will go away into a garage)
19. *lauta..pois*	'plate..away'	(*S* looking at picture of bird on plate. May mean that bird will fly off of plate: *lautaselta pois*, 'plate-from away', or 'off of plate'. *Lautanen* is the nom. sing. form of 'plate', and *lautase-* is the inflectable stem)

Two constructions which are probably object–verb and verb–object respectively, but which are not generated because *rikki*, 'broken', is classified as an adjective rather than as a noun (it is an adverb in adult Finnish):

20. *rikki vetää*	'broken pulls'	(*S* looking at picture of tow truck towing broken car)
21. *hinaa rikki rikki*	'tows broken broken'	(same context as above)

Twelve constructions with unique structural pattern. No conclusions about the productivity of these patterns could be drawn.

22. *kenkä kuti⟨ttaa⟩*	'shoe tickles'	(in response to *missä kutittaa*, 'where (does it) tickle?' *S* looking at picture of bird sitting on a boy's bare foot)
23. *on tädi*	'is aunt'	(*S* touching *B*'s tape recorder. Form of 'aunt' is appropriate for inflection, but a genitive -*n* is lacking)
24. *nam..piirakka*	'"goody"..pie'	(reversed imitation of *M*'s *piirakka nanna*, 'pie goody')
25. *tanssii hyppää tanssii*	'dances jumps dances'	(*S* looking at picture of people dancing)
26. *tuossa pois* (2)	'there away'	(no apparent reference. Perhaps word play)
27. *pois taas pois*	'away again away'	
28. *pois taas pois taas pois*	'away again away again away'	
29. *taas..pois..taas*	'again..away..again'	
30. *taas pois taas pois* (2)	'again away again away'	(27–30 were produced consecutively. No apparent reference. Perhaps word play)

31. *ajaa..bm..kovaa kovaa*   'drives.."car"..fast fast fast drives'
     kovaa ajaa

32. *bmbm..rikki..meni*   '"car"..broken..went' (grammatically correct. Probably a memorized routine. *Auto rikki meni*, 'car broken went', occurs often in *M*'s speech)

33. *tää kello*   'this clock'   (*S* and *M* looking at picture of a clock. The *tää* may have been a phonological·'accident' of some sort instead of a real word, since it was pronounced strangely ([tæ?] instead of [tæ:]) and neither it nor any other demonstrative pronoun occurred in the tapes for several months past the sample)

Fifteen constructions with uninterpretable syntactic structures:

34. *nalle..kan..aa-aa*   'teddy bear.."tractor".."sleeps"' (*S* looking at picture of bear driving a tractor. Follows *M*'s *nalle ajaa traktoria*, 'bear drives tractor'. Possibly a confusion between *ajaa* and *aa-aa*)

35. *talo..kovaa tuf tuf*   'house..(goes) fast "train"' (*S* looking at picture of house, with train in background)

36. *rikki..aa-aa..kaikki*   'broken.."sleeps"..all' (*S* has been talking about towing broken cars away to a garage. Probably means that the cars will sleep in the garage)

37. *pupu..pamma..tuf tuf*   'bunny.."closed"..   (*S* looking at picture in
     ..pois   "train"..away'   which there is a train and many animals doing different things)

38. *kuorma pamma..ajaa*   'truck"closed"..drives' (*S* looking at picture of steam roller)

39. *pupu laulaa..pamma*   'bunny sings.."closed"' (*S* looking at picture of a rabbit's face on a TV screen)

40. *pamma rikki rikki*   '"closed" broken broken' (*S* looking at picture of rabbit with electric train. *M* has just said 'he's preparing the train to go')

41. *ajaa..pamma..pamma*   'drives.."closed" "closed"' (*S* playing with toy car)

42. *pamma..ajaa*   '"closed"..drives'   (*S* playing with toy car)

43. *pamma bmbm*	'"closed" "car"'	(*S* trying to turn page away from pictures of cars)
44. *kovaa..pam*	'fast.."closed"'	(*S* playing with fire engine; making loud noises to indicate how fast it is going)
45. *pois..pamma*	'away.."closed"'	(*S* closing book)
46. *kuti⟨ttaa⟩ tuossa kenkä*	'tickles there shoe'	('Shoe' either locative or direct object)
47. *vetää..qa-aa*	'pulls.."sleeps"'	(*S* looking at picture of mother cat pushing baby cat in a carriage)
48. *istuu..ruoka*	'sits..food'	(*S* pointing to picture of bear sitting at table with empty plate in front of him)

Appendix H

Seppo, Mean Length of Utterance 1.81
Lexicon for the Transformational Generative Grammar

[+N, −pronoun]		[±animate]^a	[±vehicle]^a	f: type/token^b
Ari	'Ari'	+	.	4/4
Batman	'Batman'	+	.	3/3
Immi	'Immi'	+	.	4/4
isi	'daddy'	+	.	8/9
Laila	'Laila'	+	.	4/6
nukke	'doll'	.	.	1/1
peikko	'dwarf'	+	.	4/4
Pinocchio	'Pinocchio'	+	.	1/1
poika	'boy'	+	.	5/5
Robin	'Robin'	.	.	2/2
setä	'man, uncle'	+	.	8/17
täti	'lady, aunt'	+	.	7/8
ukko	'old man'	+	.	3/3
vauva	'baby'	+	.	5/6
äiti	'mother'	+	.	15/18
ammu	'moo-cow'	+	.	3/3
ankka	'duck'	.	.	1/1
apina	'monkey'	+	.	11/12
Bambi	'Bambi'	+	.	1/1
fantti	'elephant'	+	.	8/9
hauva	'doggie'	+	.	5/13
hiiri	'mouse'	+	.	18/20
kala	'fish'	+	.	6/6
karhu	'bear'	.	.	1/1
kissa	'cat'	+	.	6/8
kuak-kuak	"duck"	+	.	3/3
lintu	'bird'	+	.	5/6
nalle	'teddy bear'	.	.	2/2
possu	'piggie'	+	.	7/11
pupu	'bunny'	+	.	4/4
pöllö	'owl'	+	.	1/1
tipu	'chick'	+	.	1/1
auto	'car'	.	+	8/11
bmbm	"car"	.	+	1/1
helikopteri	'helicopter'	.	+	1/1

$^{a, b}$ See footnotes, Appendix D.

[255]

[+N, −pronoun] *(cont.)*		[±animate]	[±vehicle]	f: type/token
hinaus-auto	'tow truck'	.	+	1/1
kone	'machine'	.	.	1/1
laiva	'ship'	.	+	3/3
lento⟨kone⟩	'airplane'	.	.	1/1
loikka	"Volkswagen"	.	.	2/3
palo-auto	'fire engine'	.	+	5/7
pyörä	'wheel, bicycle'	.	.	2/2
rekka-auto	'trailer truck'	.	+	1/2
traktori	'tractor'	.	.	5/6
tuf tuf	"train"	.	+	1/1
hillo	'jam'	.	.	1/1
kahvi	'coffee'	.	.	1/1
keksi	'cracker'	.	.	1/1
omena	'apple'	.	.	1/1
porkana	'carrot'	.	.	1/1
ruoka	'food'	.	.	1/1
vettä	'water'	.	.	2/3
hattu	'hat'	.	.	2/2
kengä⟨t⟩	'shoes'	.	.	2/2
saappaa⟨t⟩	'boots'	.	.	1/1
takki	'coat'	.	.	1/1
häntä	'tail'	.	.	4/4
jalka	'foot, leg'	.	.	2/2
tukka	'hair'	.	.	1/1
avain	'key'	.	.	7/10
hiekka	'sand'	.	.	1/1
jää	'ice'	.	.	1/1
kaappi	'cupboard'	.	.	1/1
kassi	'bag'	.	.	2/4
kauppa	'store'	.	.	1/1
kirja	'book'	.	.	1/1
kivi	'stone'	.	.	2/2
koti	'home'	.	.	5/5
koulu	'school'	.	.	1/1
lanka⟨rulla⟩	'spool'	.	.	3/3
lattia	'floor'	.	.	2/2
laukku	'suitcase'	.	.	1/2
lumi	'snow'	.	.	1/1
nappi	'button'	.	.	4/5
pipi	'sore'	.	.	3/4
posti	'mail'	.	.	1/1
purkki	'can'	.	.	1/1
pussi	'bag'	.	.	1/1
ruoho	'grass'	.	.	2/2
savi	'mud'	.	.	2/2
talli	'garage'	.	.	1/1
talo	'house'	.	.	2/2
torni	'tower'	.	.	1/1
tuoli	'chair'	.	.	2/2

[+N, +pronoun]		[±——{V/N}]	f: type/token
lisää	'more'	.	2/4
sitä	'it' (partitive)	.	1/1
tämä	'this' (nominative)	+	2/2
tää	'this' (nominative)	.	1/1
tätä	'this' (partitive)	.	2/2
tämmö⟨nen⟩	'this-kind-of-thing' (see p. 126)	.	4/5

[+V]		[±——(NP)]	[±——[+animate]]	[±——[−animate, −vehicle]]	[±——[+directional]]	f: type/token
ajaa	'drives'	+	.	.	.	12/20
antaa	'gives'	.	.	.	.	1/1
asuu	'lives'	.	.	.	.	1/1
avaa	'opens'	.	.	.	.	1/1
etsii	'looks-for'	.	.	.	.	1/1
hakee	'fetches, looks-for'	+	+	.	.	3/3
hakkaa	'pounds'	.	.	.	.	1/1
haukkuu	'barks'	.	.	.	.	1/2
istuu	'sits'	.	.	.	+	4/4
itkee	'cries'	.	.	.	.	1/1
juo	'drinks'	+	.	.	.	1/1
juoksee	'runs'	.	.	.	.	2/2
kaatuu	'falls-down'	.	.	+	.	2/2
kastuu	'gets-wet'	.	.	.	.	1/1
katsoo	'watches, looks (at)'	.	.	.	.	1/1
kiipee	'climbs'	.	.	.	.	2/3
korjaa	'fixes, repairs'	.	.	.	.	2/3
kovaa	'(goes) fast'	.	.	.	.	1/1
kuorii	'peels'	+	.	.	.	1/1
kuti⟨ttaa⟩	'tickles'	.	.	.	.	2/2
käve⟨lee⟩	'walks'	.	.	.	.	6/6
laittaa	'prepares, fixes'	.	.	.	.	4/5
leikkii	'plays'	.	.	.	.	3/4
lentää	'flies'	.	.	.	.	1/1
lähtee	'leaves'	.	.	.	.	2/3
menee	'goes'	.	.	+	+	4/4
meni	'went'	.	.	+	+	3/4
nostaa	'lifts, picks up'	+	.	.	.	3/3
näyttää	'shows'	.	.	.	.	1/3

[+V] (cont.)		[±——(NP)]	[±——[+animate]]	[±——[−animate, −vehicle]——]	[±——[+directional]——]	f: type/token
odottaa	'waits'	·	·	·	·	3/3
ottaa	'takes'	·	·	·	·	2/2
paistaa	'bakes'	+	·	·	·	1/1
pelaa	'plays (a game)'	·	·	·	·	5/5
pelä⟨styy⟩	'is-afraid'	·	·	·	·	1/1
piirtää	'draws'	+	+	·	+	8/9
piirsi	'drew'	·	·	·	+	1/1
pois	'(goes) away'	·	·	·	·	3/9
pois	'(take) away'	+	+	·	·	2/2
puhuu	'speaks, talks'	·	·	·	·	2/2
putoo	'falls'	·	·	·	+	4/6
pysähtyy	'stops'	·	·	·	·	1/1
rake⟨ntaa⟩	'builds'	+	·	·	·	1/1
rikkoo	'breaks'	·	·	·	·	1/1
siivoo	'cleans'	·	·	·	·	1/1
soittaa	'plays (an instrument)'	·	·	·	·	1/1
syö	'eats'	+	+	·	·	15/19
syödään	'eat' (impersonal)	+	·	·	·	2/2
tekee	'does, makes'	·	·	·	·	1/1
toi	'brought'	+	·	·	·	1/1
tulee	'comes'	·	·	·	·	4/9
tuli	'came'	·	·	+	·	3/3
työntää	'pushes'	+	+	·	·	2/2
uffuf	"dirty, naughty"	·	·	·	·	1/1
ui	'swims'	·	·	·	·	6/6
vetää	'pulls'	+	·	·	·	15/20
viedään	'take' (impersonal)	·	·	·	·	1/1

[+Adj]		f: type/token
iso	'big'	6/7
kaikki	'all'	2/2
kiltti	'nice, good'	4/4
pikku	'little'	5/5
toinen	'other, another'	1/1
rikki	'broken'	7/8
yksi	'one'	1/2
Batman	'Batman'	1/1
auto	'car'	1/2
äiti	'mother'	1/1

[+Adj](*cont.*)		f: type/token
setä	'man'	1/1
soti⟨las⟩	'soldier'	1/1
vauva	'baby'	1/1

[+Proloc]		[±directional]	f: type/token
tuossa	'(right) there'	.	21/22
tässä	'(right) here'	.	2/2
siinä	'(right) there'	.	22/26
siellä	'(over) there'	.	3/3
tuohon	'to (right) there'	+	7/7
tuonne	'to (over) there'	+	1/1
siihen	'to (right) there'	+	1/1
sinne	'to (over) there'	+	7/7
ala⟨s⟩	'downward'	+	1/1

[+Adv]		f: type/token
kauhe⟨sti⟩	'terribly'	2/2
kohta	'soon'	6/10
kovaa	'fast'	1/1
noin	'like-that'	1/1
nyt	'now'	6/9
sitten	'then'	1/1
vielä	'still, yet'	3/3

Not classified		f: type/token
ei	'no, not'	2/2
hei	'hey, hello, goodbye'	2/2
hinaa	'tows'	1/1
ihan	'completely'	1/1
illa⟨lla⟩	'at night'	1/1
kiinni	'closed'	2/2
loppu	'finished'	2/2
mennyt	'gone'	1/1
mukaa⟨n⟩	'with' (directional)	1/1
ole	'is' (form used with negative verb)	1/1
oli	'was' (3rd sing.)	1/1
ollaan	'is' (impersonal)	1/1
oma	'own'	1/1
pamma	"closed"	1/1
pestään	'wash' (impersonal)	1/1
please	'please' (English)	1/1
päälle	'on, over' (directional)	1/2
päässä	'on (the) head'	1/1
satu	'happen' (form used with negative verb)	1/1
tuosta	'from-there'	1/1
täällä	'(over) here'	1/1
uimaan	'to-swimming' (directional)	1/1
äkki⟨ä⟩	'suddenly'	1/1

Appendix I

Seppo, Mean Length of Utterance 1.81
Constructions Generated by the Transformational
Generative Grammar [a]

1. *Subject–Verb*
   (a) N + V

äiti avaa	'mother opens'
äiti laittaa	'mother prepares (fixes, sets up)'
äiti ajaa	'mother drives'
äiti työntää	'mother pushes'
äiti näyttää (3)[b]	'mother shows'
äiti uffuf	'mother "naughty"'
isi laittaa (2)	'daddy prepares (fixes, sets up)'
Immi..laittaa	'Immi..prepares (fixes, sets up)'
Immi piirtää	'Immi draws'
Laila piirtää (2)	'Laila draws'
Ari rikkoo	'Ari breaks'
täti ottaa	'aunt takes'
täti..etsii	'aunt..looks-for'
setä ajaa (4)	'man drives'
setä korjaa (2)	'man fixes'
setä laittaa	'man prepares (fixes, sets up)'
setä pois (6)	'man (goes) away'
vauva käve⟨lee⟩	'baby walks'
vauva kiipee (2)	'baby climbs'
peikko katsoo	'dwarf watches (looks)'
peikko käve⟨lee⟩	'dwarf walks'
Batman pois	'Batman (goes) away'
Robin istuu	'Robin sits'
Pinocchio soittaa	'Pinocchio plays (an instrument)'
fantti puhuu	'elephant talks'
fantti ui	'elephant swims'
fantti kiipee	'elephant climbs'
fantti ajaa (2)	'elephant drives'
fantti pelaa	'elephant plays (a game)'

[a] Included are a few constructions which contain repeated words or vocatives, and two which seem to consist of two constructions run together without a break in intonation. These constructions are not, strictly speaking, generated by the grammar, but are closely related to those that are.

[b] Numbers in parentheses indicate the number of times the construction occurs in the sample. Numbers in parentheses preceded by 'T' indicate the transformation(s) which must be applied to derive a construction pattern or a particular construction.

hiiri syö (2)	'mouse eats'
hiiri leikkii (2)	'mouse plays'
hiiri odottaa	'mouse waits'
hiiri itkee	'mouse cries'
hiiri pelä⟨styy⟩	'mouse is-afraid'
hauva haukkuu (2)	'doggie barks'
hauva tulee (6)	'doggie comes'
hauva syö (2)	'doggie eats'
api⟨na⟩ pelaa	'monkey plays (a game)'
api⟨na⟩ juoksee	'monkey runs'
pupu tekee	'bunny makes'
pupu siivoo	'bunny cleans'
possu antaa	'piggie gives'
possu ajaa (4)	'piggie drives'
kuak-kuak..puhuu	'"duck"..talks'
pöllö ajaa	'owl drives'
kala syö	'fish eats'
tipu..syö	'chick..eats'
ammu..syö	'moo-cow..eats'
ammu..vetää	'moo-cow..pulls'
kissa (leikkii)	'cat (plays)'
kissa putoo (2)	'cat falls'
laiva vetää	'ship pulls'
auto lähtee	'car leaves'
helikopteri lentää	'helicopter flies'
rekka-auto pois (2)	'trailer truck (goes) away'
palo-auto..nostaa nostaa, äiti	'fire engine..lifts lifts, mother'
lanka menee	'spool goes'
torni kaatuu	'tower falls-down'
tämä tuli	'this came'
(b) Adj+N+V	
kiltti täti..käve⟨lee⟩	'nice lady..walks'
iso api⟨na⟩ tulee	'big monkey comes'
setä poika ajaa	'man boy drives'
vauva kuak..käve⟨lee⟩	'baby "duck"..walks'
(c) V+N (T 1d)	
tulee poika	'comes boy'
hakkaa isi	'pounds daddy'
vetää lintu	'pulls bird'
ui..api⟨na⟩	'swims..monkey'
kastuu api⟨na⟩	'gets-wet monkey'
odottaa..hiiri	'waits..mouse'
vetää tuf	'pulls "train"'
vetää hinaus-auto	'pulls tow truck'
tuli auto	'came car'
(d) V+Adj+N (T 1d)	
pysähtyy..rikki auto	'stops..broken car'
2. *Verb–Object*	
(a) V+N	
rake⟨ntaa⟩..talo	'builds..house'
syö lisää (3)	'eats more'
(b) V+Adj+N	
nostaa..iso kivi	'lifts..big stone'

(c) N + V (T 1*c*)

peikko hakee	'dwarf fetches'
kivi nostaa	'stone lifts'
kahvi juo	'coffee drinks'
porka⟨na⟩ kuorii	'carrot peels'
laiva hakee	'ship fetches'
tämmö syö (2)	'this-kind-of-thing eats'
tätä vetää	'this (partitive) pulls'

3. *Subject–Object* (T 2)

hiiri omena	'mouse apple' (see p. 98)
hiiri tämmö	'mouse this-kind-of-thing' (see p. 99)
täti kissa	'aunt cat' (see p. 97)
kissa, täti kissa	'cat, aunt cat' (see p. 97)

4. *Subject–Verb–Object*
   (a) N + V + N

äiti työntää vauva	'mother pushes baby'
setä ajaa..trakto⟨ri⟩	'man drives..tractor'
possu ajaa pyörä	'piggie drives bicycle'

   (b) N + N + V (T 1*c*)

äiti..ruoka..paistaa	'mother..food..bakes'
isi sitä toi	'daddy it brought'
isi tätä toi	'daddy this brought'
setä..kone..ajaa	'man..machine..drives'
hiiri..tämmö syö	'mouse..this-kind-of-thing eats'

5. *Modifier–Head*
   (a) Adj + N

pikku kala	'little fish'
pikku (kissa)	'little (cat)'
pikku traktori (2)	'little tractor'
pikku nalle	'little teddy bear'
kiltti täti	'nice lady'
kaikki ankka	'all duck'
toinen laiva	'another ship'
iso traktori	'big tractor'
yksi laukku (2)	'one suitcase'
rikki auto	'broken car'
rikki auto auto auto auto	'broken car car car car'
Batman setä	'Batman man'
soti⟨las⟩ nukke	'soldier doll'
äiti fantti	'mother elephant'
auto avain (2)	'car key'

   (b) N(genitive) + N

Ari palo⟨-auto⟩	'Ari fire ⟨engine⟩'
possu saappaa⟨t⟩	'piggie boots'
possu hattu	'piggie hat'
peikko tukka	'dwarf hair'
äiti nappi (2)	'mother button'
äiti tuoli	'mother chair'
Immi tuoli	'Immi chair'
hiiri..häntä	'mouse..tail'

hauva häntä   'doggie tail'

6. *Noun–Locative*
   (a) N+N
      poika savi   'boy mud'
      kengä⟨t⟩ savi   'shoes mud'
      kengä⟨t⟩ jalka   'shoes foot'
      lento⟨kone⟩ talli   'airplane garage'
   (b) N+Proloc
      Robin tuossa   'Robin there'
      karhu tuossa   'bear there'
      possu tuossa   'piggie there'
      api⟨na⟩ siinä   'monkey there'
      fantti siinä   'elephant there'
      Batman siinä   'Batman there'
      Ari siinä   'Ari there'
      Laila siinä (2)   'Laila there'
      palo⟨-auto⟩ siinä   'fire ⟨engine⟩ there'
      hillo siinä   'jam there'
      vettä siinä (2)   'water there'
      Robin..tässä   'Robin..here'
      pussi siellä   'bag there'
      äiti siellä   'mother there'
      avain..tuonne   'key..to-there' (T 2)
      avain sinne   'key to-there' (T 2)
      pupu alas alas   'bunny downward downward' (T 2)
   (c) M+N+Proloc
      täti nappi sinne   'aunt button to-there' (T2)
   (d) Proloc+N (T 1a)
      tuossa kala   'there fish'
      tuossa kissa   'there cat'
      tuossa nalle   'there teddy bear'
      tuossa loikka   'there "Volkswagen"'
      tuossa api⟨na⟩ (2)   'there monkey'
      tuossa palo-auto (2)   'there fire engine'
      tuossa auto palo-auto   'there engine fire engine'
      tuossa tuossa..lintu   'there there..bird'
      siinä Batman   'there Batman'
      siinä koti   'there home'
      siinä..lintu (2)   'there..bird'
   (e) Proloc+Adj+N (T 1a)
      tässä pikku traktori   'here little tractor'

7. *Verb–Locative*
   (a) V+N
      viedään kauppa   'take (impersonal) store'
   (b) V+Proloc
      ui tuossa   'swims there'
      pelaa..tuossa   'plays (a game)..there'
      kaatuu siinä   'falls-down there'
      putoo siinä (2)   'falls there'
      tulee..siinä   'comes..there'
      putoo sinne   'falls to-there'
      piirtää tuohon   'draws to-there'

   (*c*) N+V (T 1*c*)

talo asuu	'house lives'

   (*d*) Proloc+V (T 1*c*)

tuossa pelaa	'there plays (a game)'
tuossa kuti⟨ttaa⟩	'there tickles'

8. *Subject–Verb–Locative*
   (*a*) N+V+N (or Proloc)

pupu käve⟨lee⟩ hiekka	'bunny walks sand'
ammu..käve⟨lee⟩ ruoho	'moo-cow..walks grass'
hiiri syö lattia	'mouse eats floor'
bmbm kovaa koti	'"car" (goes) fast home'
Bambi..leikkii siellä	'Bambi..plays there'
isi ajaa siinä	'daddy drives there'
äiti istuu siinä	'mother sits there'
fantti istuu siihen	'elephant sits to-there'
Laila piirsi tuohon	'Laila drew to-there'
poika piirtää tuohon	'boy draws to-there'
lanka menee tuohon	'spool goes to-there'

   (*b*) N+N (or Proloc)+V (T 1*c*)

hiiri lattia syö	'mouse floor eats'
isi siinä ajaa	'daddy there drives'
kissa..siinä..putoo	'cat..there..falls'
Immi tuohon piirtää	'Immi to-there draws'
api⟨na⟩ sinne..istuu	'monkey to-there..sits'

   (*c*) Proloc+V+N (T 1*b*, 1*d*)

tuossa ui..api⟨na⟩	'there swims..monkey'
sinne meni (avain)	'to-there went (key)'

   (*d*) V+N+Proloc (T 1*d*)

menee nappi tuohon tuohon	'goes button to-there to-there'

   (*e*) Proloc+N+V (T 1*b*)

siinä kala ui	'there fish swims'

9. *Verb–Adverb*
   (*a*) V+Adv

vetää kohta (4)	'pulls soon'
lähtee kohta (2)	'leaves soon'
vetää vielä	'pulls still'

   (*b*) Adv+V (T 1*c*)

kohta vetää	'soon pulls'
kohta piirtää	'soon draws'
nyt vetää (4)	'now pulls'
noin syö	'like-that eats'

10. *Subject–Verb–Adverb*
   (*a*) N+V+Adv

api⟨na⟩ juoksee kovaa	'monkey runs fast'
hiiri syö kauhe⟨sti⟩ kauhe⟨sti⟩	'mouse eats terribly terribly'

   (*b*) Adv+N+V (T 1*b*)

nyt hiiri syö	'now mouse eats'
(nyt) lanka tuli	'(now) spool came'

11. *Verb–Object–Adverb*
   (*a*) Adv+N+V (T 1*b*, 1*c*)

nyt avain vetää	'now key pulls'

   sitten..ukko pois   'then..old-man (take) away'
   kohta ukko pois   'soon old-man (take) away'
  (*b*) N+V+Adv (T 1*c*)
   auto..hakee (nyt)   'car..fetches (now)'

12. *Predicate Nominative*
   tämä kala   'this fish'

13. *Predicate Adjective*
   auto rikki   'car broken'
   kala..iso   'fish..big'
   kuak-kuak iso   '"duck" big'
   täti kiltti   'aunt nice'
   äiti kiltti   'mother nice'

14. *Wh–Loc+(Modifier+) Noun* or *Verb* (See also Appendix K)
   missä loikka? (2)   'where "Volkswagen"?'
   missä kassi? (3)   'where bag?'
   missä purkki?   'where can?'
   missä lintu?   'where bird?'
   missä keksi?   'where cracker?'
   missä avain?   'where key?'
   missä auto? (2)   'where car?'
   missä missä kaikki kirja? 'where where all book?'
   missä vetää? (2)   'where pulls?'
   missä ui?   'where swims?'
   missä kuti⟨ttaa⟩?   'where tickles?'

15. *Neg+Noun* or *Verb* (See also Appendix K)
   enää palo⟨-auto⟩   'any more fire ⟨engine⟩'
   enää pipi   'any more sore'
   enää pelaa   'any more plays (a game)'
   enää vetää   'any more pulls'

16. *Conjoined sentences*
   no (ei)..syö vielä   'no (no)..eats still' (sense is 'no, he
                is still eating')
   setä nyt korjaa enää rikki 'man now fixes any more broken'

17. *Syntactic interpretation uncertain*
   vetää..pyörä   'pulls..wheel' (verb–subject or
                verb–object)

Appendix J

Seppo, Mean Length of Utterance 1.81
Single-word Utterances and their Frequencies of Occurrence

Ari	'Ari'	kengä⟨t⟩ (2)	'shoes'
Batman (2)	'Batman'	häntä	'tail'
Immi	'Immi'	*käsi	'hand'
isi	'daddy'		
Laila (3)	'Laila'	avain (3)	'key'
nukke	'doll'	hiekka	'sand'
peikko (2)	'dwarf'	kassi (2)	'bag'
setä (2)	'man, uncle'	*keinu (2)	'swing'
täti (5)	'lady, aunt'	kirja (2)	'book'
äiti (4)	'mother'	koti (4)	'home'
äidin	'mother's'	*kukka	'flower'
		*kunto	'order'
ammu	'moo-cow'	laukku	'suitcase'
api⟨na⟩ (5)	'monkey'	*maali (3)	'paint'
fantti	'elephant'	*naama⟨ri⟩	'mask'
hauva (3)	'doggie'	nappi (2)	'button'
hiiri (10)	'mouse'	*nälkä (3)	'hunger'
*humma	'horsie'	*pallo (2)	'ball'
kala (4)	'fish'	*piilo	'hiding-place'
kissa (3)	'cat'	*pilli (3)	'whistle'
kuak-kuak	"duck"	*rahaa	'money'
*lammas (6)	'sheep'	ruoho	'grass'
lintu (4)	'bird'	talli	'garage'
nalle (2)	'teddy bear'		
possu (2)	'piggie'	lisää (22)	'more'
pupu (4)	'bunny'	*se	'it' (nominative)
pöllö (4)	'owl'	tämmö⟨nen⟩	'this-kind-of-thing'
		tätä	'this' (partitive)
auto (2)	'car'		
laiva (5)	'ship'	hakee	'fetches, looks-for'
lentokone (2)	'airplane'	hinaa (3)	'tows'
loikka	"Volkswagen"	istuu	'sits'
*mooto⟨ripyörä⟩ (2)	'motocycle'	kastuu (4)	'gets-wet'
palo-auto (7)	'fire engine'	*kato (2)	'look' (imperative)
traktori	'tractor'	*keittää (2)	'cooks'
		kiipee	'climbs'
*banaa⟨ni⟩	'banana'	kovaa	'(goes) fast'
kahvi (2)	'coffee'	käve⟨lee⟩	'walks'
keksi (2)	'cracker'	*kääntää	'turns'
*mamma	"food"	*laulaa (4)	'sings'

* Starred words appear only in single-word utterances.

[266]

lentää	'flies'
lähtee (2)	'leaves'
*ompe⟨lee⟩	'sews'
pelaa	'plays (a game)'
pestään (2)	'wash' (impersonal)
piirtää	'draws'
pois	'away'
putoo (3)	'falls'
soittaa	'plays (an instrument)'
syö (5)	'eats'
*tanssii	'dances'
tuli (2)	'came'
uffuf (4)	"dirty, naughty"
ui (2)	'swims'
*väli⟨ttää⟩ (2)	'cares-about'
vetää (8)	'pulls'

kiltti	'nice, good'
*korkea	'high'
rikki (2)	'broken'
toinen (2)	'other, another'

*kaua⟨s⟩	'far' (directional)
siellä	'(over) there'
siinä (4)	'(right) there'
sinne (6)	'to over there'
tuohon (3)	'to (right) there'
*tuolla	'(over) there'
tuossa (21)	'(right) there'
tässä	'(right) here'
*ulos	'to-outside'

enää	'any more'
hei (5)	'hey, hello, goodbye'
ihan	'completely'
loppu (4)	'finished'
missä (2)	'where'
*mitä (4)	'what' (partitive)
*no (14)	'no' (English)
pamma	"closed"
please	'please'
*päivää	'hello'
*taas	'again'

Repeated words

api⟨na⟩ api⟨na⟩	'monkey monkey'
*laulaa laulaa	'sings sings'
lisää lisää	'more more'
*no no	'no no' (English)
piirtää piirtää	'draws draws'
*ui ui ui	'oh oh oh'

Appendix K

Seppo, Mean Length of Utterance 1.81
Constructions not Generated by the Transformational
Generative Grammar

Forty-nine construction types (53 tokens) in the sample are not accounted for by the grammar. These include:

Four constructions which express grammatical relations in a different order from that provided for by the grammar. (1) and (2) are probably 'mistakes', but (3) and (4) may represent productive but infrequently employed patterns.

1. *auto missä?*	'car where?'	
2. *kaappi..Ari*	'cupboard..Ari'	(noun–genitive. In response to 'from-where did Seppo take the pen, from-where?')
3. *odottaa siinä..hiiri*	'waits there..mouse'	(verb–locative–subject)
4. *koti syödään kohta*	'home eat soon'	(locative–verb–adverb. Verb is in impersonal form; could be translated as 'one-eats', or, colloquially, 'we-eat')

One construction in which the same word occurs both before and after another word:

5. *piirtää Laila piirtää*	'draws Laila draws'	(verb–subject–verb)

Two constructions which are probably object–verb and object–adverb–verb respectively, but which are not generated because *rikki*, 'broken', is classified as an adjective rather than a noun (it is an adverb in adult Finnish):

6. *rikki vetää*	'broken pulls'	
7. *rikki ihan hinaa*	'broken completely tows'	(both (6) and (7) were produced in response to a picture of a tow truck towing a broken car)

Three constructions which are similar to others generated by the grammar, but which contain a word the grammatical classification of which cannot be determined by reference to the criteria outlined in 4.2:

8. *täällä ollaan*	'here we-are'	(or: 'here one-is'. Impersonal form of verb)
9. *enää satu*	'any more happen'	(negative sense: 'It doesn't happen any more')

10. *illa⟨lla⟩ pestään*   'at-night we-wash'   (or: 'one-washes'. Impersonal form of verb)

Six constructions which either contain a negative word or have negative intent:

11. *enää piirtää tuossa*   'any more draws there'   (imperative intent, as in 'don't draw there any more', although verb form is not imperative)

12. *ei syödä tämmö*   'no eat this-kind-of-thing'.   (verb is impersonal, with sense of 'one doesn't eat...'. Sentence is grammatical except that *tämmö* should have a partitive suffix: *tämmöstä*)

13. *hiiri syö enää*   'mouse eats any more'   (negative intent, as in *hiiri ei syö enää* 'mouse doesn't eat any more')

14. *ei..toi*   'no..brought'   (*toi* is 3rd sing. past tense, used in affirmative sentences. In a negative sentence, it should be replaced by *tuonnut* 'brought', the past participle)

15. *loppu vielä*   'finished yet'   (negative intent, as in *ei ole loppu vielä*, 'no is finished yet', or '(he) isn't finished yet')

16. *ole pa—a—api*   'is mo—mo—monkey'   (negative intent: probably a very delayed imitation of *M*'s *ei ole apina täällä*, 'no is monkey here', or 'the monkey isn't here')

Thirty-three other constructions, most of which have unique structural patterns. Some of these are probably 'mistakes' from the point of view of Seppo's grammar. Others may represent productive patterns.

17. *takki hattu*   'coat hat'   (conjunction. *S* pointing out a coat and a hat in a picture)

18. *lumi jää*   'snow ice'   (conjunction)

19. *jala kiinni jala kiinni*   'leg tight leg tight'   (*M* expands as *jalasta kiinni*, 'leg-from tight', as in 'hold tight from the leg'. *Jalka* is the nominative sing. form of 'leg', and *jala-* is the inflectable noun stem)

20. *kiinni tuosta*   'tight there-from'   (see above)
21. *nyt avain* (3)   'now key'
22. *siinä..äidi(n) nappi..tuossa*   'there..mother('s) button..there'

23. *siinä isi koulu*	'there daddy school'	(sense is 'there daddy goes to school')
24. *sinne (menee) koti*	'to-there (goes) home'	
25. *vauva koti oma*	'baby home own'	(sense is 'baby goes to her own home'. 'Own' must precede noun in Finnish)
26. *possu isi..posti*	'piggie daddy..mail'	(possibly 'daddy' is indirect object: 'piggie brings daddy mail'. In response to a picture of a pig dressed as a mailman)
27. *missä tuossa*	'where there'	(probably two utterances)
28. *please lisää*	'please more'	
29. *äkki pam*	'suddenly "closed"'	
30. *(hei) häntä*	'(hey) tail'	
31. *hei hei missä auto?*	'hey hey where car?'	('where car' can be generated by the grammar, but not with the appended interjection)
32. *kassi(in) sinne*	'bag-(into) to-there'	('into the bag')
33. *vauva uimaan*	'baby swimming-into'	(*uimaan* is a nominalized verb form)
34. *lintu päässä*	'bird head-on'	('bird is on head'. This locative relationship is generated by the grammar, but not with the locative case ending)
35. *mukaa poika*	'with boy'	(should be *pojan mukaan*, 'boy with'. *Pojan* is genitive form of 'boy', required before this postposition. *Poika* is the nominative singular form)
36. *pipi päälle* (2)	'sore over'	(*M* expands as *pipin päälle tukka*, 'sore over hair', or 'hair over (the) sore')
37. *hiiri rikki häntä*	'mouse broken tail'	(could be modeled on *hiiren häntä on rikki*, 'mouse's tail is broken', or *hiirellä on rikkinainen häntä*, 'mouse has broken tail')
38. *kauhe vettä*	'terrible water'	(modeled on *kauhesti vettä*, 'terribly water'; *S* has just said *hiiri syö kauhe⟨sti⟩ kauhe⟨sti⟩*, 'mouse eats terrib(ly)', and is now adding that it is water that the mouse is eating, meaning that he is eating a lot of it)
39. *iso..ruoho..traktori*	'big..grass..tractor'	(*M* has just said *traktori leikkaa ruohoa*, 'tractor cuts grass', and *S* is adding

that it is a big tractor which
is doing the cutting. Thus,
this is a subject–object construction, with the subject
NP split by the object)

40. *setä pois..ukko*	'man away..old-man'	
41. *loppu tuohon*	'finished to-there'	
42. *(istuu) ajaa*	'(sits) drives'	(probably conjunction: 'sits and drives')
43. *vetää pois*	'pulls away' (or: 'out')	
44. *ota pois*	'take away' (or: 'out')	
45. *meni pois*	'went away' (or: 'out')	
46. *pois meni* (2)	'away (or: out) went'	
47. *pois mennyt*	'away gone' (*mennyt* is past participle)	

(Utterances 43–47 are not generated by the grammar because they are never constituents of longer utterances. Whenever an utterance contains *pois*, 'away', with the
sense of 'take away' or 'go away', the verb itself is omitted and *pois* substitutes for
it in function)

48. *hauva (oli) pipi·hiiri*	'doggie (was) sore mouse'	(reference unclear)
49. *syö..tuota..omena*	'eat..that (partitive) ..apple'	(verb–modifier–object strings are generated by the grammar, but the grammar cannot account for the appropriate partitive ending on the modifier 'that')

Appendix L

Rina, Mean Length of Utterance 1.83
Lexicon for the Transformational Generative Grammar

[+N, −pronoun]		[±animate][a]	f: type/token[b]
aave	'ghost'	+	2/4
Batman	'Batman'	.	1/2
isi	'daddy'	+	4/4
Maija-Täti	'Mary Poppins'	.	1/1
Mataami-Mimmi	'Madam-Mimmi'	.	1/1
Rami	'Rami'	.	4/4
Rina	'Rina'	+	64/93
setä	'man, uncle'	+	8/18
tyttö	'girl'	.	5/7
täti	'lady, aunt'	+	14/20
vauva	'baby'	+	1/1
äiti	'mother'	+	22/24
Aku-Ankka	'Donald Duck'	.	12/24
elukka	'creature'	.	1/1
hauva	'doggie'	.	6/8
heppa	'horsie'	.	4/8
hevonen	'horse'	.	2/3
kala	'fish'	.	1/1
kana	'chicken'	.	1/1
kissa	'cat'	.	1/1
(koira)	'dog'	.	1/1
lentokala	'flying fish'	.	2/2
lintu	'bird'	.	2/3
Mikki-Hiiri	'Mickey Mouse'	.	2/2
nalle	'teddy bear'	+	1/1
Pluto	'Pluto'	.	1/1
possu	'piggie'	.	1/1
pupu	'bunny'	.	2/3
susi	'wolf'	.	4/4
auto	'car'	.	2/3
brrä	"car"	.	4/11
bussi	'bus'	.	2/2
juna	'train'	.	1/1
lentokone	'airplane'	.	2/7

[a,b] See footnotes, Appendix D.

[+N, −pronoun] (*cont.*)		[±animate]	f: type/token
kakku (kakkua)	'cake'	.	8/14
	(nominative and partitive)		
keksi	'cracker'	.	5/6
nami	'food, goody'	.	1/1
nonna	"goody"	.	3/4
pumpkin	'pumpkin'	.	1/1
hampa⟨at⟩	'teeth'	.	1/1
käsi	'hand'	.	3/3
nenä	'nose'	.	1/1
pää	'head'	.	3/4
suu	'mouth'	.	1/1
syli	'lap'	.	1/1
tukka	'hair'	.	1/1
varvas	'toe'	.	1/1
hattu	'hat'	.	1/1
ikkuna	'window'	.	3/6
kirja	'book'	.	1/1
kukka	'flower'	.	1/1
kynä	'pen, pencil'	.	6/6
lattia	'floor'	.	1/1
lehti	'magazine'	.	1/1
nappi	'button'	.	1/2
nappeja	'buttons' (partitive)	.	1/1
ovi	'door'	.	1/1
paperi	'paper'	.	4/4
pipi	'sore'	.	7/9
porta⟨at⟩	'stairs'	.	1/1
talo	'house'	.	1/1

[+N, +pronoun]		f: type/token
lisää	'more'	3/5
näitä	'these' (partitive)	4/4
tätä	'this' (partitive)	5/6

[+V]		[±]——(NP)]	[±]——(NP)[+N, +animate]]	[±]——[+directional]]	f: type/token
ajaa	'drives'	+	.	.	2/2
antaa (anna)	'gives (give)'	+	+	.	15/15
asuu	'lives'	.	.	.	1/1
avaa	'opens'	.	.	.	2/3
hakkaa	'pounds'	.	.	.	1/1
haluu	'wants'	+	.	.	1/1
istuu	'sits'	.	.	.	2/2
katsoo	'watches, looks (at)'	+	.	+	5/5
laittaa	'puts, prepares, fixes, makes'	+	.	.	6/12
leikkii	'plays'	.	.	.	1/1
meni	'went'	.	.	.	1/1
nukkuu	'sleeps'	.	.	.	1/3
ottaa (otti)	'takes (took)'	+	.	.	6/6
panee	'puts'	.	.	+	1/1
pelleilee	'clowns, is-silly'	.	.	.	1/2
pestään	'wash' (impersonal)	+	.	.	1/1
piirtää	'draws'	+	.	+	9/17
pois	'(take) away'	+	.	.	3/3
putoo	'falls'	.	.	.	1/1
repii	'tears'	+	.	.	2/2
saa	'gets, is allowed'	+	.	.	8/22
siivoo	'cleans'	.	.	.	1/1
syö	'eats'	+	.	.	3/5
tulee	'comes'	.	.	.	3/3

[+Adj]		f: type/token
iso	'big'	4/4
lisää	'more'	5/8
punaise⟨t⟩	'red' (plural)	1/1
pää	'head'	1/2
tuo	'that' (nominative)	1/1
tätä	'this' (partitive)	1/1

[+Proloc]		[±directional]	f: type/token
tuolla	'(over) there'	.	3/3
tuossa	'(right) there'	.	3/3
tässä	'(right) here'	.	46/87
täällä	'(over) here'	.	22/28
tuohon	'to (right) there'	+	1/1
tänne	'to (over) here'	+	3/3

Unclassified		f: type/token
aa-aa	"sleeps"	2/2
itse	'self' (his-, her-, my-, etc.)	1/2
katso	'look' (imperative)	1/1
lika⟨inen⟩	'dirty'	2/2
(nämä)	('these') (nominative)	1/1
paha	'bad'	1/1
siellä	'(over) there'	1/1
tuttii	"sleeps"	1/1
ty⟨kännyt⟩	'liked' (past participle)	1/1
viereen	'next-to' (directional)	1/1

Appendix M

Rina, Mean Length of Utterance 1.83
Constructions Generated by the Transformational
Generative Grammar[a]

1. *Subject–Verb*

Rina repii	'Rina tears'
Rina pelleilee (2)[b]	'Rina clowns'
Rina avaa (2)	'Rina opens'
Rina istuu	'Rina sits'
Rina siivoo	'Rina cleans'
Rina ottaa	'Rina takes'
Rina katsoo	'Rina watches (looks)'
Rina leikkii	'Rina plays'
Rina syö	'Rina eats'
Rina laittaa (6)	'Rina prepares (fixes, sets up)'
Rina piirtää (7)	'Rina draws'
Rina putoo	'Rina falls'
Rina saa (9)	'Rina gets (is allowed)'
täti piirtää (2)	'aunt draws'
täti tulee	'aunt comes'
äiti laittaa	'mother prepares (fixes, sets up)'
äiti, isi tulee	'mother, daddy comes'
vauva avaa	'baby opens'
aave nukkuu (3)	'ghost sleeps'
nalle..katsoo	'teddy bear..watches (looks)'

2. *Verb–Object*

   (a) V + N

ajaa brrä	'drives "car"'
ottaa hampa⟨at⟩	'takes teeth'
pestään käsi	'wash hand'
piirtää tätä (2)	'draws this'

   (b) V + Adj + N

saa lisää kakku	'gets more cake'

   (c) N + V (T 2c)

hauva pois	'doggie (take) away'
tätä pois	'this (take) away'

[a] Included are a few constructions which contain repeated words or vocatives and one which seems to consist of two constructions run together without a break in intonation. These constructions are not, strictly speaking, generated by the grammar.

[b] Numbers in parentheses indicate the number of times the construction occurs in the sample. Numbers in parentheses preceded by 'T' indicate the transformation(s) which must be applied to derive a construction pattern or particular construction.

3. *Subject–Object* (T 3)

  (a) N + N

Rina kynä	'Rina pencil' (see p. 99)
Rina hauva (2)	'Rina doggie'
Rina näitä näitä	'Rina these these'

  (b) N + Adj + N

Rina lisää kakku	'Rina more cake' (see p. 99)

4. *Subject–Verb–Object*

  (a) N + V + N

Rina syö kakku (2)	'Rina eats cake' (nominative)
Rina syö kakkua	'Rina eats cake' (partitive)
Rina syö..keksi	'Rina eats..cracker'
Rina saa kakkua (2)	'Rina gets cake'
Rina saa kakku kakku	'Rina gets cake cake'
Rina saa nonna (2)	'Rina gets "goody"'
Rina saa lisää (2)	'Rina gets more'
Rina saa..tätä	'Rina gets..this'
Rina otti kynä	'Rina took pen'
Rina katsoo Aku-Ankka	'Rina looks-at Donald Duck'
Rina laittaa hevonen (2)	'Rina makes horse'
Rina laittaa..nonna	'Rina prepares.."goody"'
Rina piirtää Mataami-Mimmi	'Rina draws Madam-Mimmi'
Rina piirtää näitä	'Rina draws these'
täti ajaa brrä	'aunt drives "car"'
täti..(ottaa) kakku	'aunt..(takes) cake'
äiti antaa..paperi	'mother gives..paper'
äiti antaa kynä	'mother gives pen'
äiti (ottaa) nonna	'mother (takes) "goody"'

  (b) N + V + Adj + N

Rina saa lisää kakku (2)	'Rina gets more cake'

5. *Modifier–Head*

  (a) Adj + N

iso kynä	'big pen'
lisää kakkua (3)	'more cake'
punaise⟨t⟩ pipi	'red sore'
pää pipi (2)	'head sore'

  (b) N(genitive) + N

setä tyttö	'man girl'
isi tyttö	'daddy girl'
Rina tyttö	'Rina girl'
äiti.. syli	'mother..lap'

6. *Demonstrative–(Copula)–Noun phrase*

  (a) Predicate Nominative

tää täti	'this aunt'
tää hevonen	'this horse'
tää Aku-Ankka	'this Donald Duck'
tää setä	'this man'
äiti, tää bussi	'mother, this bus'

  (b) Proloc + N

tässä setä (11)	'here man'
tässä täti (3)	'here lady'

tässä Rami	'here Rami'
tässä Batman (2)	'here Batman'
tässä aave	'here ghost'
tässä elukka	'here creature'
tässä Aku-Ankka (10)	'here Donald Duck'
äiti, tässä Aku-Ankka	'mother, here Donald Duck'
äiti, tässä on Aku-Ankka	'mother, here is Donald Duck'
tässä kana	'here chicken'
tässä kala	'here fish'
tässä hauva (2)	'here doggie'
tässä..possu	'here..piggie'
tässä heppa (4)	'here horsie'
tässä lintu	'here bird'
tässä tässä lintu	'here here bird'
tässä (koira)	'here (dog)'
tässä on susi	'here is wolf'
tässä kalalento	'here fish flying' (reversal of *lentokala*, 'flying fish')
tässä brrä (8)	'here "car"'
tässä bussi	'here bus'
tässä juna	'here train'
tässä lentokone (6)	'here airplane'
auto, tässä auto	'car, here car'
tässä kukka	'here flower'
tässä ikkuna (3)	'here window'
tässä kirja	'here book'
tässä lehti	'here magazine'
tässä pipi (2)	'here sore'
tässä keksi	'here cracker'
täällä tyttö (2)	'here girl'
täällä setä	'here man'
täällä täti (2)	'here lady'
täällä Aku-Ankka	'here Donald Duck'
täällä Mikki-Hiiri	'here Mickey Mouse'
täällä hauva	'here doggie'
täällä lentokala	'here flying fish'
täällä heppa (2)	'here horsie'
täällä on heppa	'here is horsie'
täällä nappi (2)	'here button'
täällä varvas	'here toe'
tuossa..Rina	'there..Rina'
tuossa pipi	'there sore'
tuolla nappeja	'there buttons' (partitive)
(c) Proloc+M+N	
tässä..lisää kakku	'here..more cake'
tässä pää pipi	'here head sore'
tässä täti käsi	'here aunt hand'
täällä Rina käsi	'here Rina hand'
täällä Rina tukka	'here Rina hair'
(d) N+Proloc (T 2d)	
Mikki-Hiiri tässä	'Mickey Mouse here'
brrä tässä	'"car" here'
Aku-Ankka täällä	'Donald Duck here'

pupu täällä	'bunny here'
suu täällä	'mouth here'
ovi täällä	'door here'
ikkuna täällä (2)	'window here'
hattu täällä	'hat here'
ikkuna tuolla	'window there'

(e) Cop + N

on nami	'is goody'
on lintu	'is bird'
on lentokone	'is airplane'

7. *Subject–Locative* (T 3)

Rina paperi	'Rina paper'
Rina tänne	'Rina to-here'

8. *Subject–Verb–Locative*

Rina hakkaa tässä	'Rina pounds here'
Rina piirtää tässä (2)	'Rina draws here'
Rina (laittaa) tässä	'Rina (makes) here'
Rina piirtää tänne	'Rina draws to-here'
Rina laittaa paperi	'Rina puts (makes) paper' (sense is 'onto paper')

9. *Verb–Indirect Object*

(a) V + N

anna Rina	'give Rina'
Rina, anna Rinalle	'Rina, give to-Rina' (T 1)

(b) N + V (T 2b)

Rina anna	'Rina give'

10. *Indirect object–Modifier–Direct object*

tätille tätä keksi	'to-aunt this cracker' (T 1, T 2a, T 3) (see p. 139)
tätille (tuo) keksi	'to-aunt (that) cracker' (T 1, T 2a, T 3) (see p. 139)
täti, Rina iso (kynä)	'aunt, Rina big (pen)' (T 2a, T 3) (see p. 139)

11. *Subject–Verb–Direct object–Indirect object*

äiti antaa paperi Rina	'mother gives paper Rina'

12. *Wh–Loc + Noun*

missä kynä?	'where pen?'
missä keksi? (2)	'where cracker?'

13. *Neg + Noun or Verb or Proloc*

ei Pluto	'no Pluto'
ei susi	'no wolf'
ei täti (2)	'no aunt'
ei Aku-Ankka (2)	'no Donald Duck'
ei saa	'no get' (grammatical)
ei tässä	'no here' (grammatical)
ei täällä (2)	'no here' (grammatical)

14. *Run-together sentences*

tässä susi tää susi	'here wolf this wolf'

Appendix N

Rina, Mean Length of Utterance 1.83
Single-word Utterances and their Frequencies of Occurrence

Batman (4)	'Batman'	*aurinko	'sun'
isi	'daddy'	*kello	'clock'
*Melissa (9)	'Melissa'	*kukkia (2)	'flowers' (partitive)
*(poika)	('boy')	kynä (11)	'pen, pencil'
Rina (13)	'Rina'	lehti (2)	'magazine'
setä (14)	'man, uncle'	*lusi⟨kka⟩	'spoon'
tyttö (4)	'girl'	ovi (2)	'door'
täti (11)	'lady, aunt'	paperi (2)	'paper'
äiti (4)	'mother'	*(piilo)	('hiding-place')
		pipi (4)	'sore'
Aku-Ankka (6)	'Donald Duck'	*puu	'tree'
hauva (17)	'doggie'	*valo (3)	'light'
kala	'fish'		
kissa (2)	'cat'	*niitä (2)	'these' (partitive)
lintu (7)	'bird'	*tuo	'that' (nominative)
		*tuota	'that' (partitive)
auto (8)	'car'	tätä (2)	'this' (partitive)
brrä (18)	"car"		
bussi (2)	'bus'	aa-aa	"sleeps"
juna (3)	'train'	anna (4)	'give' (imperative)
*laiva	'ship'	antaa	'gives'
lentokone (12)	'airplane'	katso (3)	'look' (imperative)
		katsoo	'looks, watches'
kakku (3)	'cake' (nominative)	leikkii	'plays'
kakkua	'cake' (partitive)	nukkuu	'sleeps'
keksi (3)	'cracker'	on (5)	'is'
nami (2)	'food, goody'	ottaa	'takes'
*sokeri (3)	'sugar'	piirtää (3)	'draws'
*vettä (2)	'water'	pois	'(take) away'
		*putsaa	'cleans'
hattu (9)	'hat'		
*käsi⟨neet⟩	'mittens'	iso (2)	'big'
*takki	'coat'	lika⟨inen⟩	'dirty'
*hammas	'tooth'	tässä (21)	'(right) here'
*silmä	'eye'	täällä (4)	'(over) here'
syli	'lap'	tänne	'to-here'

* Starred words occur only in single-word utterances.

ei (13)	'no'
*joo (19)	'yes'
*kiitos (4)	'thank you'
*loppu	'finished'
*no niin	'well!'

Repeated words

äiti äiti	'mother mother'
hevo⟨nen⟩ hevo⟨nen⟩	'horse horse'
kakkua kakkua	'cake cake'
kynä kynä	'pen pen'
*laiva laiva	'ship ship'
paperi paperi	'paper paper'
Rina Rina	'Rina Rina'
täti täti	'aunt aunt'

*tuo tuo	'that that'

anna anna	'give give' (imperative)
anna anna anna	'give give give'
anna anna anna anna	'give give give give'
piirtää piirtää	'draws draws'

tässä tässä	'here here'
täällä täällä (2)	'here here'

ei ei ei	'no no no'
ei ei ei ei	'no no no no'

Appendix O

Rina, Mean Length of Utterance 1.83
Constructions not Generated by the Transformational
Generative Grammar

Fifty-four construction types (59 tokens) in the sample are not accounted for by the grammar. These include:

Twelve constructions which express grammatical relations in a different order from that provided for by the grammar:

1.	*otti Rina*	'took Rina'	(verb–subject)
2.	*tätä äiti antaa*	'this (partitive) mother gives'	(object–subject–verb)
3.	*Rina kissa..(haluu)*	'Rina cat..(wants)'	(subject–object–verb)
4.	*Rina tuohon panee*	'Rina to-there puts'	
5.	*Rina..tänne.. (katsoo)*	'Rina..to-here..(looks)'	
6.	*tässä..tässä porta⟨at⟩ meni*	'here..here stairs went'	
7.	*tätä anna tässä*	'this (partitive) give (imperative) here'	
8.	*(tuossa) anna..näitä*	'(there) give (imperative) ..these (partitive)'	
9.	*pumpkin tää*	'pumpkin this'	
10.	*repii..Aku Rami*	'tears..Donald Rami'	(in response to 'what is Rina doing?', as *R* tears her brother Rami's Donald Duck comic book)
11.	*Rina täällä nenä*	'Rina here nose'	(in response to *missä Rinan nenä on, missä?*, 'where Rina's nose is, where?')
12.	*Rina tuolla nappi*	'Rina there button'	(in response to *missäs Rinan nappi on, missä?*, 'where Rina's button is, where?')

Twelve two-word utterances, one word of which is a vocative:

13.	*äiti, isi*	'mother, daddy'
14.	*äiti, Aku-Ankka* (3)	'mother, Donald Duck'
15.	*äiti, setä*	'mother, man'
16.	*äiti, pipi pipi*	'mother, sore sore'
17.	*äiti, (lisää)*	'mother, (more)'
18.	*äiti, katso*	'mother, look' (imperative)

19. *äiti, anna*	'mother, give' (imperative)
20. *äiti, tässä*	'mother, here'
21. *hauva, äiti*	'doggie, mother'
22. *lisää, äiti*	'more, mother'
23. *täti, auto* (2)	'aunt, car'
24. *täti, anna*	'aunt, give' (imperative)

Two utterances with a word which occurs both before and after another word:

25. *tässä anna tässä* 'here give (imperative) here'
26. *saa Rina..saa lisää* 'gets Rina..gets more'

Two constructions which are similar to others which are generated by the grammar, but which contain words the grammatical classification of which cannot be determined by reference to the criteria outlined in 4.2:

27. *ei tyy* 'no like' (should be *ei tykännyt*. Response to *M*'s comment, *ai, et sä tykännyt siitä*, 'oh, no you liked it' ('you didn't like it'). Verb form is the past participle, appropriate for past tense following the negative verb. Rina omits most of the participle in her rendition, and changes the negative verb from second to third person singular)

28. *ei (nämä)* 'no (these)'

Twenty-one constructions with unique structural patterns. No conclusions could be drawn about the productivity of these patterns.

29. *Rina saa ottaa (lisää) kynä* 'Rina gets to-take (more) pen'
30. *täti tulee istuu Rina viereen* 'aunt comes sit Rina next-to'
31. *äiti, (iso) Rina anna..piirtää* 'mother, (big) Rina give.. draws' (or:'to-draw'. R trying to get *M* to give her the larger of two pens)
32. *tässä setä susi (on)..susi* 'here man wolf (is)..wolf'
33. *ei Aku-Ankka o(n)* 'no Donald Duck is' (see p. 64)
34. *ei oo tyttö* (2) 'no is girl' ('isn't (a) girl'. Grammatical. In response to 'is Rina a bad girl?')
35. *Ramilla on Aku-Ankka* 'Rami has Donald-Duck' (see pp. 137–8)
36. *tytöllä on* 'girl has' (see pp. 137–8)
37. *tässä on* 'here is'
38. *tää on* (2) 'this is'

39. *paha on*	'bad is'	(in response to *onko pahaa?*, 'is (it) bad?')
40. *on lika⟨inen⟩*	'is dirty'	(in response to *onko likainen?*, 'is (it) dirty?')
41. *Rina lika⟨inen⟩*	'Rina dirty'	(in response to 'who is dirty?')
42. *Rina lattia*	'Rina floor'	(in response to 'who is on the floor?')
43. *tää..setä täti*	'this..man lady'	(conjunction: *R* pointing out a man and a woman in a picture)
44. *tässä (oli) heppa*	'here (was) horsie'	(this corresponds to the Demonstrative–copula–NP pattern of the grammar, but 'was' was not yet a productive form of the copula and so was not included as a possible rewriting of Cop)
45. *Rami..äiti*	'Rami..mother'	(conjunction: *R* pointing out Rami and her mother in a picture)
46. *setä asuu täällä talo*	'man lives here house'	
47. *Rina itse*	'Rina (her)self'	
48. *Rina itse itse*	'Rina (her)self (her)self'	
49. *iso anna*	'big give'	(*R* trying to get *M* to give her the larger of two pens. Adjectives can be used as substantives in adult Finnish)

Five constructions with uninterpretable syntactic structures:

50. *on siellä aa-aa pois*	'is there "sleeps" away'	(in response to 'what is there?' *R* pointing to picture of baby in carriage)
51. *pupu hauva* (2)	'bunny doggie'	(in response to *mitäs tää pupu-äiti tekee?* 'what this bunny-mother does?' *R*'s meaning is not clear)
52. *Rina..Rami*	'Rina..Rami'	(in response to 'what is Rina doing?')
53. *Rina isi äiti*	'Rina daddy mother'	(reference unclear)
54. *aa-aa tuttii*	'"sleeps" "sleeps"'	(reference is to a picture of Caspar the Ghost in bed)

Appendix P

Seppo, Mean Length of Utterance 1.42

Case Grammar Lexicon: Verbs Classified According to Frame Features

---

[+V, +——(A)]

aa-aa	"sleeps"	*laulaa*	'sings'
avaa	'opens'	*leikkii*	'plays'
hakkaa	'pounds'	*lentää*	'flies'
heittää	'throws'	*lukee*	'reads'
itkee	'cries'	*pippaa*	'injures'
katsoo	'watches, looks (at)'	*pois*	'(goes) away'
korjaa	'fixes, repairs'	*polttaa*	'burns'
kovaa	'(goes) fast'	*tanssii*	'dances'
kuorii	'peels'	*tuu*	"blows horn"
kuti⟨ttaa⟩	'tickles'	*uffuf*	"dirty, naughty"
käy	'goes'	*ui*	'swims'

[+V, +——(A) (O)]

ajaa	'drives'
juo	'drinks'
kiinni	'(put) closed, fasten'
laittaa	'prepares, fixes, sets up'
pois	'(take) off, away'
rake⟨ntaa⟩	'builds'
vetää	'pulls'

[+V, +——(O)]

pikku	'little'
rikki	'broken'

Appendix Q

Seppo, Mean Length of Utterance 1.42
Constructions Generated by the Case Grammar[a]

---

1. V + A

äiti..avaa	'mother..opens'
äiti lukee (3)[b]	'mother reads'
isä itkee (2)	'father cries'
setä tuu	'man "blows horn"'
setä polttaa	'man burns'
setä tanssi	'man dances'
vauva aa-aa	'baby "sleeps"'
tipu laulaa (2)	'chick sings'
tipu katsoo (2)	'chick watches'
tipu..lentää	'chick..flies'
tipu..ui	'chick..swims'
tipu kuti⟨ttaa⟩	'chick tickles'
tipu pois (3)	'chick (goes) away'
pupu ajaa (2)	'bunny drives'
pupu heittää (3)	'bunny throws'
pupu leikkii	'bunny plays'
pupu korjaa	'bunny repairs'
hauva..pippaa	'doggie..injures'
hauva pois (2)	'doggie (goes) away'
kissa pois	'cat (goes) away'
ammu pois	'moo-cow (goes) away'
nöf pois	'"piggie" (goes) away'
nöf..hakkaa	'"piggie"..pounds'
fantti..lukee	'elephant..reads'
fanttii uffuf (2)	'elephant "naughty"'
nalle aa-aa	'teddy bear "sleeps"'
humma aa-aa	'horsie "sleeps"'
bmbm..käy (2)	'"car"..goes'
bmbm kovaa (2)	'"car" (goes) fast'
auto auto auto..käy	'car car car..goes'

---

[a] Headings such as V + A and D + O indicate the deep structure combinations of cases with each other and with verbs. The symbols are to be considered unordered; therefore, they do not necessarily correspond to the order of elements in the utterances listed. Below the broken line in each category are listed utterances which are not generated by the grammar for various reasons, but which seem to express the case relations in question.

[b] Numbers in parentheses indicate the number of times the construction occurs in the sample, if more than once.

– – – – – – – – – – – –	– – – – – – – – – –
pois api⟨na⟩	'(goes) away monkey'
laulaa tipu	'sings chick'
kuorii äiti	'peels mother'
kovaa kovaa kovaa kovaa..bmbm	'(goes) fast fast fast fast.."car"'

2. V+O

ajaa bmbm (2)	'drives "car"'
laittaa..bmbm	'sets-up.."car"'
kirja..pois	'book..(take) away'
takki pois	'coat (take) off'
mamma pois (2)	'"food" (take) away'
takki kiinni	'coat (put) closed, fasten'
pikku kala	'little fish'
rikki auto	'broken car'
– – – – – – – –	– – – – – –
auto vetää	'car pulls'
rikki vetää	'broken pulls'
hinaa rikki rikki	'tows broken broken'
rikki..auto..rikki	'broken..car..broken'
rikki bmbm rikki	'broken "car" broken'

3. A+O

tipu mamma (2)	'chick "food"' (see p. 90)
täti mamma (2)	'lady "food"' (see p. 90)
humma kukka	'horsie flower' (see p. 90)

4. D+O

täti auto	'aunt car'
isä kello (5)	'father clock'
setä kello	'man clock'
– – – – – – – –	– – – – – –
hauva..tädi(n)	'doggie..lady('s)'

5. L+O

auto talli	'car garage'
ankka vettä	'duck water'
ankka puu	'duck tree'
tipu kenkä (2)	'chick shoe'
pipi tuossa	'sore there'
tipu..tuossa	'chick..there'
tuossa kenkä	'there shoe'
tuossa ammu	'there moo-cow'
tuossa..tuf tuf	'there.."train"'
– – – – – – – –	– – – – – –
talli bmbm	'garage "car"'
ulo⟨s⟩ takki	'to-outside coat'
kuorma..talli..kuorma	'truck..garage..truck'

6. V+L

– – – – – – – –	– – – – – –
kenkä kuti⟨ttaa⟩	'shoe tickles'

7. O+E

– – – – – – – –	– – – – – –
tää kello	'this clock'

8. V + A + O

nalle ajaa kan	'teddy bear drives "tractor"'
pupu ajaa bmbm (2)	'bunny drives "car"'
kissa ajaa bmbm	'cat drives "car"'
pupu ajaa tuf tuf	'bunny drives "train"'
pupu laittaa bmbm	'bunny sets-up "car"'
äiti juo kahvi	'mother drinks coffee'

– – – – – – – – – – –

bmbm pupu ajaa	'"car" bunny drives'

9. *Case Relations uncertain*

tyttö hauva	'girl dog' (D + O or conjunction)
täti..täti kahvi	'aunt coffee' (D + O or A + O)
täti..vauva	'lady..baby' (D + O or A + O)

Appendix R

*Constructions of Kendall (English), Sipili (Samoan),
and Luo children, classified according to deep
structure case relations*[a]

<table>
<tr><td colspan="2" align="center">Kendall, Mean Length of Utterance 1.48</td></tr>
<tr><td>

1. V+A
   Kendall bark
   Kendall swim
   Kendall bite
   Kendall break
   Kendall turn
   Kendall fix-it (2)[b]
   Kimmy spit
   Kimmy come
   Kimmy swim
   Kimmy blow (2)
   Kimmy bite
   Kimmy running
   Kimmy eat (2)
   Mommy bounce
   Mommy sleep
   Mommy read
   Mommy break-it
   Daddy pick-up
   Daddy break-it
   Melissa bounce
   Melissa read
   cow moo (4)
   Phil running
   Pam running
   Scott scream
   doggie bark
   Kendall Kristin sit
   hug Mommy ('Mommy hugs')
2. V+O
   look Kendall ('look at Kendall')
   read..book
   bite..finger
   open..lotion
   see running

</td><td>

   leave-it heel
   shoe off ('take shoe off')
   hat on ('put hat on')
   lotion away ('take lotion away')
   doggie sew ('sew doggie')
   Kimmy kick ('kick Kimmy')
   Kendall pick-up ('pick-up
     Kendall')
   doggie look-it ('look at
     doggie')
   break Fur-Book
   poor doggie (2)
   red Kendall
   blue Mommy
   big bed
   dear..horsie
   more lotion
   hair wet
   pillow fell
   thread break
3. V+F
   writing book
4. V+D
   see Kendall ('Kendall sees')
5. V+L
   play bed (2)
   sit pool
   sit here (2)
6. A+O
   Kendall bath (6) ('Kendall takes
     a bath')
   Kendall shower ('Kendall takes a
     shower')
   Kendall book ('Kendall reads a
     book')

</td></tr>
</table>

---

[a] See footnote *a*, Appendix Q.   [b] See footnotes, Appendix C.

Kendall, Mean Length of Utterance 1.48 (*cont.*)

Kendall spider ('Kendall looked
at a spider')
doggie woof (3) ('doggie says
woof'. Alternatively, could be
V + A, as in 'doggie woofs',
equivalent to 'doggie barks')
7. D + O
Kendall rocking-chair
Kimmy bike
papa door (2)
Kendall turn
Kimmy pail (3)
Kendall pail
Kendall birthday
pig tail
cow tail
doggie hole (4)
Kendall presents
Kendall dinner
Kendall doggie
Kimmy doggie
8. L + O
Kendall bed ('Kendall is in bed')
Kendall water
Kendall pool
lotion tummy
ear outside
towel bed (2)
Kendall innere
Kendall innere bed
Kendall down
mess here
pillow here
there cow
here mess
9. O + E
that Kimmy (2)
that Scott
that lady
that hole
that..candy
that Daddy's
Mommy lady

Daddy Shawn
Kendall monkey
Kimmy monkey
boy, Kurt boy
10. V + A + O
Mommy..sew doggie
Kimmy ride bike
Kendall turn page
Kimmy eat hand
Mommy pick-up..Kendall
Mommy fix-it..ear
Mommy hit Kendall ('Kendall
hit Mommy')
11. V + A + L
Ben swim pool
Kristin sit chair
Kendall play bed (2)
Kendall crying there
12. V + O + L
Kimmy change here (2) ('change
Kimmy here')
Kimmy kick there ('kick Kimmy
there')
13. O + E, E = D + O
that Kimmy ball
14. *Case Relations uncertain* (see
Appendix C)
Kendall book (2) (A + O or D + O)
doggie pillow (D + O or L + O)
Mommy kiss (V + A or V + O)
that blow (V + A or V + O)
Kimmy look-it Kimmy (2)
(probably V + O)
Daddy read Kendall (V + A + D or
V + A + C)
Kendall read Daddy (V + A + D or
V + A + C)
water Ben (L + O or L + C)
Kendall see Kendall (A + V + A or
A + V + O or O + V + O)
read Kendall (V + A or V + D)
15. *Miscellaneous and uninterpretable*
(see Appendix C)

Sipili (Samoan), Mean Length of Utterance 1.52[a]

1. V+A
    brought Keith
    brought Tasi
    goes Va
2. V+O
    spank me
    take me
    hit you ⎱
    hit you ⎰ (two construction types)
    do work
    nurse girl
    children older
3. V+L
    go home
4. D+O
    boat mine
    candy mine
    balloon mine
    thing mine
    lessons mine
    ball mine
    bicycle mine
    swing mine
    candy yours
    ball yours
    this yours ⎱ (two construction
    this yours ⎰ types)
    pie Tafale
    our thing

house Sina
balloon mama
balloon of mine
ball of mine
thing of mine
tricycle of mine
candy of mine
Joshua, ball of mine
the nose of mine
balloon for Fai

5. L+O
    ball there
6. L+O, O = D+O
    candy yours there
    candy mine there
7. *Modality (Neg)+V*
    not eat
8. *Modality (Neg)+V+A*
    not eat you
    not eat Upia
9. *Modality (Neg)+V+O*
    not eat candy
10. *Not Classified*
    yes, not eat
    whine word-no
    car whose that?
    want to defecate
    we children

Luo, several children, MLU not known[b]

1. V+A
    he-brought
    car runs
    European comes
    I-refuse
2. V+O
    eat medicine
    give-me potato

give-me milk
give-me water
give-me banana
give-me porridge
give-me candy
drink porridge
cover-me
see candy

[a] Sipili's 12 constructions consisting of the morpheme translated as 'and', 'for', or 'with' plus a noun might be considered instances of nouns in isolation which are marked for case. 'For'+N would be Dative or Benefactive, and 'with' +N would be Comitative. The construction 'in (the) shirt' is marked as a noun in the Locative case. Twenty-seven construction types of 'the' +N or 'sign of the nominative' +N seem to be equivalent in semantic function to the O+E constructions of the Finnish and American children ('this fish', 'that Kimmy', etc. (see 3.4.3)), but they cannot be classified as such because 'the' and 'sign of the nominative' are noun markers rather than nouns or pronouns.

[b] See footnotes, Table 9, p. 112.

Luo, several children, MLU not known (*cont.*)

hand (over)-it
see that-there
food give-me
it-has-hole
pepper hot
thing-that good
3. V+D
    I sick
    I know
4. D+O
    this one his
    hand-mine
    head-mine
    shoes-mine
    leg-mine
5. L+O
    she here
    she there
    cigarette down
6. O+E
    it European
    it clock
    it thing-this
    this one
    this one European
    this visitor
    that-there it chicken

7. V+A+O
    I-burned-him
    I-drink water
    hunger bites-me
    he-brought this one
8. V+D+O
    I-see-them
    I-see European
    I-want food
    I-want water
9. V+A+L
    he-went Ulanda
    he-goes river
10. V+O+L
    here it-has-hole
11. O+E, E = D+O
    that-there box-ours
12. *Modality (Neg)*+V+D
    I-not-know
13. *Modality (Q)*+V+A
    you-eat?
14. *Not Classified*
    father cigarette (A+O or D+O)
    I-want to-go to-sleep
    Mamma goes to-wash
    absent/without

Bibliography

Aaltio, Maija-Hellikki. (1967). *Finnish for foreigners*. Helsinki: Otava.

Atkinson, J. (1961). *A Finnish grammar*. Turku: The Finnish Literary Society.

Bellugi, Ursula. (1967). 'The acquisition of negation'. Unpublished doctoral dissertation, Harvard University.

Bever, T. G., Fodor, J. A., and Weksel, W. (1965). 'On the acquisition of syntax: A critique of "Contextual generalization"'. *Psychological Review*, **72**(6), 467–82.

Bloom, Lois. (1968). 'Language development: form and function in emerging grammars'. Doctoral dissertation, Columbia University.

(1970). *Language development: Form and function in emerging grammars*. Cambridge, Mass.: M.I.T. Press.

Blount, B. G. (1969). 'Acquisition of language by Luo children'. Unpublished doctoral dissertation, University of California at Berkeley.

Braine, M. D. S. (1963). 'The ontogeny of English phrase structure: The first phase'. *Language*, **39**(1), 1–14.

(1971). 'The acquisition of language in infant and child'. In C. Reed (Ed.), *The learning of language*. New York: Scribners, pp. 7–95.

Brown, R. (1968). The development of Wh questions in child speech'. *Journal of Verbal Learning and Verbal Behavior*, **7**(2), 279–90.

(1970). 'The first sentences of child and chimpanzee'. In R. Brown, *Psycholinguistics: selected papers*. New York: The Free Press, pp. 208–31.

(in press). 'Stage I: Semantic and grammatical relations'. Draft of a chapter for *A first language: The early stages*. Cambridge, Mass.: Harvard University Press.

Brown, R. and Bellugi, Ursula. (1964). 'Three processes in the child's acquisition of syntax'. In E. H. Lenneberg (Ed.), *New directions in the study of language*. Cambridge, Mass.: M.I.T. Press, pp. 131–61.

Brown, R., Cazden, Courtney B. and Bellugi-Klima, Ursula. (1968). 'The child's grammar from I to III'. In J. P. Hill (Ed.), *Minnesota Symposia on Child Psychology*. Minneapolis: University of Minnesota Press, II, 28–73.

Brown, R. and Fraser, C. (1963). 'The acquisition of syntax'. In N. Cofer, Barbara S. Musgrave (Eds.), *Verbal behavior and learning: Problems and processes*. New York: McGraw-Hill, pp. 158–97.

Brown, R. and Hanlon, Camille. (1968). 'Derivational complexity and the order of acquisition in child speech'. Paper presented at the Carnegie–Mellon Symposium on Cognitive Psychology, 1968. In J. R. Hayes (Ed.), *Cognition and the development of language*. New York: John Wiley & Sons, 1970, pp. 11–53.

Burling, R. (1959). 'Language development of a Garo and English speaking child. *Word*, **15**, 45–68.

Cazden, Courtney B. (1968). 'The acquisition of noun and verb inflections'. *Child Development*, **39**(2), 433–48.

Chomsky, N. (1957). *Syntactic Structures*. The Hague: Mouton.

(1959). Review of *Verbal Behavior* by B. F. Skinner. *Language*, **35**, 26–58.

(1964). 'Formal discussion on W. Miller and Susan Ervin's presentation, 'The development of grammar in child language'. In Ursula Bellugi and R. Brown (Eds.), *The acquisition of language*. Monographs of the Society for Research in Child Development, **29** (1), 35–9.

(1965). *Aspects of the theory of syntax*. Cambridge, Mass.: M.I.T. Press.

(1968). *Language and mind*. New York: Harcourt, Brace, and World, Inc.

Fillmore, C. (1968). 'The case for case'. In E. Bach and R. T. Harms (Eds.), *Universals in linguistic theory*. New York: Holt, Rinehart & Winston, Inc., pp. 1–88.

Fodor, J. A. (1966*a*). Comments in the general discussion on the McNeill and Slobin presentations. In F. Smith and G. A. Miller (Eds.), *The genesis of language: A psycholinguistic approach*. Cambridge, Mass.: M.I.T. Press, pp. 93–103.

(1966*b*). Comments in the general discussion on the Slobin presentation. In F. Smith and G. A. Miller (Eds.), *The genesis of language: A psycholinguistic approach*. Cambridge, Mass.: M.I.T. Press, pp. 149–52.

(1966*c*). 'How to learn to talk: some simple ways'. In F. Smith and G. A. Miller (Eds.), *The genesis of language: A psycholinguistic approach*. Cambridge, Mass.: M.I.T. Press, pp. 105–22.

Fodor, J. A. and Garrett, M. (1966). 'Some reflections on competence and performance'. In J. Lyons and R. J. Wales (Eds.), *Psycholinguistic papers*. Edinburgh: Edinburgh University Press, pp. 135–79.

Fraser, C., Bellugi, Ursula and Brown, R. (1963). 'Control of grammar in imitation, comprehension, and production'. *Journal of Verbal Learning and Verbal Behavior*, **2**(2), 121–35.

Gvozdev, A. N. (1961). *Voprosy izucheniya detskoy rechi*. Moscow: Akad. Pedag. Nauk RSFSR.

Harris, Z. S. (1951). *Methods in structural linguistics*. Chicago: University of Chicago Press.

Katz, J. J. (1966). *The philosophy of language*. New York: Harper.

Katz, J. J. and Postal, P. (1964). *An integrated theory of linguistic descriptions*. Cambridge, Mass.: M.I.T. Press, Research Monograph no. 26.

Kernan, K. T. (1969). 'The acquisition of language by Samoan children'. Unpublished doctoral dissertation, University of California at Berkeley.

(1970). 'Semantic relations and the child's acquisition of language'. *Anthropological Linguistics*, **12**(5), 171–87.

Klima, E. and Bellugi, Ursula. (1966). 'Syntactic regularities in the speech of children'. In J. Lyons and R. J. Wales (Eds.), *Psycholinguistic papers*. Edinburgh: Edinburgh University Press, pp. 183–208.

Lees, R. (1964). Formal discussion of R. Brown and C. Fraser's presentation, 'The acquisition of syntax', and R. Brown, C. Fraser, and U. Bellugi's presentation, 'Explorations in grammar evaluation'. In Ursula Bellugi and R. Brown (Eds.), *The acquisition of language.* Monographs of the Society for Research in Child Development, **29**(1), 92–8.

McCarthy, Dorothea. (1954). 'Language development in children'. In L. Carmichael (Ed.), *Manual of child psychology.* New York: John Wiley & Sons.

McNeill, D. (1966a). 'The creation of language by children'. In J. Lyons and R. J. Wales (Eds.), *Psycholinguistic papers.* Edinburgh: Edinburgh University Press, pp. 99–115.

(1966b). 'Developmental psycholinguistics'. In F. Smith and G. A. Miller (Eds.), *The genesis of language: A psycholinguistic approach.* Cambridge, Mass.: M.I.T. Press, pp. 15–84.

(1970). 'The development of language'. In P. A. Mussen (Ed.), *Carmichael's manual of child psychology.* 3rd edn., vol. 1, New York: John Wiley & Sons, Inc., pp. 1061–1161.

(1971). 'The capacity for the ontogenesis of grammar'. In D. I. Slobin (Ed.), *The ontogenesis of grammar.* New York: Academic Press, pp. 17–40.

McNeill, D. and McNeill, Nobuko. (1966). 'What does a child mean when he says "no"?' In E. Zale (Ed.), *Proceedings of the conference on language and language behavior.* New York: Appleton-Century-Crofts, pp. 51–61.

Miller, W. and Ervin, Susan. (1964). 'The development of grammar in child language'. In Ursula Bellugi and R. Brown (Eds.), *The acquisition of language.* Monographs of the Society for Research in Child Development, **29**(1), pp. 9–34.

Schlesinger, I. M. (1971). 'Production of utterances and language acquisition'. In D. I. Slobin (Ed.), *The ontogenesis of grammar.* New York: Academic Press, pp. 63–101.

Shipley, Elizabeth F., Smith, Carlota S. and Gleitman, Lila R. (1968). 'A study in the acquisition of language: Free responses to commands'. *Language*, **45**(2), 322–42.

Slobin, D. I. (1966a). 'The acquisition of Russian as a native language'. In F. Smith and G. A. Miller (Eds.), *The genesis of language: A psycholinguistic approach.* Cambridge, Mass.: M.I.T. Press, pp. 129–48.

(1966b). Comments on McNeill's 'Developmental psycholinguistics'. In F. Smith and G. A. Miller (Eds.), *The genesis of language: a psycholinguistic approach.* Cambridge, Mass.: M.I.T. Press, pp. 85–91.

(1966c). 'Early grammatical development in several languages, with special attention to Soviet research'. Working Paper no. 11, Language-Behavior Research Laboratory, Berkeley.

(1968). 'Questions of language development in cross-cultural perspective'. Paper prepared for symposium on language learning in cross-cultural perspective, Michigan State University.

(1970). 'Universals of grammatical development in children'. In W. Levelt and G. B. Flores d'Arcais (Eds.), *Advances in psycholinguistic research.* Amsterdam: North Holland Publishing Co., pp. 174–86.

Smith, F. and Miller, G. A. (1966). *The genesis of language: A psycholinguistic approach.* Cambridge, Mass.: M.I.T. Press.

Tuomikoski, Anne and Deans, Helen. (1952). *Elementary Finnish.* Helsinki: The Society of Finnish Literature.

Watt, W. C. (1970). 'On two hypotheses concerning psycholinguistics'. In J. R. Hayes (Ed.), *Cognition and the development of language.* New York: John Wiley & Sons, Inc., pp. 137–220.

Weir, Ruth. (1962). *Language in the crib.* The Hague: Mouton.

Index

adjectives, 82; *see also* modification of nouns

adverbs, 58, 82, 233
  in case grammar, 198; for child language, 211, 215
  in Stage I speech, 110, 132, 147, 150, 152–3, 170

agent, *see* case grammar, outline of; subject, semantic functions of

ambiguity, structural, 70–1, 166

animate and inanimate nouns, *see* noun forms, animate and inanimate

Bellugi(-Klima), Ursula, 7, 8, 10, 12, 14, 19, 25, 33, 107, 159, 161, 165, 171, 174

Bever, T. G., 192

Bloom, Lois, 7, 9, 14, 20, 39, 43–5, 55–6, 57, 62, 66, 68, 69, 70, 72, 73, 74, 81–2, 90–4, 96, 100, 101, 105, 106–7, 109–10, 116n, 130–1, 153–4, 172, 174, 179, 189, 209, 210, 219, 222

Blount, B. G., 1, 8, 9, 65, 111–13

Braine, M. D. S., 3, 10, 27, 28, 30, 32, 33, 34, 35, 36, 37–8, 39, 41–2, 46, 47, 54, 159, 181

Brown, R., 3, 7, 8, 9, 10, 11, 12, 14, 19, 21, 22, 24, 25, 27, 30, 32–3, 34, 37, 38, 41, 45–6, 49, 51–2, 54, 58, 60–1, 62, 67, 68, 69, 72, 73, 92, 101, 106, 107, 108, 127, 150–1, 152, 159, 161, 165, 167, 171, 175, 177, 178–9, 219

Bulgarian, 48

Burling, R., 117

case endings, 7, 231–2
  Finnish children's failure to distinguish between nominative and partitive, 104–5, 148–9
  for indirect objects (allative), 142, 144
  for locative meanings, 20, 142–3, 144, 207, 232, 233–4
  order of emergence of functions of, 142–3
  for possessive meanings (adessive), 138, 142–3, 144

for subjects and direct objects (nominative, partitive, genitive/accusative), in adult Finnish, 125, 126–7, 235; in child Finnish, 125–7, 141, 144, 185–6
  see also functors, inflections

case grammar
  adequacy of as representation of children's linguistic knowledge, 10, 73–4, 196; advantages, 15, 206–8, 216, 224, 226–7; disadvantages, 211–16, 225–7
  case relations, 197–8, 202; rewriting of symbols for, 202–3, 207, 224; present in Stage I speech, 206, 209–11, 224
  frame features for verbs, 204, 205
  modality and proposition in, 198, 200–1, 207–8, 211, 214–16, 226
  outline of, 197–9
  for Seppo, 199–206

catenative verbs, 103, 110, 118, 159, 169

Cazden, Courtney B., 7, 8, 10, 11, 14, 19, 24, 107, 159, 161, 165, 171

child language learner
  as formulator and tester of hypotheses, 3, 5, 6, 160, 165
  as theory constructor, 3

Chomsky, N., 1, 2, 3, 4, 10–11, 14, 15, 74, 75, 77–80, 88, 94, 175, 176, 178, 192, 193, 194, 197, 214, 217, 222, 224

cognition
  as basis of linguistic expression, 187, 190, 192

competence and performance, 10–13; *see also* verb deletion transformation

comprehension, 11, 12–13, 133, 149

constituent structure
  in case grammar, 198; as improvement over transformational grammar account of, 15, 206, 216, 224; inadequacy of account of noun phrases in, 203, 214, 225–6
  information about contained in answers to substitutions and Wh questions, 11, 178–9
  in optimal grammar for child language, 227
  in pivot grammar, 43, 44